INTRODUCTION TO THE HEBREW BIBLE

An Inductive Reading of the Old Testament

Michael Brennan Dick
Siena College

Prentice Hall, Englewood Cliffs, New Jersey 07632

Library of Congress Cataloging-in-Publication Data

Dick, Michael Brennan
  Introduction to the Hebrew Bible.

  Includes bibliographies and index.
  1. Bible. O.T.—Introductions. 2. Bible as
literature. I. Title.
BS1140.2.D53 1988   221.6'1   87-7283
ISBN 0-13-484486-6

Editorial/production supervision
  and interior design: Virginia L. McCarthy
Cover design: Ben Santora
Interior sketches: Gregory J. Zoltowski, O.F.M.
Manufacturing buyer: Margaret Rizzi
Page layout: Karen R. Salzbach

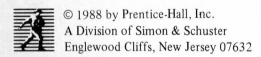 © 1988 by Prentice-Hall, Inc.
A Division of Simon & Schuster
Englewood Cliffs, New Jersey 07632

Printed in the United States of America

10 9 8 7 6 5 4 3 2 1

ISBN 0-13-484486-6 01

Prentice-Hall International (UK) Limited, *London*
Prentice-Hall of Australia Pty. Limited, *Sydney*
Prentice-Hall Canada Inc., *Toronto*
Prentice-Hall Hispanoamericana, S.A., *Mexico*
Prentice-Hall of India Private Limited, *New Delhi*
Prentice-Hall of Japan, Inc., *Tokyo*
Simon & Schuster Asia Pte. Ltd., *Singapore*
Editora Prentice-Hall do Brasil, Ltda., *Rio de Janeiro*

To Donna
and our family,
Christopher and Jonathan

CONTENTS

THE PENTATEUCH OR TORAH

THE PROPHETS

THE WRITINGS
Psalmist, Sage, and Short Story

ACKNOWLEDGMENTS

page 18   *Mother and Child*, **Pablo Picasso, 1922**

The Baltimore Museum of Art: The Cone Collection, formed by Dr. Claribel Cone and Miss Etta Cone of Baltimore, Maryland. BMA 1950.279.

page 19   *Guernica*, **Pablo Picasso, 1937**

Copyright ARS (Artists Rights Society, Inc.), New York/SPADEM 1987.

page 114   **Route of the Exodus**

Adapted from *Westminster Historical Atlas to the Bible* (Revised Edition), edited by George Ernest Wright and Floyd Vivian Filson. Copyright 1956, by W. L. Jenkins. Adapted and used by permission of The Westminster Press, Philadelphia, PA.

page 126   **Jerusalem from the South**

Biblisch-historisches Handwörterbuch, Göttingen, Vandenhoeck & Ruprecht.

page 143   **Hammurabi's Stele**

Cliché des Musées Nationaux—Paris. Justicatif demandé.

page 181   **Ivory Sphynx from Samaria**

Courtesy of the Israel Department of Antiquities and Museums.

page 182   **Orthostat of Sargon II**

Courtesy of Museo de Antichità, Torino.

page 195   **Stele of Baal from Ugarit**

Cliché des Musées Nationaux — Paris. Justicatif demandé.

page 206   **Interior of Solomon's Temple**

Drawing by Edward S. Winters.

page 207   *At That First Eucharist* (hymn A)

Text © copyright 1970 by the American Catholic Press, 1223 Rossell, Oak Park, IL 60302. Reprinted with permission from *The Johannine Hymnal*. All rights reserved.

page 208   *Father, God of All Things Living* (hymn C)

Members of the One Mystic Body (hymn D)

© Copyright, World Library Publications, Inc. Used with permission.

page 209   *We Come To Join in Your Banquet of Love* (hymn E)

© Copyright, World Library Publications, Inc. Used with permission.

Feed On Me (hymn F)

Copyright © 1976 by Damean Music. Published exclusively by North American Liturgy Resources (NALR), 10802 N. 23rd Ave., Phoenix, AZ 85029. All rights reserved. Used with permission.

I Am the Bread of Life (hymn G)

By Sr. Suzanne Toolan. Copyright © 1966 by G.I.A. Publications, Inc., Chicago, Illinois. All rights reserved.

Bread That Was Sown (hymn H)

From the album *Spirit Alive,* © 1977, Gregory Norbet, O.S.B., composer. The Benedictine Foundation of the State of Vermont, Inc.

page 210   *God and Man at Table Are Sat Down* (hymn I)

By Robert Stamps. © copyright 1972 by Dawn Treader Music. All rights reserved. Used by permission of Gaither Copyright Management.

page 295   **Mesopotamian Flood Story**

James B. Pritchard, *Ancient Near Eastern Texts: Relating to the Old Testament*, 3rd Edition with Supplement. Copyright © 1969 by Princeton University Press. Excerpt, pp. 93-95, reprinted with permission of Princeton University Press.

page 301   **Treaty Between Mursillis and Duppi-Tessub of Amurru**

James B. Pritchard, *Ancient Near Eastern Texts: Relating to the Old Testament*, 3rd Edition with Supplement. Copyright © 1969 by Princeton University Press. Excerpt, pp. 203–205, reprinted with permission of Princeton University Press.

pages 324-25   **The Ancient Near East**

Adapted from *Westminster Historical Atlas to the Bible* (Revised Edition), edited by George Ernest Wright and Floyd Vivian Filson. Copyright 1956 by W. L. Jenkins. Adapted and used by permission of The Westminster Press, Philadelphia, PA.

PREFACE FOR STUDENTS AND TEACHERS

A few years ago while I was at a convention of Old Testament scholars, several of us at dinner were discussing the various academic projects on which we were currently working. When I mentioned that I was just completing the first draft of a new introductory textbook on the Old Testament/Hebrew Bible (this very book), I was greeted by general but polite disbelief. "Just what we need! Another introduction to the Old Testament." I tried to defend what I felt was (and still is) a legitimate need for "yet another introduction to the Old Testament."

Because even professionals in the field believe that there are already a number of excellent books to acquaint the student with the Hebrew Bible/Old Testament[1]—and indeed there are—I feel that from the very outset I should justify my perceived need for *this particular book* and should clearly present its goals and objectives.

There are indeed several excellent texts on the Hebrew Bible. Each of them pursues a slightly different approach to its subject matter, which is so vast that one would expect there to be multiple approaches. Not only is the Hebrew text extensive, but the various critical skills used by scripture critics are so complex, and the history of the ancient Near East during the biblical period so foreign, that the textbook that introduces all these issues must appear overwhelming to the beginning student. Furthermore, the Hebrew Bible can be approached from so many different *interests*. To some it represents a major cultural influence on Western art and literature; to others it constitutes the basis of faith for three of the world's major religions (Judaism, Christianity, and Islam). There are then so many topics to be covered that most current textbooks used in the average one-semester introductory course become themselves the focus of the course; this leaves very little time for the student to read the Bible itself.

---

[1] In this text I shall use "Hebrew Bible" rather than its equivalent "Old Testament" because the latter term views this literature from the Christian perspective of the "*Old* and *New* Testaments." Because this text envisions a broad readership, I prefer broader terminology. In this text only the Book of Judith treated in Chapter 11 is not strictly part of the Hebrew Bible; preserved only in Greek, Judith is found only among the Protestant apocryphal or Roman Catholic deuterocanonical books.

The 24[2] books that comprise the Hebrew Bible cover almost 1,500 years and were written in at least two languages (Hebrew and Aramaic), or in three languages if one includes the Greek of books such as Wisdom of Solomon and Judith, which are included only in the Roman and Orthodox Catholic lists of authoritative (that is, **canonical**) books.[3] As you can readily see, any textbook that will introduce the student over a semester to each of these books (dealing with its history of composition, literary outline, theology, Near Eastern comparative literature, etc.) will not only overwhelm the student but also leave the reader with little time for studying the Bible itself.

In over a decade of teaching beginning courses, generally to college freshmen and sophomores, I have seen the need for a different type of textbook for the typical one-semester introductory course as found in many colleges or universities. This textbook does not intend to be a comprehensive and encyclopedic introduction to the entire Hebrew Bible (book by book) with full coverage of such ancillary issues as Hebrew manuscripts, archaeology, and ancient Near Eastern history. The function of *An Inductive Reading of the Hebrew Bible* more modestly seeks to expose its beginning reader to both the main critical methodologies and the major religious topics in the Hebrew Bible and to do so by using an *inductive* approach that guides the student in the achievement of these goals.

What follows is an outline of the philosophy that lies behind this inductive approach to teaching the Hebrew Bible.

1.   The textbook intended for the beginning college/university course should be governed by the needs of pedagogy as much as by its biblical subject matter.

2.   The text should not replace reading the Bible; in fact, it should serve to bring the student unavoidably to the biblical text.

3.   The text should sharpen students' reading skills by having them read manageable amounts of biblical texts *carefully,*[4] thereby acquiring a sensitivity to how the passages work to convey their meaning.

My experience has taught me that the average student is overwhelmed by reading a biblical book such as Genesis or Exodus at one sitting. There is also a tendency to read with excessive naiveté, as if the biblical author only intended to be taken on one level (*referentially*; but more about this in Chapter 1) and that the text

---

[2] In the Jewish list of books (canon), books that come in two sections (for example, Samuel, Kings, and Chronicles) are both counted as one; the 12 minor prophets are considered one book. The Protestant canon, which lists these books separately, totals 39 books. See Appendix A for a list of canonical books.

[3] The books of Tobit/Tobias, Judith, Wisdom of Solomon, Ben Sirach/Ecclesiasticus, Baruch (Roman Catholics only), 1 and 2 Maccabees, and the Greek additions to Esther and the supplements to Daniel (Susanna, Song of the Three Young Men, Story of Bel and the Dragon) constitute the *Deuterocanonical books* for Orthodox and Roman Catholics and the *Apocrypha* for Protestants. For a list of the canonical books of the Hebrew Bible for Jews, Protestants, and Roman and Orthodox Catholics, see Appendix A at the back of this text. Furthermore, a Glossary at the back of the text defines or explains all of the major terms used throughout this book.

[4] For this reason I have preferred to have the student study smaller—although *representative*—prophetic texts such as Amos rather than such massive books as Jeremiah and Isaiah, and wisdom texts such as Qoheleth (Ecclesiastes) rather than Job. I fully realize that those books that are not covered represent treasures of world literature; however, I think that beginning students should be exposed to amounts of texts that can be handled critically. Furthermore, the texts chosen generally represent the main themes and issues represented by the larger works.

merely means what it *apparently* says. On any given day, the average college student easily adjusts his or her response to the reading of a textbook on biology, a newspaper editorial, rock lyrics, a magazine ad, or a conversation with a friend. Each of these "communication situations" is normally responded to in a different fashion; that is, the biology text is accepted differently from the magazine ad. Too often, however, this same "communication" sophistication is not transferred to the reading of the Bible.[5] By having the reader carefully cover small, but crucial, passages, I hope to be able to sensitize the reader to the biblical author's clues for how a particular passage functions. I have found that students do not come to such a course already possessing this attention to critical details.

I shall, of course, relate these small key passages to broader issues in the Bible so that the student acquires the broad appreciation of the Hebrew Bible expected from an introductory textbook.

4.   Together, these first several criteria mean that such a textbook can cover only a few passages from the Hebrew Bible, which must be chosen because they represent either major movements or literary genres in the Bible as a whole.

5.   This textbook focuses on the Bible's *literary dimension*. (In more critical language, the methodology used in this text is heavily influenced by current biblical literary or rhetorical criticism.) This choice has been made for several reasons.

First of all, a literary approach to the Bible can claim a certain priority over the more historical or religious approaches, for much of what we know about the history of the biblical period is derived from the Bible itself. But before we can mine the Bible as a quarry for historical reconstruction, we first must assess the nature and reliability of our records, and that is a *literary* judgment based on the type (or genre) of literature we are reading (for example, court records, short story, satire, myth, etc.).

Also, as we shall see in Chapter 1, before the Bible can ever be appreciated as *religious* literature, it must first be read with consideration for its *literary* dimension. Some may see the Bible as a divine communication; but it certainly is clothed in human language,[6] and thus conveys its meaning similarly to other examples of human language. And so, even for the believer, the literary dimension assumes a certain priority. For only in reading the text with sensitivity to such literary features as style, structure, and genre can the religious dimension fully emerge. Nevertheless, students should appreciate the fact that no matter what their own religious stance might be, the Bible really is *religious* literature; that is, it is totally taken up with a people's relationship with its God.

---

[5] Because of this need for the reader to reflect on all the different functions of communication in order to read the Bible with perception, I have begun this text with a chapter on the various processes and functions involved in all communication. As you will quickly appreciate, this description is hardly exhaustive, but it does seek to expand the student's sensitivity to the broad spectrum of written communication encountered in the Bible.

[6] That is, even if the Bible is accepted as the "Word of God," it still has all the characteristics of *human* speech: grammar, syntax, the structure of the story, plot, character development, poetry, etc. To understand this word of God, the reader would first of all have to comprehend Hebrew grammar (or the language of the particular translation being used), have an adequate vocabulary, etc.

This focus on the literary, however, does not exclude consideration of the historical and comparative dimensions. Throughout this text, passages will be related to different historical situations from which they might have emerged. They will also be related to similar literatures elsewhere in the Near East, especially Mesopotamia. In general, I shall defer historical information until after the literary study of a biblical text; in this way I hope to raise the importance of historical concerns in the student's mind so that the later examination of ancient history will be seen as essential and clearly relevant.

6. The approach used by this book is *inductive*. Because it is important that the beginning student primarily reads the Bible itself and not the secondary thinking of scholars, this text uses detailed questions to guide the reader through a *close reading* of the biblical passages. Even when unsure about answers, students should try to write responses to all the questions. This forces students to notice many subtle features of the passage, even when uncertain about how to interpret them.

First off, some observations about the questions themselves. Students quickly realize that two main types of questions are used in the classroom. The first type is the "real" question, the inquiry that prompts students freely to mull over an issue without precharting where they should go. The second type of question is best termed the "Guess what *I*'m (that is, the teacher) thinking?" question. In this latter case, the question really serves to guide the student in fairly specific directions predetermined by the teacher. In this book I have tried to chart a path between these two types of questions. The questions in this text should suggest new ways of looking at the biblical text and open the student up to entirely different paths of inquiry (Question Type One); however, many of the questions, quite frankly, guide the student in a specific direction determined by the author ("Guess what I'm thinking" questions). In other words, a particular reading of the biblical passage has influenced the very formulation of the questions. The results of this type of inquiry become the bases for many of the observations in the chapters that follow. Still, even these questions should focus students' attention on important features of the text that will occasion altogether new questions on the part of students. Furthermore, even here, students should feel utterly free to depart from the direction the questions are leading them and to strike out on their own. Remember: The interpretations of the biblical text found in this book depend totally on their persuasiveness and clarity. (Indeed, many scholars would disagree on some of the issues presented here, as references in the Further Readings will make clear.) If the reader finds these interpretations unconvincing, then he or she should feel free to use the literary features of a passage to develop one's own structures and interpretations. Just be sure that the student can verbalize in the spaces provided in this book the reasons for such deviation. If students acquire the skills to strike out on their own, to isolate relevant literary features, to arrange them into a coherent pattern, and to verbalize their proposals, then this book will have been most successful.

There should be no anxiety about writing answers directly into the book. First of all, the questions *are* challenging (read *difficult*). Many of them introduce the student to different and unfamiliar ways of looking at a text. Most readers are new to the close, detailed reading of passages expected by the questions. But even if the reader has difficulty responding to the questions, the questions still will have served their vital role in highlighting important features in the biblical text. Secondly, one of the features of great literature is its inherent ambiguity. No one can define the *exact and only meaning* of a piece of writing (poem, novel, play) with the same certitude as a chemist can perform a laboratory analysis. The reading of each passage results in different meanings depending on the background and questions that the reader brings to this complex encounter. Although this does not mean that a passage can mean absolutely anything, it does allow for a great variety of responses to any of the questions contained in this book. Even when answers differ, the process of responding to all the questions does slow down the student and force a close reading of the text.

I generally follow each "inductive" chapter with a chapter that ties together all of the students' answers. Such chapters will also show what hypotheses different biblical scholars have formed using the same data. These "tie-in" chapters also function to relate the small biblical text to broader issues; for example, they will sketch the historical context in which a passage was written and will relate the text to broader religious and literary movements within the Hebrew Bible. This latter function acquires importance, for this text purports to be an independent, adequate introduction to the Hebrew Bible as a whole; therefore the student's reading of small passages has to be tied to larger portions of the Bible.

7.   There is considerably more material here than can usually be covered in an introductory course to the Hebrew Bible/Old Testament. Thus, the instructor should feel free to choose various sections as he or she wishes. However, the first four chapters are particularly important because they cover methodology, biblical history, and some of the dominant religious themes of the Hebrew Bible. If students understand these chapters well, then they should be equipped with the main tools for an independent reading of the rest of the Bible (and of this textbook).

8.   At the beginning of each chapter is a statement of Goals and Objectives, which will state what I intend to accomplish in that particular chapter. This should keep the broader picture before the reader's eyes as he or she becomes involved in smaller textual details. Most chapters will also contain a list of Further Readings, which will either expand on ideas found in that chapter or present different scholarly positions. Most of these references are suitable to the average college student. However, these readings are not meant to be comprehensive. Rather, they seek especially to introduce the student to material that will not only expose students to broader ideas and opinions but also introduce them to a more comprehensive bibliography. There are, however, two standard works that should be readily available to all students: *The Interpreter's Dictionary of the Bible*, 4 vols. and supplement (Nashville, Tenn.: Abingdon, 1962–1976); and Y. Aharoni and M. Avi-Yonah, *The Macmillan Bible Atlas* (London: The Macmillan Co., 1968).[7] The *Interpreter's Dictionary* contains articles on such topics as the various criticisms, biblical fauna and flora, individual books of the Bible, or on such documentary sources as the Elohist. Each entry has been written by an expert on that topic and includes a bibliography. The *Macmillan Bible Atlas* contains excellent maps and text detailing such subjects as the political divisions of the Near East, Israelite tribal distributions at various periods, battles, etc.

[7] This textbook uses as its Bible the Revised Standard Version (RSV), of which there are many outstanding student editions complete with notes and maps. Although many other Bible translations exist, the RSV has the advantage of being fairly literal in its representation of the ancient texts. Obviously, more literal translations are necessary for our type of study. Paraphrase translations may cause the student difficulties in following the biblical passages discussed in this text.

Throughout this text I have been caught in a dilemma. On the one hand, I have the obligation to acquaint the reader responsibly with the status of various academic debates (for example, theories for the conquest of Palestine and for the development of the Pentateuch) and about the extent of disagreement of these theories. At the same time, I feel that a *beginning* text cannot become a listing of rival positions on every single issue, which can overpower the student. I hope, therefore, that the practical bibliography at the end of chapters will help achieve this delicate balance.

WHY THESE BIBLICAL PASSAGES?

Because this text deals with so few biblical passages (and in such detail), I feel that I should comment thus: Why these particular selections? How do they relate to the Hebrew Bible as a whole? In general, I have tried to select readings from all three divisions of the Hebrew Bible (*Pentateuch/Torah, Prophets,* and the *Writings*). Secondly, I have tried to incorporate representatives of many of the various literary forms or genres—prose and poetry—found within the Hebrew Bible: myth, saga, law, hymns, prophetic oracles, laments, proverbs, short story, etc. Thirdly, I hope the passages chosen portray the major theological movements within the Hebrew Bible as a whole.[8]

Genesis, Chapters 1-11

For the treatment of the Pentateuch I focus on Genesis, Chapters 1-11. These chapters were probably intended by their later editor as an introduction or preface to the entire first five or six books of the Bible. They serve to present both the major thesis of that editor and the theological perspective according to which the editor details the origins of Israel and the occupation of the promised land of Canaan. So if the student can understand these important chapters, then the heart of the Hebrew Bible, the Pentateuch, becomes intelligible.

These 11 chapters are also important because they are currently so often in the news. The debate between creationism and evolution hinges on how these crucial chapters of Genesis are read. These chapters then can readily provide the foundation for a careful reading of the Hebrew Bible with sensitivity to its various literary styles and genres.

Chapters 1-11 of Genesis were composed over centuries and represent the constant adaptation of the story of Israel's religious origins throughout trials and setbacks. By tracing the development of the final biblical text of Genesis 1-11 from its oral recitals to its final editing, we can mark the major movements within biblical history. (This process is called the *History of Traditions.*)

The Book of the Covenant (Exodus 20:22—23:33)

Israel perceived its relationship to God as governed by a *covenant,* a legally binding contract. This covenant made by Moses on Mount Sinai carried with it stipulations that obligated the people of Israel. If they were to maintain their relationship to

---

[8] Perhaps the major movement *not* represented here is the *apocalyptic,* such as found in Isaiah 24-27 and the Book of Daniel.

God, they must be faithful to their obligations. And so the concept of law plays an important role in the Hebrew Bible. This selection from Exodus illustrates the Israelite religious thinking on law and covenant[9] and also introduces the important role in the Hebrew Bible of Moses, the Lawgiver.

These passages from Exodus also demonstrate Israel's relationship with its cultural environment, for the Code of the Covenant is a literary amalgam of legislation borrowed from the legal tradition of the ancient Near East and of laws derived from Israel's own religious consciousness of a covenant with her God. The study of Exodus 20:22–23:33 reveals the adaptation of foreign material to a different religious setting. This section also guides the student through the use of the important critical tools of *form* and *redaction* **criticisms**.

The Prophets: Deuteronomy, 1 Kings 17-19, Amos

Selections from the Book of Deuteronomy link the Pentateuch with the second division in the Hebrew Bible, namely, the Prophets. Deuteronomy 18:9–22 represents a classical understanding of Israelite prophecy from a movement for which prophecy was a central institution that continued and actualized generation after generation the religious authority of Moses. This selection is from a section of that seventh-century B.C.E. (before the common era) book, which defines all of the major institutions of Israel's ideal theocracy: judge, priest, prophet, and king. However, Deuteronomy 34:10-12 seems to sound a counterpoint; this passage reveals another reflection on the status and authority of the prophet and seeks to diminish the prophet's status in relationship to Moses, who thereby was considered a unique religious figure.

The saga about the northern prophet Elijah (1 Kings 17–19) portrays this ninth-century B.C.E. prophet as the prophetic ideal who guarantees the orthodoxy of Mosaic religion and the Sinai Covenant against the deviations of King Ahab and his Canaanite wife, Jezebel. This story exploits the link between the theology of covenant and the role of the prophet. And so in the story about Elijah we actually find an important biblical statement about the nature of prophecy (at least according to the theology prevalent in the north).

Questions about the Book of Amos move the reader from consideration of the prophet as an individual (Elijah) to the prophetic *book*. Amos was chosen both because it represents the first written work attributed to a prophet (about a century after Elijah) and because it is of manageable length. The Book of Amos also illustrates an important fact about the 15[10] biblical books attributed by name to prophets. The canonical prophetic books as we now have them represent the end of a long editorial process, usually lasting three to four centuries. The process began with the oracles of an Amos, but then generations of believers adapted these authoritative words to ever-new situations. The study of Amos attempts to guide the student through at least three of these major redactional (editing) stages and to focus upon the religious crises that spawned these editorial activities and the "updatings" of Amos' original words.

---

[9] This thinking forms the basis for the legal accusations leveled by the prophets against Israel.

[10] This number includes the *major prophets* Isaiah, Jeremiah, and Ezekiel and the 12 *minor prophets*, among which we find the Book of Amos.

The Psalms

This section of the textbook, which begins the treatment of the third major division of the Hebrew Bible—the Writings—studies some of the major types of Psalms found in the Psalter: the individual lament and thanksgiving psalm, the Zion hymns, and the royal hymns. These poems, or psalms, are placed in the context of Israel's temple worship. The treatment of the Psalter also exercises the student in the critical tool of *form criticism.*

Wisdom Literature: Proverbs and Qoheleth

This chapter of the text introduces the student to the wisdom movement within Israel, which is represented by two very different literary genres. The Book of Proverbs portrays a world ordered and harmonious from its creation. The "skillful person" (that is, the "wise" person) survives and prospers in such a world by participating in and controlling its order and predictability. Such an individual acquires the good "life." The Book of Qoheleth (also called Ecclesiastes), on the other hand, describes a far less optimistic universe. Here chance, fate, and unpredictability seem to preclude human control and exploitation. In the absence of power to manipulate the environment, the author of the Book of Qoheleth recommends enjoyment of the present moment, which God has given as a gift.

The Short Story: Esther, Ruth, and Judith

These writings illustrate the appearance of a different literary genre, namely, the short story. Curiously, these three stories involve women who come to power when men prove inadequate. The books demonstrate religious developments appropriate for the survival of an Israel that had lost all political control: In apparent weakness there can be strength.

CHAPTER 1
INTRODUCTION TO READING THE HEBREW BIBLE

GOALS OF THE BOOK

This book is intended as an introduction to the Hebrew Bible/Old Testament (OT). It presupposes no specific historical or religious background for the student other than the abilities to read, question, and wonder about one of the masterpieces of religious literature. This book avoids replacing the student's direct contact with the biblical text; rather, its goal is to develop each student's own literary sensitivities by having the student isolate many of the principal literary features of representative Hebrew Bible passages and by helping the student formulate theories about the meaning(s) of those texts. It is hoped that the end result of this approach will be that the student acquires a methodology for a sensitive reading of the remainder of the Hebrew Bible.

Reading the Bible Itself

First of all, the workbook approach is designed to place you in direct contact with the biblical text itself. All too often introductions to the Bible deluge readers with information about the creation and history of the text, the literature and history of the ancient Near East, and with an encyclopedic array of data about each biblical book. This approach is better suited for a reference work than for a true introduction. The sheer quantity of reading makes it thoroughly impossible for a student to read such a textbook along with any significant amount of material from the Bible itself. Furthermore, the avalanche of unfamiliar and strange-sounding people and places from distant times makes the Bible seem even more remote than when students first handed in their course cards.

Rather than talking *about* the Bible, this book directly guides the reader through the text itself. Only indirectly will the opinions of scholars intrude into the text—and then only after you have formed your own ideas about the meaning(s) and origins of passages.

This approach consciously addresses what I have long felt is a major difficulty experienced by students. Students resist the detailed and careful reading that many texts seem to require. Although students prefer only the most general *ideas* found in great literary works, this minimal approach can rarely help students acquire a sense of how meaning is conveyed and condemns students to total dependence on meanings distilled through others.

All too often students are ill-prepared to read a biblical passage as carefully and closely as this textbook requires. It will not be enough to know that Genesis 2, 3 is about Adam and Eve, a tree, and a talking snake. You will be expected to look at the words for nuances and hints of meaning, for repetitions, and for inconsistencies as carefully as a contract negotiator studies an opponent's every word and gesture. The key phrase here is *close reading.*

When the textbook suggests several readings of a passage, this is certainly optimal. (Although my experience certainly teaches me that shortcuts will be attempted; however, *one* reading will rarely be adequate.) The first time through a text, you should read it all at once and fairly quickly. Your limited goal is to get a rough idea about the topic of a passage. The second time through, read the text carefully, underlining and marking your Bibles. Only at this reading will you bring to the Bible the questions asked in this book. Your third time through ties together any loose ends while double-checking to see if any theories that you have developed about the meaning of the text actually fit. This last reading is fairly swift. If you suspect that this request for three readings is an extravagance that might easily be dispensed with, then wait until you see the questions. The purpose here is not to overburden you, but to sensitize you to the text itself and to how it works.

The Inductive Approach

Because this book is a *work*book, you cannot approach the Bible passively nor can you use this book as a reference tool. The exercises must be worked through. Even if you are hesitant about the quality of your answer, it is essential that you attempt to reply to each question in writing. Please make your responses *clear* (complete sentences generally) and *specific* (that is, always refer to those specific parts of the biblical text—chapter and verse—that support your answer; no generalities, please). If you are not sure what the question is asking, then begin your response by rephrasing the question *as you understand it*; then proceed to answer your reformulation. Perhaps it would be best to use pencil so that you can return later to enhance or correct earlier answers. In my experience using this book, I have found that students should work in groups on the questions; this procedure helps students acquire confidence in their own reading of the passage.

In many cases there would seem to be several answers that are equally possible. This does not necessarily reveal a vagueness in the question asked; rather, it illustrates the nature of literature. For is there only *one* single meaning to a poem or short story? You have seen ads for perfumes that are "unique" because they supposedly react with an individual's body chemistry to produce a unique scent. Well, literature is similar. The reader always brings unique experiences and questions to whatever he or she is reading; and so the communication ("the meaning") that occurs between reader and literary work has to be individualized.

We have either forgotten the essential role that the reader/listener plays in all human communication (literature or speech) or else we have diminished it as totally passive. However, the experiences and interests of the reader play an active part. The questions and concerns that the reader brings to a literary work, or even the total lack of interest—"It's only an assignment!"—determine the reading process as much as the creativity of the writer. If we want to be mathematical about it, then *M*eaning results from the interaction of a *R*eader with the ideas of a *W*riter communicated either through the written or spoken word ($M = R + W$). The implication of this is that the text cannot insist that you derive a single, predictable meaning from your own interaction with a text.

Now all this emphasis on the individual reader does not suggest that anything goes, that any meaning that the reader suggests is allowable. (The perfume cited in the example above could hardly be expected to react with an individual to generate *any* scent whatsoever.) In both cases, there are clear boundaries of meanings (and scents) to be expected. Anything outside these boundaries is recognized as bizarre. Although we all might react differently to reading a Shakespearean sonnet, we would wonder about anyone who stretched this subjectivism to the point of finding within the sonnet an Elizabethan recipe for brownies. The only test for anyone's interpretation, including those in this textbook, must remain the text itself—in this case the Bible: Does my reading agree with all the features of the text? If my understanding cannot account for certain features of the text, then I should try to formulate a more comprehensive interpretation.

As you work further through this book you will be tempted to return and change earlier ideas and answers. This is to be expected. Literature and literary study are cases of trial and error. Often you will posit an hypothesis to explain the text read up to that point only to read further and discover a more comprehensive theory. The best litmus test for any theory about what the text means is: *Does it explain all the text? Does the hypothesis explain and render purposeful all of the sections, even such seemingly useless passages as genealogies ("So and so begat so and so"), contradictions, and repetitions?* But more about this later.

In most cases a chapter containing questions will be followed by a chapter explaining and tying together the preceding exercises: (1) It will discuss the significance of the data that you yourself have already uncovered; (2) it will place your theories in the context of what other scholars have discovered (in most cases you will be gratified—or disturbed—to know that most of your ideas have been anticipated); (3) this explanatory chapter will also present information that is not easily taught by the more inductive approach, such as the ancient Near Eastern background of the passage or historical issues of authorship, etc. (This latter type of background information is studied by *historical-cultural criticism*.) In the more traditional introductions, the student encounters these issues *before* they can be assimilated or *before* their relevance has been established: The effect of this best resembles drowning. In this book, however, it is hoped that such information, which, after all, is external to the text, will only be presented *after* the student has already become aware of its helpfulness; (4) this explanatory chapter will also place the passages that you have previously studied in the broader context of the Hebrew Bible/ Old Testament. This textbook has carefully chosen passages representative of the entire Hebrew Bible; and in this "orientation" chapter you will see how the text you have labored over ties in with more extensive biblical sections. In this way, even though you will only study a few texts carefully, you will still acquire a familiarity with the entire Hebrew Bible.

A Methodology to Be Mastered

The approach outlined thus far serves yet another purpose: to give the student a sense of *how* to read the text. Obviously the entire Bible cannot be read in a one-semester course. Hence, the purpose of this book is at least to communicate the skills (methods) necessary for an intelligent reading of all portions of the Bible.[1] Thus, you will read sections that represent or introduce the major sections of the Hebrew Bible. For example, in the chapter on Genesis 1–11, you will see how a close reading of these 11 biblical chapters introduces you to the major motifs and themes of the entire Pentateuch, Torah, or first five books of the Hebrew Bible. This is important for these five books are the heart of the Hebrew Bible, which is divided into the three parts: the Torah (Pentateuch), the Prophets, and the Writings. You will also be exposed to almost all the major literary types (genres) in the Bible (for example, different types of poetry, historical writing, wisdom, and legal texts).

Because these methods of close reading are hardly unique to the Bible, most of these skills will readily be applicable to other areas in which you, the student, ask: What does that text mean?

As you learn such tools as source, literary, and form criticisms by actually using them, you will experience both their strengths and their weaknesses. It is the author's hope that the approach adopted here will not only strengthen your natural confidence in your abilities to work with the Bible but also equip you to evaluate critically the work of others no matter what their academic credentials.

Problems in Teaching the Bible

There are some obvious difficulties about introducing students to the Bible—few people have a neutral attitude about the subject matter. To some the Bible is God's very word; to others, it is merely a curious instance of an ancient religious text. The emotional attitudes about the Bible range all the way from total commitment in faith to hostile suspicion. The combination of such a broad spectrum of views about the nature of the Bible coupled with so much emotional involvement on the part of almost all students would seem to preclude the possibility of writing an introduction for the broad cross section of students this book envisions. How can a book address the interests of students with such diverse motivations? Some are interested in the Bible because of deep religious sentiment; others perhaps only because of its import in either the history of religion or in Western literature.

The answer to this dilemma involves finding a common ground: No matter what attitudes about the Hebrew Scriptures that you bring to this book, there remains the common denominator that the Bible is scripture, that is, it is *writing*. Whether it is God's own word or only regarded as the religious heritage of an ancient people, the basic fact remains that here we encounter human writing. I use the word "human" here not in any minimalist or derogatory sense that would preclude an interpretation based on divine inspiration; rather, human here means that no matter what the ultimate origin claimed for the Bible, it is similar, at least in respect to language, to other *human* written communication. That is, the books that comprise the Bible communicate using words grouped into sentences governed by rules of syntax; they conform to common literary genres such as lyric poetry, narrative, genealogies, etc. The Bible, as well as other literature, employs standard literary devices such as puns, repetition, references to other stories, ring structure (more about this later), step patterns ("on the first day . . . on the second . . . but on the third day . . .").

This common ground provides the basis for this textbook. Even if you main-

---

[1] These methods are often called "criticisms" by scholars; for example, literary criticism, historical criticism, source criticism, etc. Perhaps a better term would be *critical tools*.

tain that the Book of Genesis conveys a supernatural message from God, *because it is writing* it still must conform to the nature of that human vehicle of communication—writing. Consequently, we may legitimately ask, what does it mean? How does it mean? These two questions are basically *literary* questions. It is hoped that the literary approach adopted by this textbook will not be perceived as a threat to any student's view about further levels of meaning that he or she might attribute to the Bible.

No one, not even a militant atheist, could deny that the Hebrew Bible is a collection of religious literature. No matter what attitude(s) you might bring to your study of the Bible, it still contains inescapably religious writings. This book in no way seeks to diminish that fact; it merely seeks to discover what that message is and how it is conveyed. What *personal* stance a student might take regarding that message is clearly beyond the intent of this text.

I propose to develop this literary analysis first of all by talking about some of the rudiments of the *nature* and *purpose* of all human communication, whether oral, written, or by sign language. The purpose of this is to highlight some aspects about literature that—though at times self-evident—are too often neglected when people come to read the Scriptures. Second, I would like to outline some of the methods ("criticisms" or "critical tools") that are used by scholars (called *exegetes*) when they study this particular literature. Most of these criticisms flow naturally from the very nature of communication. In the next chapter we shall be more concrete and shall apply these principles to actual texts: first to a so-called secular passage and then to a biblical selection.

THE NATURE OF HUMAN COMMUNICATION

The Process of Human Communication

There is another way of approaching a literary study of the Hebrew Bible. Let us look for a moment at the structure of human communication. A quick overview of the nature and functions of communication will reinforce the importance of a "literary sensitivity" for an adequate reading of the Bible no matter what your religious background is. I should stress that the short lesson in communication that follows, which has been derived from that of Roman Jakobson's communication model, is hardly all-encompassing. Its purpose is to expose the reader to the complexity of human communication and to the myriad uses to which we put it. I hope that this exposure will better prepare readers of the Bible to notice the different purposes or functions for which a biblical passage might have been written. Communication is more involved than just taking a text at "face value."

Although much of this is really quite obvious, it will be helpful to stop and diagram both the **processes of communication** involved when humans communicate and some of the different *functions and uses* of language so that we can apply these observations to our study of the Bible.

In every exchange between people there will be a speaker (*addresser*);[2] the person spoken to (*addressee*); the actual physical vehicle used in the communication, whether written or oral (*means*); and, lastly, the thing talked about (*referent*).

---

[2] I will present this diagram using terminology from the most rudimentary communication act: *speech*. The terminology can easily be switched when it is applied to writing, which is a secondary act; for example, writer, reader, text, etc.

Process of Communication

Referent

Addresser ———————————————————————— Addressee

Means

It is virtually impossible to imagine any communication that does not contain all these elements. Even an Indian smoke signal has an addresser, the intended addressee, the physical means of exchange (smoke puffs), and a referent ("The bison are coming"). Even when a person talks to oneself, the components are still there, even though now the addresser and addressee are one and the same. The hand signs used to communicate with the deaf display all these elements; only the means of communication differ.

The Functions of Human Communication

Clearly, however, not all communication serves the same purpose. Sometimes we speak to share our emotions; at other times we want to discuss the news of the day; there are occasions when we try to influence the opinions and actions of the listener. We can understand the different **functions of human communication** by looking at the figure above titled "Process of Communication." Whenever we communicate we tend to emphasize one of the four elements over the others. For example, if the conversation stresses the speaker, we call that **emotive** language; this type of exchange often—but not invariably—focuses on the first grammatical person "I" and is primarily interested in revealing the status of the speaker: "*I* really feel terrible" or "*I'm* excited about . . . ." I say "not invariably" because sometimes the speaker has purposefully disguised emotive speech. For example, when the speaker says, "This weather is much too hot and humid," the speaker is really suggesting the speaker's own discomfort.[3]

Should conversation, however, focus on the addressee (the person spoken to), then we have *persuasive* (**conative**) speech. This type of communication frequently uses the second grammatical person "you." We encounter examples of this type of exchange every time we sit through an advertisement on television or listen to a political speech. Persuasive speech tries to affect the addressee; it can also appear in the format of a direct command (the imperative): "Close the door!" or "Listen to me!" Once again, as you are already quite aware from advertising, this can also appear disguised without a specific "you": For example, "Any intelligent person would buy this product."

Referential communication mainly talks about things. Into this category fall most textbooks, user manuals, etc. When you read a guide to a computer language such as BASIC, you are solely concerned with the programming being talked about and are not concerned about the health or well-being of the author. Nor would you consider a lot of persuasive rhetoric to be appropriate.

---

[3] "Emotive" is not the same as "emotional," which means "markedly aroused or agitated in feeling or sensibilities" (Webster's *Ninth New Collegiate Dictionary*). All of the functions could be "emotional"; for example, a referential description of the plight of the peoples bordering the Sahara desert could be "emotional." Also, an emotive statement may not really be "emotional," that is, "aroused or agitated."

Can you think of a type of communication that would focus our attention on the *means,* on the shape or sound of the words themselves? This is actually the function of *poetry*. Poetry calls attention to the sound and flavor of the words by such devices as alliteration, assonance, rhyme, meter, etc. In no other type of exchange do we become so conscious of the actual means itself. A comparison can be made between a McDonald's hamburger and a gourmet dinner. In the latter we actually savor what we are eating; we don't just eat to sustain ourselves; the food itself becomes an object of attention. In a real sense, anything that calls attention to the physical means of exchange, whether it be the gestures of a mime or Indian smoke signals, constitutes poetry.

If we continue our diagram, which we began above, then we can structure language according to *function* as follows:

Functions of Communication

Referential

Emotive ——————————————————————————— Conative

Poetry

As you can already sense, different circumstances call for appropriate types of speech whether it be emotive, conative, referential, or poetic. It is very important that we be able to distinguish which function is being used and to expect only what is appropriate for each type of communication. To put it more simply, when someone yells to you, "You're full of it!," this is probably neither referential nor conative speech but emotive, and it suggests that the speaker is angry. When we quickly distinguish this statement from the more obviously referential "This cup is full of milk" (although the two sentences are structurally similar), we are showing that we think it important in our day-to-day living to distinguish such speech functions. You should realize, however, that in day-to-day speech these functions are often intricately intermixed, so that actual communication is rarely cut-and-dried.

Truth in Literature

How a communication is intended to function will be important for the question, Is it true? We can apply criteria or rules for truth most obviously in cases of referential speech. For example: Is this my telephone number or not? There are clear ways to decide that question. But when we attempt to judge emotive speech, matters become more complex. If I say that I have a headache, there are medical tests to determine the truth of that assertion. When an addresser states that he or she is depressed, then we have even more difficulty in determining whether that emotive statement is true. The ways we decide that are different from those used to validate my telephone number. When we ask whether an instance of conative speech is true, what exactly are we asking? "Please, close the door!" True or false? Do we mean, has it *effectively* changed the addressee's mind or determined his or her activities?

I have mentioned all this because one of the most frequent questions asked of the Bible is, Is it true? Is what the Bible says here or there true? (I can already sense many readers getting nervous.) But a little reflection should tell us that the question about truth is applied quite differently to the various functions of speech.

It is applied most obviously to referential literature and less clearly to poetry. ("Is this Shakespearean sonnet true or not?") Let's apply this question to *Gulliver's Travels.* Is this work by Jonathan Swift true? If you mistakenly interpret its function as referential ("Swift thinks that there really are such lands and places"), then you answer "It's false." But if you correctly perceive that the novel is a satire that tries to convince the reader (conative) of the absurdity of many contemporary social and religious customs, then you can answer, "Yes, it's a true study of contemporary customs and foibles."

Disguised Functions

An endless variety of literature can be fashioned simply by playing with these functions or by combining them. For example, many times a speaker/writer might wish to camouflage his or her intent by clothing speech (or writing) in the guise of another function. Thus, satire frequently is achieved precisely by attributing absurd positions to fictional characters—positions that are so outrageous that the addressee/listener reacts by adopting the stance that the real speaker already intended from the beginning. Satire, then, seen in this light can be analyzed as a type of conative literature in that it often seeks to convince others (the "you") of an argument that "you" might otherwise shy away from were it proposed more directly. You will see this more clearly when you have studied "A Modest Proposal" in the next chapter.

Can you give other examples of similar plays on speech functions or disguised speech? (These are cases in which the addresser tries to disguise the real *function* of his or her speech.) Write down at least two examples, and then explain why a speaker might resort to such games:

Is this difficult? Then let's work backwards. Describe a situation in which speech that appears to be emotive or that talks about the speaker/writer is in reality conative or an attempt to move and influence the reader/listener. What would be the purpose in such a communication deception?

Using your newly acquired acquaintance with communication functions, explain how love poetry works. What functions does it combine?

Codes

How can we tell how a speaker wishes to be taken? What are some of the devices we use in conversation to help the listener understand our real intent? We communicate our real (but perhaps disguised) purpose by the choice of a word, a voice inflection, or by such body language as a wink or shrug. We call these clues to meaning **codes**. All communication includes codes, which tell the listener/reader how the addressee wishes to be understood. Sometimes even a social setting could function as a code in that it suggests how we wish to be understood. Thus, the university classroom situation (a code) suggests that the teacher's speech is mainly referential.

Let's use the example in the paragraph above. How might a satirist suggest to the reader that he or she is writing satire and not referential speech? In other words, what codes might the writer use when the distance between the reader and writer precludes body language or voice inflection used so often by speakers and listeners? List a few examples of these literary codes for satire:

I know what you're thinking: "We seemed to have diverted from our main path. How does all this fit in with an introduction to the Hebrew Bible?" To answer quite simply, What is the literary function of Genesis 1 (the Creation story)? Is it referential, that is, does it tell about the factual origin of the cosmos *or* is it cona- tive, that is, is the main purpose of this chapter to convince the reader to adopt a certain position or belief? If you don't think this distinction is important, then you have been missing the endless debates between the creationists and the evolutionists. Whenever we ask whether a passage in the Hebrew Bible is true or not, we need first to make the necessary literary determinations; for as you recall, the question of truth is asked differently of the various functions of language.

In summary, if it is legitimate to read the Bible as human literature, then it is also important that we bring to that task all of the sensitivity that we accept as necessary for understanding all other human communication and that we acknowl- edge many of the distinctions discussed above. If we misunderstand what a biblical passage intends, if we miss its speech function and take a passage as referential or factual when it is not really so intended, then we are missing the meaning of the Bible. Too much of the Bible is wrongly classified as referential, almost as if the Bible were a textbook. The Bible actually runs the entire gamut of literature: poetry (lyric and narrative), history, narrative, myth, saga, satire, etc. When we ignore these distinctions we risk misunderstanding the text—whether we claim that it is God who ultimately speaks or only an ancient Israelite. Often our results are as ludicrous as if we read Swift's *Gulliver's Travels* as a true-life travel adventure. As long as the reader is in quest of the Bible's *meaning,* then he or she must begin with literary considerations; and this is true whether the reader is a fundamentalist believer or an avowed atheist.

WAYS WE READ THE BIBLE: THE CRITICAL TOOLS

Let's look for a moment at how we look at the Bible from the viewpoint of literature, at how we apply our sketchy knowledge of the process and function of communication.

Literary and Rhetorical Criticism

When we analyze a biblical passage and ask how it functions as a literary piece and what devices (repetition, inclusion, puns, etc.) it uses in order to convey its meaning(s), we are using what scholars call **literary** or **rhetorical criticism**.[4] This approach is clearly the focus of this workbook.

Because this is a college-level course, we are not simply interested in what we think (intuition) a passage means but in learning ways or skills by which we can actually see *how* such meaning is effected.

Literature is in many ways like painting or architecture: What the artist communicates by means of paint, the writer conveys with words. Because both artist and writer have the disadvantage of being absent when their works are appreciated by the viewer or reader, they have to plant various devices within their works in order to guide readers or viewers in their appreciation and understanding of what the artist or writer intended. Please study carefully the two works by Pablo Picasso that are contained in this section of the chapter (*Mother and Child* and *Guernica*). The questions that follow are designed to help the student relate the organization and structure of the paintings to what the two convey (meaning).

Mother and Child

[4] I use "literary" and "rhetorical" interchangeably. Several years back, biblical scholars used (or misused) the phrase "literary criticism" to refer to what I call here *source criticism.* However, throughout this book—indeed, throughout most modern books—"literary criticism" refers to a study of a passage from its perspective as literature.

1.   Structure refers to the arrangement and placement of the various devices used in a painting (or in a story, film, music, statue, photograph, etc.). For example, a painter could use such devices as choice of colors, texture of paint, placement of figures, size and shape of canvas, choice of paints (oil, pastels, watercolor, etc.). The actual devices being organized or structured will vary from work to work. What are some of the devices Picasso uses in the two works found here?

2.   In the drawing *Mother and Child,* where does the artist direct your eye?

Relate the position of the child in relation to the mother's body to the artist's purpose. Where are both subjects positioned in the painting? What type of a geometrical shape do the two subjects make? Where does this shape focus your attention? Explain your answer.

Guernica

3.   Now look at *Guernica,* a painting that depicts the suffering of the inhabitants of Guernica following a savage bombing of the town during the Spanish Civil War. Where does the artist direct your eye?

Let's look at the "geometry" of the painting; what geometrical shape(s) dominate the picture? Trace them with a pencil on the picture. Relate this to what you think the artist is communicating.

On the lower left there is a mother and child. How does the position of the two figures relate to the overall meaning of the work?

Notice the position of the child in relation to its mother's body. Compare this to the child's position in the other painting. Relate any differences to both paintings as a whole.

4.   Now list some concrete ways how a painter can use organization and structure in a work to manipulate your attention and to convey meaning.

Let's try one more example of the interplay among (1) devices that focus or direct attention, (2) the arrangement or structuring of these devices, and (3) the meaning conveyed by this structure. Imagine that you are a movie director and are filming a meeting of a man and a woman on the street. Name some of the devices ("tricks of the trade") that a film director might use.

List below five different ways by which this meeting of a man and a woman on the street might be filmed, describing camera angle, distance of camera from the subjects, lighting, etc. To the right of these describe what meaning or attitude each of these techniques (ordering of devices) conveys.

CAMERA TECHNIQUE   MEANING

1.

2.

3.

4.

5.

Now let us return to our original analogy. List below some ways (at least five) by which a *writer* can guide the attention of the reader. (These are the devices that tell us how a writing functions, how it is to be understood.) Then show how each of these five techniques might be used to express a meaning.

WRITING TECHNIQUES   MEANING

1.

2.

3.

4.

5.

When we try to isolate the patterns or structure in a biblical passage, when we analyze how its parts have been assembled, and when we relate this organization to meaning, then we are using rhetorical or literary criticism. Remember, when we read a biblical passage that was written thousands of years ago, such patterns are our main clues to what the literature means.

One of the first things that we have to do before describing the structure of a passage is to be sure that we are working with a self-contained unit, that we have a natural unit. The pattern isolated will obviously depend on how much of the text we bracket off for study. For example, the pattern of Genesis 1 might be different from Genesis 1-11; Genesis 1-11 from the entire Pentateuch; the entire Pentateuch from the overall pattern of the Hebrew Bible—if such be found. The biblical author frequently brackets off such segments using the device of *inclusion,* by which a segment begins with the same words or phrase with which it ends (see Amos 5:4–14). Inclusion then serves the same purpose in an oral society as paragraphing does in our print-oriented world and can be used as a clue to a basic unit. Inclusion will be used to separate what amounts to small paragraphs or even entire books. This device serves the same function as the frame does in a picture: It directs our attention to what is enclosed within its borders.

Form and Historical-Cultural Criticisms[5]

Besides all of the characteristics of language discussed above, it is clear that all communication takes place in a broader context. For example, there are *social dimensions*; that is, communication corresponds to social expectations ranging from a common language to certain speech patterns appropriate to set social situations. No speaker is able to talk using his or her own invented language; the speaker uses a known language (German, Russian, Chinese, Swahili) in common with the listener. Language is thus a social construction. Moreover, the type of speech used depends on such social factors as the social context. Language (grammar, vocabulary, etc.) that is appropriate with friends over a beer might well be *inappropriate* in a university seminar. This remains true even if the topic of conversation is the same in both instances; for example, the presidential election.

Form criticism studies the social dimensions of biblical literature. Form criticism begins with the observation that the actual *format* of speech (vocabulary and syntax) depends on what is being expressed (content) and the social context.[6] Simply put, the power of the Davidic king in Jerusalem, a power that was believed to be confirmed directly by God (content), would be described differently (format) when described in a hymn to be recited in the royal temple, in an historical saga, or in a hostile diatribe of a prophet (context). The form critic wants to compare all biblical passages with similar vocabulary and format to try to theorize about the social context within which such speech was at home: Was it legal language, cultic, or religious language? In most cases these hypotheses remain highly speculative, for we know so little about biblical Israelite society. Furthermore, how the reader uses such information is quite important. A passage might indeed be an example of legal speech, but it might be used ironically and thus not indicate a primary legal context. (I do the

---

[5] I use the unusual term "historical-cultural" rather than the more common "historical" because I have found that too often students limit the idea of "history," a concept often restricted to dates and rulers. "History" as used in historical criticism encompasses the entire culture (literary, religious, economic, etc.) of an age.

[6] Here scholars often use the German phrase *Sitz im Leben* to describe the social context or particular life situation within which speech takes place.

same thing when I say to my wife, who is angry at my being late, "I solemnly swear that I shall never again be late, so help me God.")

Historical-cultural criticism investigates questions about the historical context in which a work was written. What about the author? When did he or she live? What historical events are either referred to in the work or else might have influenced the writing of the piece? Are there references to other writings? To other contemporary intellectual movements? Will a knowledge of other contemporary literatures from Egypt, Babylon, or Phoenicia help us understand the background of a biblical book and thus aid our understanding? We ask similar questions about contemporary works. For example, what was the background of J.R.R. Tolkein, author of *The Lord of the Rings*? Did this background affect his writing? Do contemporary world events—the period between the two world wars in Europe—find mention in his stories? These questions become more difficult when the gap between us and a literary work approaches two and a half millennia. And questions about the author(s) of a biblical book are most often guesswork, for the ancients in general tended toward anonymity and very few names of ancient authors have been preserved.

Historical-cultural criticism makes use of our knowledge of ancient texts that have been discovered and deciphered over the last century as well as the results of the archaeologist's shovel. On occasion I shall have you read a few passages from ancient texts from Egypt or Mesopotamia in order to help you see the literary background against which the biblical author worked. Texts that are not included in this book can be read in James B. Pritchard's *Ancient Near Eastern Texts* (abbreviated *ANET*).

Source, Redaction, and Tradition Criticisms

So far all of the methods we have studied can be visualized along a *horizontal* plane. Literary/rhetorical criticism, form criticism, and historical-cultural criticism all ask questions about either the act of communicating or about the social or cultural influences behind such an act. These exegetical tools are equally of use for study of any modern literary work. However, biblical literature differs from contemporary writing in an important respect. Almost all books in the Hebrew Bible are the end product of centuries of anonymous composition. For example, the present text of the Book of Genesis was arrived at around 450 B.C.E.; however, that book had been made up of several earlier oral and written sources, some of which go back almost a millennium earlier. The final version of the Pentateuch was the product of oral traditions and written documents dating back to the time of the Patriarchs, the early forefathers of the Israelite nation (Abraham, Isaac, and Jacob).

The following two criticisms can be visualized along a *vertical* plane inasmuch as they examine the successive stages behind the biblical book being studied.

Source criticism attempts to divide a finished passage or book into its component written sources. It then tries to characterize each of these hypothetical documents[7] as to its theology, date, geographical location, etc. Source criticism has been used especially in the study of the Pentateuch—the first five books of the Hebrew Bible. The source critic employs such criteria as repetition, doublets (twin passages), different outlooks or theologies, and contradictions to isolate sources. We'll see more of this in the next two chapters.

---

[7] Always keep in mind that the results of source criticism are entirely theoretical. No one has ever discovered a manuscript or text that corresponds to one of these sources.

Redaction criticism takes up where source criticism leaves off. Once the source critic has dissected a book or passage into what he or she thinks are its component sources, the original passage closely resembles a cadaver after a thorough autopsy. The question remains, however, as to why these preexisting documents were arranged in their final form. According to what editorial principle were they joined together? Even such a loose literary unit as the anthology is usually put together according to some editorial criterion: Anthology of Canadian Poets, Anthology of Short Stories by Women, Anthology of Nineteenth-Century British Love Poetry, etc. The redaction critic looks for this criterion in the assembly/editing[8] of the final edition of a biblical book. According to what editorial viewpoint were source A and source B joined together even though they seemingly contradict each other? Why were they arranged in a certain order, etc.?

Tradition criticism studies the entire historical process of change and adaptation from the earliest oral stage of a tradition (for example, the story of the Exodus from Egypt), through the writing stage of various versions (for example, the Yahwist, Elohist), through final redaction (or editing) into books as we now have them, and on through their later use (and frequently) readaptation by Jews and Christians. Thus, this critical tool is easily the most comprehensive because it covers the entire "history" of the tradition from its beginning up to the present. (Some tradition critics, however, will stop the study at some earlier point; for example, at the point when a book was accepted as authoritative or canonical by either Jews or Christians.) Chapter 4 in this text represents an example of tradition criticism.

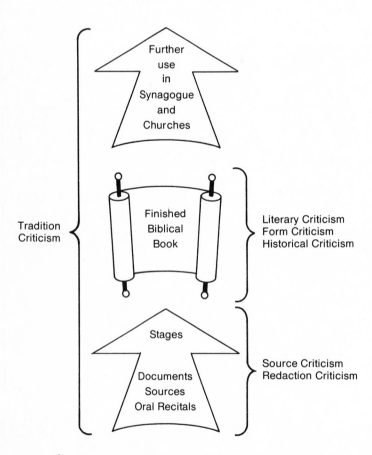

[8] "Redact" is a synonym for "edit."

OUTLINE OF THE BOOK

What follows is a brief outline of the chapters of this book and the sections of the Hebrew Bible that are covered. In most cases a chapter of questions on a select group of passages will be followed by a chapter that will both integrate the answers to those questions and relate them to broader sections of the Hebrew Scriptures. These "integrating" chapters will also refer to the state of current biblical scholarship on these topics. The reader may gain still further appreciation of contemporary scholarship by consulting the works cited in the Further Readings at the conclusion of most chapters. At the end of the book the student will find appendices containing (1) those ancient Near Eastern texts that have been mentioned in the text, (2) maps, (3) chronological tables, (4) a short treatment of biblical Hebrew poetry, and (5) a glossary of terms used in the book.

The biblical passages have been chosen to give the student a sampling of different literary types as well as selections from all three divisions of the Hebrew Scriptures. Chapters 3 through 6 are mainly concerned with the Pentateuch/Torah; Chapters 7 and 8 deal with the biblical Prophets; Chapters 9 through 11 are chosen from the generally postexilic Writings.

CHAPTER 2: Exercises in Biblical Criticisms

THE PENTATEUCH/TORAH

CHAPTER 3: Genesis 1–11 as an Introduction to the Pentateuch

CHAPTER 4: The Theme and Growth of the Pentateuch

CHAPTER 5: Israel's Legal Tradition and the Book of the Covenant

CHAPTER 6: Law and Covenants in Israel

THE PROPHETS

CHAPTER 7: Inquiry into Prophecy in Ancient Israel

CHAPTER 8: Survey of Israelite Prophecy

THE WRITINGS

CHAPTER 9: An Exercise in Form Criticism: The Psalms

CHAPTER 10: Wisdom Literature (Proverbs and Qoheleth)

CHAPTER 11: The Biblical Short Story (Ruth, Esther, and Judith)

APPENDIXES: Near Eastern Texts, Maps, Chronological Table, Glossary, Biblical Poetry

FURTHER READINGS

Norman K. Gottwald, *The Hebrew Bible: A Socio-Literary Introduction* (Philadelphia: Fortress Press, 1985). Pages 6–31 contain a good treatment of the various critical methods introduced in this chapter and further elaborated upon in Chapter 2.

John H. Hayes and Carl R. Holladay, *Biblical Exegesis: A Beginner's Handbook* (Atlanta: John Knox Press, 1982).

Norman R. Petersen, *Literary Criticism for New Testament Critics (Guides to Biblical Scholarship*; Philadelphia: Fortress Press, 1978). Especially read pp. 33–48 for a treatment of the Roman Jakobson communication model used in this chapter.

CHAPTER 2
EXERCISES IN LITERARY, HISTORICAL, AND FORM CRITICISMS

GOALS AND OBJECTIVES: This chapter contains exercises that illustrate the critical tools or criticisms introduced in the previous chapter. For most of the criticisms there will first be a non-biblical example and secondly an example taken from the Hebrew Bible. This sequence is designed to assure the student that most of these critical skills apply to all literature, religious as well as nonreligious, and to demystify the criticisms by showing how they really derive from common-sense insights about language.

As we established in the previous chapter, the Bible means different things to different people. To some it is God's word dictated to humans; to others it represents nothing more than interesting, but ancient, writings. But no matter what position a reader takes—from religious fundamentalism to atheism—the Bible is first of all *literature*; that is, the Bible may be more than just literature, but it is that. To believer as well as nonbeliever the Bible is a collection of writings that conveys its meaning no differently from other writings of a similar literary type. Hence, before the believer inquires about how God is speaking in the Bible, that person must first ask *literary* questions such as, What type of literature am I reading?

Our first task is to put into practice—using the workbook approach—many of the principles of rhetorical or literary criticism that we described in the previous chapter. Our eventual goal is to become familiar with (1) literary criticism, (2) source criticism, and (3) form criticism. We shall also pose the question of the importance of historical and cultural issues in reading ancient texts like the Bible. In each of these three cases, we shall start with a "nonreligious," more modern, writing and dissect *how* we read it; our purpose is to make explicit our usually unconscious literary presuppositions and to illustrate that the procedures for reading secular and religious texts are quite similar. Next we shall apply these same literary techniques to a biblical passage.

LITERARY/RHETORICAL CRITICISM

Our first selection is a bizarre work called "A Modest Proposal." After reading this selection there will be some study questions that you will be expected to answer in writing. It will be helpful for you to look at the questions *prior* to at least one of your several readings of "A Modest Proposal." Next you will read the Book of Jonah and apply many of the insights that I hope you have gained from your close reading of "A Modest Proposal."

Reading "A Modest Proposal"

I want you to read the following selection quite carefully. Some of you might be familiar with it, some not. It doesn't matter. The questions relating to the text are designed to bring out *how* a piece of writing conveys its meaning; only secondarily are they interested in meaning itself. In other words, I am interested in *how it means* rather than *what it means*, although the two issues are not completely separable.

Although we are of course interested in what "A Modest Proposal" is saying, I want you to pay particular attention to the techniques and devices that the author uses to communicate meaning. We have to acquire a concrete sense of how literature expresses itself.

Please write your answers to the questions in the spaces provided. Always explain your answer with reference to the text. You can refer to the text by using the paragraph numbers.

A MODEST PROPOSAL
for

Preventing the Children of Poor People in Ireland from Being a Burden to Their Parents or Country; and for Making Them Beneficial to the Public.

1.   It is a melancholy object to those who walk through this great town or travel in the country when they see the streets, the roads and cabin-doors crowded with beggars of the female sex, followed by three, four, or six children, all in rags, and importuning every passenger for an alms. These mothers, instead of being able to work for their honest livelihood, are forced to employ all their time in strolling to beg sustenance for their helpless infants; who, as they grow up, either turn thieves for want of work, or leave their dear native country, to fight for the Pretender in Spain or sell themselves to the Barbadoes.

2.   I think it is agreed by all parties, that this prodigious number of children in the arms, or on the backs, or at the heels of their mothers, and frequently of their fathers, is, in the present deplorable state of the Kingdom, a very great additional grievance; and, therefore, whoever could find out a fair, cheap, and easy method of making these children sound and useful members of the commonwealth, would deserve so well of the public, as to have his statue set up as a preserver of the nation.

3.   As to my own part, having turned my thoughts for many years upon this important subject and maturely weighed the several schemes of other projectors, I have always found them grossly mistaken in their computation. It is true, a child, just dropt from its dam, may be supported by her milk for a solar year with little other nourishment; at most, not above the value of two shillings, which the mother may certainly get, or the value in scraps, by her lawful occupation of begging; and it is exactly at one year old that I propose to provide for them in such manner, as, instead of being a charge upon their parents, or the parish, or wanting food and raiment for the rest of their lives, they shall, on the contrary, contribute to the feeding and partly to the clothing of many thousands.

4.   There is likewise another great advantage in my scheme, that it will prevent those voluntary abortions, and that horrid practice of women murdering their bastard children, alas, too frequent among us, sacrificing the poor innocent babes, I doubt more to avoid the expense than the shame, which would move tears and pity in the most savage and inhuman breast.

5.   The number of souls in Ireland being usually reckoned one million and a half, of these I calculate there may be about two hundred thousand couple whose wives are breeders; from which number I subtract thirty thousand couple, who are able to maintain their own children (although I apprehend there cannot be so many under the present distresses of the Kingdom); but this being granted, there will remain an hundred and seventy thousand breeders. I again subtract fifty thousand, for those women who miscarry or whose children die by accident, or disease, within the year. There only remain a hundred and twenty thousand children of poor parents annually born. The question therefore is how this number shall be reared and provided for? Which, as I have already said, under the present situation of affairs, is utterly impossible by all the methods hitherto proposed. For we can neither employ them in handicraft or agriculture; we neither build houses, (I mean in the country) nor cultivate land: they can very seldom pick up a livelihood by stealing until they arrive at six years old; except where they are of towardly parts; although I confess, they learn the rudiments much earlier; during which time, they can, however, be properly looked upon only as probationers; as I have been informed by a principal gentleman in the County of Cavan, who protested to me that he never knew above one or two instances under the age of six, even in a part of the Kingdom so renowned for the quickest proficiency in that art.

6.   I am assured by our merchants that a boy or a girl before twelve years old is no saleable commodity; and even when they come to this age, they will not yield above three pounds or three pounds and a half-crown at most, on the exchange; which cannot turn to account either to the parents or the Kingdom, the charge of nutriment and rags having been at least four times that value.

7.   I shall now, therefore, humbly propose my own thoughts, which I hope will not be liable to the least objection.

8.   I have been assured by a very knowing American of my acquaintance in London that a young healthy child, well nursed, is at a year old a most delicious, nourishing, and wholesome food, whether stewed, roasted, baked, or broiled; and I make no doubt that it will equally serve in a fricassee or ragout.

9.   I do therefore humbly offer it to public consideration that of the hundred and twenty thousand children already computed, twenty thousand may be reserved for breed, whereof only one-fourth part to be males; which is more than we allow to sheep, black cattle, or swine; and my reason is that these children are seldom the fruits of marriage, a circumstance not much regarded by our savages; therefore one male will be sufficient to serve four females. That the remaining hundred thousand may, at one year old, be offered in sale to the persons of quality and fortune through the Kingdom; always advising the mother to let them suck plentifully in the last month, so as to render them plump and fat for a good table. A child will make two dishes at an entertainment for friends; and when the family dines alone, the fore or hind quarter will make a reasonable dish, and, seasoned with a little pepper or salt, will be very good boiled on the fourth day, especially in winter.

10.   I have reckoned upon a medium, that a child just born will weigh twelve pounds; and in a solar year, if tolerably nursed, increaseth to twenty-eight pounds.

11.   I grant this food will be somewhat dear, and therefore very proper for landlords, who, as they have already devoured most of the parents, seem to have best title to the children.

12.   Infants' flesh will be in season throughout the year; but more plentiful in March, and a little before and after: For we are told by a grave author, an eminent French physician, that fish being a prolific diet, there are more children born in Roman Catholic countries about nine months after Lent than at any other season: Therefore, reckoning a year after Lent, the markets will be more glutted than usual, because the number of popish infants is at least three to one in this Kingdom, and therefore it will have one other collateral advantage, by lessening the number of papists among us.

13.   I have already computed the charge of nursing a beggar's child (in which list I reckon all cottagers, laborers, and four-fifths of the farmers) to be about two shillings per annum, rags included; and I believe no gentleman would repine to give ten shillings for the carcass of a good fat

child, which, as I have said, will make four dishes of excellent nutritive meat, when he hath only some particular friend, or his own family to dine with him. Thus the squire will learn to be a good landlord, and grow popular among his tenants; the mother will have eight shillings net profit and be fit for work until she produces another child.

14.   Those who are more thrifty (as I must confess the times require) may flay the carcass; the skin of which, artificially dressed, will make admirable gloves for ladies, and summer-boots for fine gentlemen.

15.   As to our city of Dublin, shambles may be appointed for this purpose in the most convenient parts of it; and butchers we may be assured will not be wanting; although I rather recommend buying the children alive and dressing them hot from the knife as we do roasting pigs.

16.   A very worthy person, a true lover of his country, and whose virtues I highly esteem, was lately pleased in discoursing on this matter to offer a refinement upon my scheme. He said that many gentlemen of this Kingdom, having of late destroyed their deer, he conceived that the want of venison might be well supplied by the bodies of young lads and maidens, not exceeding fourteen years of age, nor under twelve; so great a number of both sexes in every county being now ready to starve for want of work and service; and these to be disposed of by their parents, if alive, or otherwise by their nearest relations. But, with due deference to so excellent a friend, and so deserving a patriot, I cannot be altogether in his sentiments. For as to the males, my American acquaintance assured me from frequent experience that their flesh was generally tough and lean, like that of our schoolboys, by continual exercise and their taste disagreeable; and to fatten them would not answer the charge. Then as to the females, it would, I think, with humble submission, be a loss to the public, because they soon would become breeders themselves: and besides it is not improbable that some scrupulous people might be apt to censure such a practice (although very unjustly) as a little bordering upon cruelty; which, I confess, has always been with me the strongest objection against any project, how well soever intended.

17.   But in order to justify my friend, he confessed that this expedient was put into his head by the famous Psalmanazar, a native of the island of Formosa, who came from thence to London about twenty years ago and in conversation told my friend that in his country when any young person happened to be put to death, the executioner sold the carcass to persons of quality as a prime dainty; and that in his time the body of a plump girl of fifteen who was crucified for an attempt to poison the emperor was sold to his imperial majesty's prime minister of state and other mandarins of the court in joints from the gibbet at four hundred crowns. Neither indeed can I deny that if the same use were made of several plump young girls in this town who without a single groat to their fortunes cannot stir abroad without a chair, and appear at the Playhouse and assemblies in foreign fineries, which they never pay for, the kingdom would not be the worse.

18.   Some persons of a desponding spirit are in great concern about the vast number of poor people who are aged, diseased, or maimed; and I have been desired to employ my thoughts what course may be taken to ease the nation of so grievous an incumbrance. But I am not in the least pain upon that matter, because it is very well known that they are every day dying, and rotting, by cold, and famine, and filth, and vermin, as fast as can reasonably be expected. And as to the younger laborers, they are now in almost as hopeful a condition: They cannot get work, and consequently pine away for want of nourishment to a degree that if at any time they are accidentally hired to common labor, they have not strength to perform it; and thus the country and themselves are in a fair way of being soon delivered from evils to come.

19.   I have too long digressed, and therefore shall return to my subject. I think the advantages by the proposal which I have made are obvious and many as well as of the highest importance.

20.   For *first,* as I have already observed, it would greatly lessen the number of papists with whom we are yearly overrun; being the principal breeders of the nation as well as our most dangerous enemies, and who stay at home on purpose with a design to deliver the Kingdom to the Pretender, hoping to take their advantage by the absence of so many good Protestants, who have chosen rather to leave their country than stay at home and pay tithes against their conscience to an idolatrous Episcopal curate.

21.   *Secondly,* the poorer tenants will have something valuable of their own which by law may be made liable to distress and help pay their landlord's rent, their corn and cattle being already seized and money a thing unknown.

22.   *Thirdly,* whereas the maintenance of a hundred thousand children, from two years old and upwards, cannot be computed at less than ten shillings a piece per annum, the nation's stock will be thereby increased fifty thousand pounds per annum; besides the profit of a new dish, introduced to the tables of all gentlemen of fortune in the Kingdom who have any refinement in taste; and the money will circulate among ourselves, the goods being entirely of our own growth and manufacture.

23.   *Fourthly,* the constant breeders, besides the gain of eight shillings sterling per annum by the sale of their children, will be rid of the charge of maintaining them after the first year.

24.   *Fifthly,* this food would likewise bring great custom to taverns, where the vintners will certainly be so prudent as to procure the best recipes for dressing it to perfection, and, consequently, have their houses frequented by all the fine gentlemen who justly value themselves upon their knowledge in good eating; and a skillful cook who understands how to oblige his guests will contrive to make it as expensive as they please.

25.   *Sixthly,* this would be a great inducement to marriage, which all wise nations have either encouraged by rewards or enforced by laws and penalties. It would increase the care and tenderness of mothers towards their children, when they were sure of a settlement for life to the poor babes provided in some sort by the public to their annual profit instead of expense. We should soon see an honest emulation among the married women, which of them could bring the fattest child to the market. Men would become as fond of their wives during the time of their pregnancy as they are now of their mares in foal, their cows in calf, or sows when they are ready to farrow; nor offer to beat or kick them (as is too frequent a practice) for fear of a miscarriage.

26.   Many other advantages might be enumerated. For instance, the addition of some thousand carcasses in our exportation of barrelled beef; the propagation of swine's flesh, and improvement in the art of making good bacon, so much wanted among us by the great destruction of pigs, too frequent at our tables, which are no way comparable in taste or magnificence to a well-grown fat yearling child, which, roasted whole, will make a considerable figure at a Lord Mayor's feast, or any other public entertainment. But this, and many others, I omit, being studious of brevity.

27.   Supposing that one thousand families in this city would be constant customers for infants' flesh, besides others who might have it at merry meetings, particularly weddings and christenings, I compute that Dublin would take off, annually, about twenty thousand carcasses; and the rest of the Kingdom (where probably they will be sold somewhat cheaper) the remaining eighty thousand.

28.   I can think of no one objection that will possibly be raised against this proposal, unless it should be urged that the number of people will be thereby much lessened in the Kingdom. This I freely own, and it was indeed one principal design in offering it to the world. I desire the reader will observe that I calculate my remedy for this one individual kingdom of Ireland, and for no other that ever was, is, or I think ever can be, upon earth. Therefore, let no man talk to me of other expedients: of taxing our absentees at five shillings a pound: of using neither clothes nor household furniture except what is of our own growth and manufacture: of utterly rejecting the materials and instruments that promote foreign luxury: of curing the expensiveness of pride, vanity, idleness, and gaming in our women; of introducing a vein of parsimony, prudence and temperance: of learning to love our country, wherein we differ even from Laplanders, and the inhabitants of Topinamboo: of quitting our animosities and factions; nor act any longer like the Jews who were murdering one another at the very moment their city was taken: of being a little cautious not to sell our country and consciences for nothing: of teaching landlords to have at least one degree of mercy towards their tenants. Lastly, of putting a spirit of honesty, industry, and skill into our shopkeepers, who, if a resolution could now be taken to buy only our native goods, would immediately unite to cheat and exact upon us in the price, the measure, and the goodness; nor could ever yet be brought to make one fair proposal of just dealing, though often and earnestly invited to it.

29.   Therefore, I repeat, let no man talk to me of these and like expedients, till he has, at least, a glimpse of hope that there will ever be some hearty and sincere attempt to put them in practice.

30.   But, as to myself, having been wearied out for many years with offering vain, idle, visionary thoughts, and at length utterly despairing of success, I fortunately fell upon this proposal;

which; as it is wholly new, so it has something *solid* and *real*, of no expense, and little trouble, full in our own power; and whereby we can incur no danger of disobliging England: for this kind of commodity will not bear exportation; the flesh being of too tender a consistence, to admit a long continuance in salt, although perhaps I could name a country which would be glad to eat up our whole nation without it.

31.   After all, I am not so violently bent upon my own opinion as to reject any offer proposed by wise men, which shall be found equally innocent, cheap, easy, and effectual. But before something of that kind shall be advanced in contradiction to my scheme, and offering a better, I desire the author, or authors, will be pleased maturely to consider two points: First, as things now stand, how they will be able to find food and raiment for a hundred thousand useless mouths and backs? And, secondly, there being a round million of creatures in human figure throughout this Kingdom, whose whole subsistence, put into a common stock, would leave them in debt two millions of pounds sterling; adding those who are beggars by profession, to the bulk of farmers, cottagers, and laborers, with their wives and children who are beggars in effect; I desire those politicians who dislike my overture and may perhaps be so bold to attempt an answer, that they will first ask the parents of these mortals, whether they would not at this day think it a great happiness to have been sold for food at a year old, in the manner prescribed; and thereby have avoided such a perpetual scene of misfortunes as they have since gone through by the oppression of the landlords, the impossibility of paying rent without money or trade, the want of common sustenance, with neither house nor clothes to cover them from the inclemencies of weather, and the most inevitable prospect of intailing the like, or greater miseries upon their breed for ever.

32.   I profess, in the sincerity of my heart, that I have not the least personal interest in endeavoring to promote this necessary work, having no other motive than the public good of my country, by advancing our trade, providing for infants, relieving the poor, and giving some pleasure to the rich. I have no children by which I can propose to get a single penny; the youngest being nine years old, and my wife past child-bearing.

Study Questions for "A Modest Proposal"

1.   Describe the style in which this work was written. You may wish to illustrate your reply by comparing its style to a contemporary one: Is it the sensational style of writing found in the *National Inquirer* or the more sober style found in a textbook? Be sure to explain your reply in detail, and refer to all features that helped you form your answer.

2.   Is the actual writer of this piece (its author) identical with the narrator, that is, with the person who speaks in the first person ("I") throughout? In other words, are the opinions or proposals expressed by the narrator necessarily those of the author? Explain your answer and tell why this question is important.

If there is a difference between the author and the narrative "I," why would the author resort to this fiction?

Describe the narrator as carefully as possible: (1) What type of person is he? (2) What is his nationality? (3) Describe his profession *based upon the style of writing he uses* (that is, is he a mathematician, a preacher, an economist, a chef or what?). To help formulate your answer, you might ask yourself: If this were a movie, whom would I cast for the narrator? Be sure to show from the text itself how you have arrived at your answer.

Notice how many statistics (numbers and facts) are used by the narrator in support of his "modest proposal." Be sure to mark examples of these facts. How do these affect your understanding of the portrayal of the narrator? Of the work as a whole?

Do you find any instances in which you suspect that so-called facts have been made up? How does this affect your reading of the proposal? Does this suggest the *type* of literature you are reading?

Where in the work do you sense that the views of the actual author (as opposed to those of the narrator) surface?

Describe in some detail (1) the "modest" proposal of the narrator and (2) what you suspect is the actual proposal of the author.

Why should an author present two different—even contradictory—views in a work: the author's own (under the surface) and the views of a fictional narrator (on the surface)? What clues might warn the reader of this possibility?

3.   Try to create in your mind (and then here on paper) the types of readers who most likely would read this work. Describe their probable economic status, nationality, religion, etc. This exercise is not really an *historical* investigation. I want you to portray this readership based solely on clues and information contained within the *literary* text not on external evidence such as publisher's sales records, etc.

Against whom was the author writing? What is the relationship between the reader and the group against which the author was writing? In other words, relate the *reader* to the work's *target*.

Describe how the reader would react to this work. Would the reader's reaction be uniform? Would it be the same attitude (for example, revulsion) throughout the reading or would it change at a certain point? (If so, where exactly would the reader's sympathies be likely to change?) Explain your answer in detail.

Read 2 Samuel 12:1–9 in your Bible. How is the effect of the parable on King David in this passage similar to the effect that "A Modest Proposal" had on its original reader?

4.   Could the author have used a different type of writing; for example, a speech or technical report? Describe what other type(s) of writing the author could have used. Why do you think the type used was chosen?

5.   What kind of literature are we reading here? Detail the evidence in the work (remember *code*?) that supports your answer.

Why is this question so important to answer in order to understand a piece of writing?

Many people have isolated the following characteristics (codes?) for satire:

a.   Satire is humor based on the exaggerated, fantastic, and absurd.

b.   Satire always is interested in morality; that is, it has a target of some significant vice against which it wishes to fight.

c.   Satire always attacks indirectly through the backdoor.

Do you find examples of these characteristics in "A Modest Proposal"? If so, give examples of each. Does an awareness of these codes for satire help you better understand this work?

What is *irony*? If you need help, look up the definition in the dictionary, but be sure you understand what you write down here. How can the presence of irony serve as a code?

Can you give examples of irony from "A Modest Proposal"?

Study the narrator's references to the "feeding" and "clothing" of people. Mark all the places where these occur. Does the author use these phrases in an unexpected (*ironical*) way? Explain your answer. Suggest how this theme might help you understand the story as satire.

6.   Using the terms we learned in the previous chapter, is the *function* of this work emotive, conative, referential, or poetic? Be sure to explain and justify your answer.

7.   Are there any internal references to historical events in the work (historical criticism)? What are they?

Would a knowledge of the history and culture of the time of its writing help our understanding? Explain your answer with reference to the text itself.

Is a knowledge of the historical circumstances behind the writing of "A Modest Proposal" absolutely necessary for our understanding of the text?

How would a better knowledge of the historical and socioeconomic circumstances behind the writing of this literary work help our understanding of it?

8. Is this work true? (Remember what we said in Chapter 1 about truth.)

What would have to be clarified before you could answer this question adequately?

A Literary Reading of the Book of Jonah

Carefully read through the Book of Jonah twice. (Also read the RSV introduction.) You might want to make a photocopy of the four chapters so that you can mark it up and experiment visually with colored pens and pencils, etc.

Too often people ask the wrong questions about the Book of Jonah. They thus become totally caught up in either *historical* ("Was Nineveh actually converted by a Hebrew prophet?") or *ichthyological* questions ("What kind of a 'big fish' could have swallowed and held a man for three days in its gullet?"). Such questions should only be asked if the Book of Jonah functions as *referential* communication; but the function of the Book of Jonah has yet to be determined. Thus it is clear from the beginning that we are immediately confronted not by historical but by *literary* questions.

Questions on the Book of Jonah

Answer the following questions, which are designed to help you uncover the literary structure (or structures) of the Book of Jonah; you will then be asked to relate what you find to meaning(s).

1. Let's try to discover the *type* of literature we are reading. The Book of Jonah looks like an historical account of what an Israelite prophet accomplished. And yet it is quite different from the other prophetic books. In general, the prophetic books were quite interested in *dating* their oracles, that is, in providing a reference to the reign of the kings during which the prophecy was uttered. (Read, for example, Micah 1:1, Amos 1:1, Hosea 1:1, Zephaniah 1:1.) How does Jonah differ from these prophetic books? Does that help us evaluate its literary type?

Recall the three characteristics of satire in our previous reading (exaggerated humor, interest in morality, indirect attack). The fantastic and absurd humor usually provides the initial code to what is being read. How many examples of the exaggerated, fantastic, and absurd can you uncover in the Book of Jonah?

2.   Let's look especially at the first verses in Chapter 1.

This is a typical scene in the Bible, for Yahweh[1] is commissioning a prophet.[2] It will help to look at a few of these passages from elsewhere in the Bible.[3] Read Exodus 4:10–20, Judges 6:12-22, Jeremiah 1:4-10, Isaiah 6:5-8. How is the commissioning scene in Jonah 1:1-2 similar to and different from these other passages?

Hebrew narrative almost never adds unimportant filler. What is the significance of the detail in Jonah 1:3–"and he *paid the fare*"? Why is it significant to mention that Jonah actually bought a ticket to go on board the boat?

---

[1] The proper name for the God of Israel was Yahweh, the meaning of which is uncertain. Although the original Hebrew text did not write vowels and only wrote the four consonants YHWH (the tetragrammaton or "Four Letters"), we can vocalize these consonants with fair reliability based on early Greek transcriptions. Late in the biblical period, this name became so sacred that its pronouncement was avoided. Late texts preferred such phrases as the "God of Heaven" or "My Lord" (Hebrew "Adonai") rather than the sacred "Yahweh." This practice has been followed by the RSV, which translates the original Hebrew "Yahweh" into "Lord."

[2] To speak a bit more technically, according to form criticism this is an example of the typical form of prophetic commission, although with a twist.

[3] This is a case where it is helpful to have a larger literary perspective.

Jonah is told "to arise, call/cry out, and go" to Nineveh. (Find Nineveh on the map at the end of this text.) Who else in this chapter issues a similar order to Jonah, thus echoing Yahweh? Describe any significance that this repetition might have for the reader's understanding of the characters in the Book of Jonah.

What does Jonah do in response to this divine imperative? How is this response significant in determining the type of literature we are reading?

Show how often chapters 1 and 2 of Jonah use words marking the directions "up (arise)" and "down (descend)." How are these words significant in characterizing the type of literature?

3. All of the clues we have gathered so far suggest that the Book of Jonah is a study in "opposites of what is to be expected." To test this hypothesis, list several examples of how people behave differently from how we would expect them to behave.

Does even prayer behave differently from how it should be expected? Look closely at chapter 2 of Jonah. How would you characterize Jonah's prayer? Is the prayer consistent with the spirit of the book as you read it up to this point? Is the Jonah who prays consistent with the character of Jonah elsewhere in the book? (This question is an example of *literary criticism.*) Be sure to explain your reply.

Let's put the question another way. We can rephrase our original question in terms of *source criticism.* Many scholars think that chapter 2 is a later source added to the book, which interrupts the mood of the narrative. Do you agree?

LITERARY STRUCTURES OF THE BOOK OF JONAH

Now let us examine the overall anatomy of the Book of Jonah. This inquiry becomes more complicated. What we are seeking to do is to discover the literary organizations or structures for the book.[4] In looking for literary structure, the first thing the critic does is to discover those component elements which are going to make up the organization. (A lot of hit and miss!) An architect might use windows, brick patterns, or columns as structural devices; a painter might use color and light or the placement of subjects. Because the Book of Jonah is clearly divisible into four scenes, which roughly correspond to the present chapters, organization will possibly be along the lines of the relationships between these chapters. The second task for the critic is to show the overall organization of these parts; thirdly, the critic must show what is communicated by this structure. We are not after organization for its own sake, and we shall always relate any literary structure uncovered to meaning. (If there is more than one structure, there will be more than one meaning.)

Many people think that the four chapters of the Book of Jonah have an interlocking relationship, that is, that chapter 1 relates to chapter 3, and chapter 2 with chapter 4. Let us test this out. First we shall examine this structure and then

[4] I have used the plural *structures* because often there are several different structures in a work, each one communicating a separate idea. Don't be surprised by this; the same is true of architecture, music (counterpoint!), and painting.

consider the meaning that might be conveyed by such a pattern. (Looking at the book this way will highlight some of the main themes and conflicts within the work.)

1.   List ways in which chapters 1 and 3 are related (related in geographical location, main characters "on stage," words or phrases in common, etc.).

Describe the relationships between the main characters, who are highlighted when we juxtapose chapters 1 and 3. In other words, who in Jonah 1 are like characters in Jonah 3? Who are different? What are the main conflicts or themes that are similar in these two chapters?

2.   List ways in which chapters 2 and 4 are related.

Describe the relationship between the main characters in chapters 2 and 4. Especially relate them to the issue of "salvation/deliverance" (*from* whom and *for* whom).

3.   This organization in chapters 1 and 3 and chapters 2 and 4 highlights certain issues or themes. Structure conveys meaning by focusing the reader's attention on certain aspects of the story. To what issues in the Book of Jonah does this structure draw our attention? (In other words, combine the main issues in chapters 1 and 3 with the main issues isolated in chapters 2 and 4 into one single statement.)

4.   If these four chapters are so related (1 and 3, 2 and 4), there are also ways in which chapters 1 and 2 and chapters 3 and 4 form a structural unit. List some ways (words, phrases, ideas, etc.) in which these can be so grouped (1, 2 and 3, 4).

FACTORS LINKING CHAPTERS 1 AND 2   FACTORS LINKING CHAPTERS 3 AND 4

It can be helpful to divide a passage into such binary groupings, because it often serves to highlight significant literary motifs when they appear as polar contrasts. If these two groups (1, 2 and 3, 4) are related to each other, then what conflict does that emphasize?

5.   However we divide the book (1, 3 and 2, 4 *or* 1, 2 and 3, 4), there is a strong break between chapters 2 and 3. Let's look at it closely. Regarding the end of chapter 2, a preacher once joked that it was appropriate that the fish vomited after Jonah said, "Deliverance belongs to the Lord!" What's the joke? Why is the quip helpful in understanding one of the main ideas in the book?

6.   Why was Jonah reluctant to go to Nineveh? And when exactly do we first learn the reason for his resistance?

Notice the irony in Jonah 4:2. How is this important to the book?

7.   In a sense the entire book emerges as a study of *change*. Mark how each character in the book changes. Who does *not* really change?

8.   Now tie all of these questions together. What do you think is the main thesis of the book? (State it in a *complete* sentence.)[5] The best statement of a thesis will be that which incorporates as many of the motifs you have uncovered as possible from your study of the juxtaposition of chapters 1 and 3, 2 and 4; 1 and 2, 3 and 4.

---

[5] I shall always insist on the important difference between *theme* and *thesis*. The theme is the *general* subject area or topic about which the author is writing; the thesis is the *exact point* or *statement* that the author is trying to make. Certainly, Jonah is about a runaway prophet and the salvation of the heathens at Nineveh, but these all constitute a theme. What exactly is the author saying about these events (thesis)?

9.   Now evaluate the relative importance of the *literary* issues in the book and such *historical* questions as "Did Jonah really preach and convert the Assyrian capital?"

In order to understand the historical attitude of the Israelites about Nineveh and the Assyrians, read the Hebrew prophet Nahum's joy at the destruction of Nineveh in 612 B.C.E. How does the introduction of this historical information affect your reading of the Book of Jonah?

It is very difficult to date the Book of Jonah. Try to imagine a religious situation for which the book might have been composed. Against what type of problems in the community might it have been directed?

10.   Is this book *true*? Why is this seemingly straightforward question so complicated?

EXERCISES IN FORM CRITICISM

When we read Jonathan Swift's "A Modest Proposal" we agreed that it was important to know what *type* of writing (scholars sometimes call it the *genre*) we were reading; otherwise we could easily miss the meaning of the piece. (In the previous chapter we used the example of mistaking another of Swift's works, *Gulliver's Travels,* for a travelogue—you can imagine the results in how the work would be understood!) We learned next that much of the Book of Jonah parodies the typical *form* of the prophet's commissioning, although the normal reluctance of the prophet was rather exaggerated.

Detecting the type of writing might be important, but it is also a little tricky. For example, clearly it is important to realize that "A Modest Proposal" is a satire, otherwise its meaning could easily be missed. But it is also important to note that the author *imitates* the genre, or type, of an economic treatise with all his pompous style complete with facts and economic figures. And so Swift's satirical proposal also mimics the scholarly economic *type*—in fact, it's this imitation that supports its satire, for Swift is satirizing precisely those whose style he imitates with their cold, inhuman calculations.

Social Context and Communication

Form criticism is the literary tool we use to help us detect the types of writing used in the Bible. (*Form* is another word for literary type/genre.) However, form criticism has more to say about human communication than merely pointing out its literary type or form (no matter whether the communication be written or oral). Form criticism is also sensitive to the fact that the type of communication we choose is often related to our social circumstances. Society dictates that we adopt a different letter form for a business correspondence than for a letter to a close friend.

The following exercises help you notice certain correspondences between a form or type of writing and the social context in which that style is most appropriate. In the first example we shall see the close link between form and content. We shall keep the same content (description of a house) in the second exercise but vary the context in which we describe it. Watch how this affects the *form*ulation of our words.

Exercises in Form Criticism

Part One

Content and verbal *form* are closely linked. You all know the doggeral form "Roses are red, violets are blue . . . ." The verbal form of this *poetry* is quite strict; but also notice how linked this particular *form* is with *content.* There are a limited number of ideas that could legitimately be expressed by "Roses are red . . . ." Just try writing a condolence to a friend on the loss of his or her parent using this poetic form.

You will also note that this verbal format is only appropriate in certain fixed social circumstances (context). You would hardly expect it to be used by a politician, a judge, a preacher, etc.

Part Two

I want you to write a description of your home, but I want your description to be appropriate to the following circumstances: (1) Describe your home as you would in a *real estate advertisement* in the classified section of the *Local Gazette*.

(2) Describe the same home as you would in response to any inquiry from your county tax assessor, who is trying to determine your annual property tax.

(3) Describe your home as you would in a letter to a close friend whom you haven't seen in years.

(4) Describe your home to an architect.

Part Three

Now let's see how well you can work backwards. Below in the left column you will find a short phrase or sentence that illustrates a common contemporary literary type/form. In the columns to the right, briefly describe *what specifically is being talked about* (content) and the exact *social circumstances* in which that type of writing would be used (context).

FORM	CONTENT	CONTEXT
1. . . . so help me God.		
2. Dear Ms. Petersen:		
3. . . . and they lived happily ever after.		
4. There was a young woman from Nantucket . . .		
5. Dear Occupant of 105 Avon Dr.		
6. 4 out of 5 doctors recommend Brand X		
7. I will do my best to see a hold on taxes		
8. Gene Kelley presents 3 new reasons to buy an RCA		
9. He is survived by his wife, Lisa, three daughters, and a brother in Peoria.		
10. What has three eyes, two heads, and is green?		
11. Complete assignments early and you can pick up some extra cash. Those in broadcasting enjoy good luck.		
12. Dlx, beautiful room, laundry, phone, cable, etc. 482-0132 eves.		
13. Her dress was trimmed with French lace and caught at the waist with a satin bow. She carried a cascade of yellow roses.		

Part Four

Now I want you to reflect on the significance of both these exercises. First of all, comment on the relation between the exact form our writing (or speaking) takes and the social circumstances in which it is written or uttered. Secondly, describe how this relationship could help us better understand the Bible and biblical society.

A few years ago I had a foreign student in my class who was quite fluent in English, although it was not his native language. Despite his fluency, he did very poorly on the exercise above. Even though he knew the meaning of all the words, he had difficulty detecting the specific social *context* from which all the examples were taken. As you can imagine, some of the subtle shadings of language were quite lost! In order to detect the form and its inseparable social context, the listener/ reader must notice that a passage is *typical,* that is, not only do its individual words and phrases have meaning, but also that the passage actually acquires meaning from being associated with texts of a similar pattern. Thus, the phrase ". . . so help me God" not only has meaning from the sum of its words (form), but it also acquires meaning from the fact that it evokes in the listener the picture of the courtroom (context). Form criticism *only* comes into play when a passage is an instance of typical speech, when it is an example of a recurrent speech pattern or form. Hence, if a passage is unique, that is, if it is not an example of a *recurring* form of speech, then form criticism is not applicable. Try to link the words "The blue one goes on the left" with a specific context! Remember that all of the 13 examples in the exercise above were of "typical speech" and so we could easily attach each of them to a specific social context. But the phrase "I don't like pickles on my hamburgers" does not fit into that category; thus, it is not of interest to the form critic.

The biblical form critic must first be sure that the words being examined are a verbal formula (form), that they are a recurrent speech pattern. This can be done by checking the words in a biblical Hebrew concordance to see if the exact same phrases are found elsewhere in the Bible. If there truly is a speech form, then the critic examines all the instances of this pattern (form) to see if they share a common content, that they all talk about the same thing. Finally, the critic looks for clues in the passages about the original social context in which these phrases would be used. There are clues to the context in the Bible itself and in comparisons with literature elsewhere in the ancient Near East.

Biblical Exercises in Form Criticism

In very few instances in the Bible do we have all of the above elements (form, content, and context) clearly linked. Normally we can easily detect recurrent speech forms just by noticing formal similarities in vocabulary and syntax. But it is rare that the biblical passage explicitly reveals the exact context in which such phrases were at home in Israelite society.

The exception is in Deuteronomy 26:1–11. Here we have the words of a prayer (actually an historical recollection) in verses 5b–10.[6] Because many of the phrases in this creedal recital are quite traditional and recurrent, we have an example of speech that is of interest to the form critic. But this passage from the Book of Deuteronomy also describes the exact *context* in which this recital would be appropriate: the ceremony thanking God for the successful harvest by offering God the first fruits in the temple in Jerusalem. You can see how difficult it would have been to reconstruct the ceremonial context just from the words of the prayer.[7]

But now let us work with a more common example in which we have only indirect information of the social context with which a speech form is associated. In the exercise that follows we shall methodically go through each of the steps followed by the form critic: First, we shall isolate the *form*ula, for we want to make sure that it is a recurrent speech pattern and to determine its extent and literary features; secondly, we want to link several examples of the formula with a shared content; last, and most difficult of all, we shall try to reconstruct the *implied* social context from subtle clues throughout both the Bible and the rest of the ancient Near East.

1.   Read the first two chapters of the Book of Amos, one of the oldest prophets (eighth century B.C.E.) after whom a biblical book has been named. Notice the frequent speech pattern (the *form*) beginning with the phrase "Thus says the Lord . . . ." From all of the examples of this pattern in these two chapters mark down recurrent characteristics: Who is speaking? What does the speaker announce? How grammatically does the speaker introduce the reasons or causes behind the message? What is the grammatical tense of the message? How is the end of the message indicated? And so forth.

Who is the "I" in each example?

---

[6] The "b" in verse 5b–10 means that the citation begins in the middle of the verse. This implies, as is the case, that verse 5 can easily be divided into two grammatical parts and that the quotation begins with the second part.

[7] We should not be surprised that an historical account of origins played a role in a religious ceremony; in many cases in the Christian liturgy, for example, there are references to what Jesus did or said. Similarly, the Jewish Passover seder recalls Israel's deliverance from Egypt.

2.   Just to ensure that this is not peculiar only to Amos, read Jeremiah 9:7–26, which was written several centuries later. Mark the characteristics of the "Thus says the Lord . . ." pattern in Jeremiah.

Now let us see if the characteristics discovered in Amos also apply to this later prophet (sixth century B.C.E.). List all of the characteristics of this literary form that are more or less in common with Amos and Jeremiah. In other words, sift out the details specific to each, leaving behind only the *common* pattern/form.[8]

3.   What is the *content* of this formula? In other words, what subject matter do the passages from Amos and Jeremiah that use this formula have in common?

4.   We have a form (or patterned speech) that was used over at least three centuries. But the form critic is particularly interested in the natural social context of this pattern. In this case such findings would be particularly helpful because this form is common to all prophetic speech; if we can discover the *context* of the pattern, then perhaps we can uncover how prophets regarded their role in Israelite society. Read Genesis 32:3–4 and 2 Kings 18:19–25.

Show how many of the characteristics of the form found in Amos and Jeremiah are also found in the pattern occurring in 2 Kings 18 and Genesis 32.

[8] Notice that in Jeremiah 9:22 the prophet is even instructed to recite the "Thus says the Lord," which strongly suggests that this pattern was immediately recognized as a formula.

Do you think that this form was first used in a religious context (Amos and Jeremiah) or in a nonreligious one (Genesis and 2 Kings)? Be sure to explain your answer and show its significance for determining the context of biblical literary forms.

How do these passages from 2 Kings and Genesis help explain the context of the "Thus says X . . ." pattern?

5.   Now form an hypothesis: Based on the evidence from speech patterns and the context from which the speech patterns were taken, how did Israelite prophets view their role? In what social context do these language patterns situate the prophet?

Read 1 Kings 22:1-28 (especially verses 19–23), Isaiah 6, and Jeremiah 23: 18–22. At first glance these passages, all of which mention a prophet, are very different. However, they all describe the commissioning or summoning of a prophet. Describe the exact situation (context) portrayed in each of these scenes. How do these commissioning scenes support your hypothesis about how the prophets see their role?

THE REUSE OF BIBLICAL FORMS

We saw in our reading of "A Modest Proposal" that a form could be reused—often for a comical or satirical effect. Thus, Swift mimics the form of the technical economics paper to make a statement on human insensitivity. The reader should always be aware of the possibility that a literary form might have been *reused* in a different (secondary) literary context. This placement in a secondary context can clearly affect meaning.[9] To be technical for a moment, the reemployment of a form could function as a code, that is, it is an indication of how the author/speaker wants to be understood. If a witness on the stand in an important murder trial were to begin testifying with the words (form), "Once upon a time . . . ," the fact that the witness had borrowed a form from another context would certainly color the value of the testimony. If a juror were unaware of this reuse, he or she might mistake the witness's testimony.

Let us mark a similar result in the following biblical passages.

1.   Read Psalm 8 and answer the following questions regarding its literary form, content, and context.

Note the refrain (verses 1, 9). What kind(s) of literature uses the refrain?

In what social context do you think this type of literature would be appropriate? In other words, where would these words normally be recited?

How is God portrayed in Psalm 8? How would you describe God's relationship to humans? What is the nature of God's care for humans?

---

[9] Think how jokes depend on this same feature: Language or speech patterns from one situation are (inappropriately and thus effectively) reused in a secondary situation. If you did not understand this you could never appreciate (or really hate) the *National Lampoon* or *Saturday Night Live.*

2.   Now read Job 7:17–21 and answer the following questions.

How is this selection from the Book of Job *similar in literary form* to Psalm 8? (List the verbal similarities.)

How is God portrayed in Job? How does God's supervision in this case affect the human? Compare the description of God in Job with that in Psalm 8.

Which passage do you think is older, Job 7:17–21 or Psalm 8? Explain your answer.

3.   How is Job 7:17–21 ironic? (Remember your earlier definition of "irony.") How does the literary form used in Job contribute to this "irony"?

How is Job a spoof on the piety of Psalm 8?

4.   How has a knowledge of the original form—witnessed in Psalm 8—helped you understand the depth of Job's bitterness? How does Job's imitation of the hymn style of Psalm 8 add force to his disenchantment with God?

EXERCISE IN SOURCE CRITICISM

We mentioned in the Introduction that many books in the Hebrew Bible were written over centuries and were comprised of several earlier written sources (often called "documents"). It can be helpful to be aware of this when reading parts of the Bible, especially the Torah/Pentateuch where this was first noticed. A rudimentary knowledge of such component parts and of the history behind them can help the reader appreciate the long process behind the editing of the final version; but, more importantly, by revealing the written building blocks used in the final text, *source criticism* can help the reader detect the architectural blueprint used by the final editor in assembling the book. In other words, if we can first isolate the sources behind the passage (source criticism), we can then ask the question about how these sources were brought together and according to what overall editorial schema (which is the work of *redaction* criticism).

You detect component sources the same way a teacher looks at a student's term paper for plagiarism. If there are internal contradictions, repetitions,[10] sudden fluctuations in levels of vocabulary or in style, these usually reveal that the final paper was made up of different written sources.

1.   Read Exodus 24 and try to isolate its component sources. (There are between two and four different sources.)

Use the criteria of repetition, contradictions (just how many times does Moses go up the mountain and with whom?), different vocabulary, different portrayals of the deity.

---

[10] Be careful! Repetition by itself is not proof of different sources. Repetition can often be used by one author effectively. Look especially at such children's stories as "Chicken Little."

How is God portrayed in each of your sources? Is God approachable in some sections, but remote and distant in others? Remember that just as people you know might have different notions of God (God as brother, or God as aloof majestic figure), so different sources often reflected pluralistic concepts about God's divinity.

How is the role of Moses described in your various sources? Is Moses a unique figure of authority in some passages but a member of a committee in others?

List the different words or phrases used to describe the document ratified between Moses and the deity. Who wrote the document?

2. None of the sources in Exodus 24 is unique to that chapter; rather, each represents a written thread that extends throughout the first several books of the Bible. Try to link your hypothetical sources with other biblical passages. Look for similarities in characters, vocabulary, descriptions of the deity, account of the law that Moses receives, etc. Which of these sources (label them A, B, etc.) is related to the following other whole chapters in the Bible? (Be sure to justify your answer.)

EXODUS 18

EXODUS 32

GENESIS 1

3.   How could a knowledge of source criticism help the reader better understand the biblical text?

How can a knowledge of sources behind a text help the *literary critic*?

FURTHER READINGS

The Book of Jonah

Terence E. Fretheim, "Jonah and Theodicy," *Zeitschrift für alttestamentliche Wissenschaft*, 90 (1978): 227-237.

Edwin Good, *Irony in the Old Testament.* (Sheffield, England: The Almond Press, 1981), pp. 39-55.

John C. Holbert, " 'Deliverance Belongs to Yahweh!' Satire in the Book of Jonah," *Journal for the Study of the Old Testament,* 21 (1981): 59-81.

The Prophetic Messenger Formula

Bernhard W. Anderson, *Understanding the Old Testament,* 4th ed. (Englewood Cliffs, NJ: Prentice-Hall, 1986), pp. 248-249. There are references here to further readings on this topic.

Psalm 8 and the Book of Job

Norman Habel, *The Book of Job* (*Old Testament Library*; Philadelphia: Westminster Press, 1985), pp. 164-165.

J. Gerald Janzen, *Job* (*Interpretation*; Atlanta: John Knox, 1985), pp. 81-83.

David Robertson, *The Old Testament and the Literary Critic* (*Guides to Biblical Scholarship*; Philadelphia: Fortress, 1977), pp. 39-40.

Exodus 24

Brevard S. Childs, *The Book of Exodus* (*Old Testament Library*; Philadelphia: Westminster Press, 1974), pp. 499-502.

Norman Habel, *Literary Criticism of the Old Testament* (*Guides to Biblical Scholarship*; Philadelphia: Fortress, 1971), pp. 1-6.

THE PENTATEUCH OR TORAH

CHAPTER 3
A LITERARY READING
OF GENESIS 1–11

GOALS AND OBJECTIVES: This chapter contains questions for a close literary reading of Genesis 1-11, which probably contains the key for understanding the first part of the Hebrew Bible. These questions seek to focus the reader's attention on several important devices whereby the meaning of these key chapters is conveyed. The important questions will center on the literary genre of Genesis' 11 chapters and their function (referential, conative, etc.). The student will employ almost all the critical skills introduced in the previous two chapters. First, there will be detailed inquiries about the various documents that make up this section (source criticism) and how the various components have been assembled and by whom (redaction criticism). There will also be a detailed literary analysis of each episode (literary criticism). Throughout this chapter will be found references to historical issues surrounding the first 11 chapters of Genesis (historical-cultural criticism), although this tool as well as tradition criticism will be most fully developed in Chapter 4 of the text, where the results of the investigation in this chapter will be tied together. This chapter seeks both to reinforce the student's experience with critical biblical tools and to acquaint the student with the "introduction to the Torah." This part of Genesis is so often discussed today, and is so often the center of controversy, that an ability to read it carefully and with sensitivity to its literary purposes will equip the student for reading the rest of the Hebrew Bible.

General Instructions for Reading: Please answer all of the following questions in the spaces provided; explain your answers in detail; always support your response by reference to the biblical text itself. Usually your answer will only be preliminary; that is, after you have worked through more questions and read sections of the text in more detail, you will be asked to rethink your initial impressions. Therefore, you should probably write your answers in pencil.

In general, much of literary analysis is "trial and error"; you will experiment with various structures and patterns and their meanings until you arrive at those structures which appear most comprehensive and meaningful.[1] Like any work of art, there is no *single* correct hidden pattern with *one* acceptable meaning, for literature has a built-in ambiguity that resists such dogmatism.

[1] I use the plural "structures" because it is often possible for there to be several operative patterns, each contributing its own meaning.

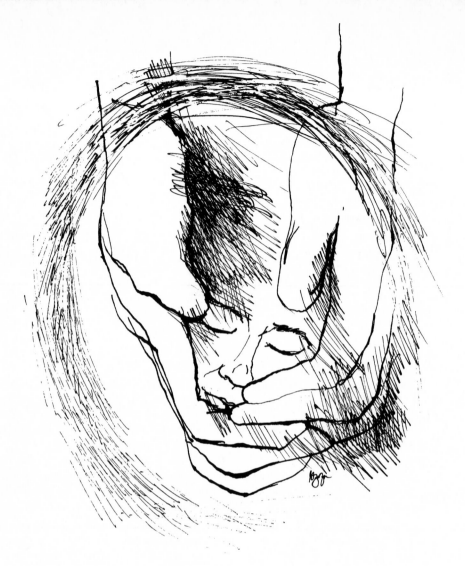

DIRECTIONS OF INQUIRY IN CHAPTER 3

We shall begin our treatment of the "Primeval History" (Genesis 1–11) by examining how it connects with chapters 12ff. The purpose of this inquiry is to verify both whether these initial 11 chapters really are a natural unit and whether in some sense chapters 1–11 introduce what follows. If these first 11 chapters of Genesis actually function as an introduction, then they should stand apart from what they introduce, just as the "introduction" to a textbook is usually set apart from the chapters that follow.

We shall then focus our attention on Genesis 1–11 and use each of the methodologies to which we were introduced in the previous chapter of this text. Our examination of the two different creation stories in Genesis 1–3 suggests that this section is made up of different *sources* (source criticism). The way in which these accounts have been combined is both evidence for who joined them and a clue to why these different accounts were placed back-to-back (redaction criticism). Next we shall look at each of the episodes in the Primeval History (Cain and Abel, Noah and the Ark, Tower of Babel, etc.) and use their literary structure to determine their isolated meanings as well as the meaning they acquire when strung together by the editor (rhetorical/literary criticism). Along the way we shall refer to similar literatures elsewhere in the ancient Near East and to such historical information as might help us better understand this crucial section of Genesis (historical-cultural criticism).[2]

OVERALL VIEW OF GENESIS 1-11 AND ITS CONTEXT

You will first note the literary context of Genesis 1-11, that is, its relationship to chapter 12 and chapters following. This is especially important because many scholars think that these first 11 chapters of Genesis function as an *introduction* to the entire first five books of the Bible (Genesis, Exodus, Leviticus, Numbers, and Deuteronomy), which are called the Pentateuch, or Torah. An introduction sets the tone for the work it introduces; it also presents the major themes and motifs that are developed in the larger piece. Because these five books traditionally form the heart of the Hebrew Bible, it would be important to detect any introduction that would tell us how this major portion of the Hebrew Bible was to be understood. However, the full implications of these 11 chapters of Genesis will not be developed until the next chapter of this text, where we place Genesis 1-11 in the broader literary context of the entire Torah, or Pentateuch.

How this possible introduction (Genesis 1-11) is to be read will depend on where it ends. (Remember how much an ending can affect your reading of a mystery novel!) For example, ask yourself the following questions (*and write down your thoughts in the space below*): (1) If this so-called preface or introduction ends with the Tower of Babel episode in Genesis 11:9, then what is the overall mood of these 11 chapters? What is your impression of the deity? (2) If, however, the introduction carries over into chapter 12 of Genesis, how in turn does this affect its spirit or dominant mood? Thus, our first task will be to mark off the exact confines of this "introduction."

A Preliminary Reading of Genesis 1-12

1. Read Genesis 1-12 through *two* times.

2. Read it through *once* quickly to acquaint yourself with the subject matter.

3. The *second* time, read it very carefully. (Be sure to read the footnotes in your Bible.) Ask yourself the following questions:

[2] However, most of the historical background for the text will be found in Chapter 4 of this book.

Most scholars see a major break between Genesis, chapters 1–11 and chapters 12ff. (If Genesis 1–11 is truly an introduction, then we would expect some type of break after chapter 11—after all, a preface is usually marked off from the first chapter in most books.) Let's test this. Write out some concrete links between the two sections. What words, characters, themes, and locations, etc., tie together chapters 1–11 and chapter 12?

LINKS

Just as important, are scholars justified in seeing a major break here? Explain differences between the two sections. These differences could be in tone, focus, scope of activity, etc.[3]

DIFFERENCES

4. What type or kind (genre) of literature do you think Genesis 1–11 is? In other words, are you reading an objective (referential) attempt to describe the origin of the world? Explain your answer in terms of the concepts explained in Chapter 1 of this text; that is, are these chapters referential ("this is the way the world came about . . ."), poetry, conative, or emotive? What codes are there to guide you in this initial impression? Try to describe in your own words what type of literature we have here. Perhaps it will help to give the name of another literary work of which you are aware that is similar.

---

[3] Remember, the full significance of your findings here will have to be postponed until the next chapter, where they will be placed in perspective.

Obviously Genesis 1-11 looks *as if* it is interested in things that happened in the distant past. In what time frame is the work *really* interested (past, present, future)? (Think in terms relative to someone reading Genesis 1-11: time before that reading is *past time*; time simultaneous to the reading is *present time*; time after the reading is *future time.*)

How does the question of the *function* of the chapters (emotive, conative, referential, etc.) help answer the question about its intended time frame? Explain your answer.

How important is it to know what *type* of literature you are reading in order to understand it correctly? Explain your answer; give particular examples where you think that people have mistaken the type of literature contained in Genesis 1-11.

Check the definition of **myth** in the Glossary. Could the definition of this genre of literature help explain Genesis 1-11?

What role do you think Genesis 1–11 played in Israelite society? In other words, who in Israelite society recited such stories and in what setting: the temple, the family, etc.? (This is just a preliminary question; you may want to modify your answer later.)[4]

5.   List the major episodes or stories in Genesis 1–11.

Do you see any common thread or threads that link these stories?

If there is a linkage, describe the pattern(s) according to which the stories have been arrayed. In other words, can you detect an overall arrangement to the individual parts (stories or episodes)?

[4] These are the main questions asked by form criticism.

6.   Read the chapters through a *third* time quickly.

At this stage in your reading, what do you think is the *thesis* of Genesis 1–11?[5]

GENESIS 1:1–3:24: THE CREATION STORIES

We shall follow the path determined at the beginning of this chapter. First we shall begin with source criticism to separate the different written documents that comprise this section. Second, we shall use redaction criticism to see who organized these different accounts of creation and kept both of them despite some tension between them. Third, we shall study the literary structures and meanings of each creation account and then look at their combined literary pattern (as the redactor, or editor, intended).

Source Criticism

1.   Read Genesis 1:1–3:24.

Let us begin by using source criticism. Notice that there are really two stories about the Creation. (For now let us just call them Account A and Account B. Where exactly do the two accounts separate? (There will be more on this later.)

[5] A thesis is the central or dominating idea in a literary work; a thesis must be *comprehensive*, that is, it must explain as much of Genesis 1–11 as possible, including the genealogies. A thesis is different from a *topic*, which is merely the subject matter being treated; the thesis is the author's complete proposal or statement about the subject matter. Therefore it should be stated in a complete sentence; for example, "the creation of the earth and the early days" constitutes only the topic; the thesis involves what the author is saying about these.

List the differences in literary style, attitudes toward the divinity, and humankind (include here different attitudes about the roles of male and female). Always illustrate your answers from the text.

DIFFERENCES IN LITERARY STYLE

DIFFERENCES IN ATTITUDES TOWARD DIVINITY

DIFFERENCES IN ATTITUDES TOWARD HUMANS

Catalogue the factual contradictions between the two accounts. A contradiction is not just something left out in one account that is mentioned in another; contradictions are elements that are present in both accounts but are mutually exclusive; for example, the order of things created.

FACTUAL CONTRADICTIONS

Redaction Criticism

1.   Genesis 2:4a reads: "These are the generations of the heavens and the earth at their creation." This phrase is typical of the language of the author of Genesis 1 and occurs elsewhere in Chapters 1–11 in Genesis 6:9, 10:1, and 11:27. There is really no dispute that the author of our Account A wrote the phrase in 2:4a; we

are not then asking who wrote it, but rather how does it function: as a summary of Account A or as an introduction to Account B? Therefore, is the expression in 2:4a a *summary* of what precedes in Account A (". . . and thus was the generation of . . .") or an *introduction* for Creation story B that follows (". . . and what follows is the story[6] of . . .")?

First of all, how is this phrase handled in Genesis 6:9, 10:1, and 11:27: Does it introduce or summarize?

Secondly, how does this broader usage of the phrase (a favorite linkage-phrase of our editor as we shall see!) help answer our question about its role in Genesis 2:4a? Explain your answer.

2. At the risk of confusing you further, there is an additional clue to help you determine the function of Genesis 2:4a. Remember that Hebrew literature loves to use *inclusion* as a device for setting off segments. The Bible uses this device much as we use paragraph indentation in our post-Gutenberg era. Now if there were an inclusion in either Account A or Account B, then this would determine the actual beginning or ending of that particular account. Look at Genesis 2:3b, which reads awkwardly in Hebrew: ". . . and he hallowed it because on it he rested from all his work which *God created* to do." What role does this phrase play in the first Creation account? Do you see any way in which this phrase could serve as one element in an inclusion? Therefore, according to the literary structure of the first story of Creation, where exactly would Account A end?

---

[6] The word "generation" can also mean "story" or "history."

How does this evidence help us determine the function of Genesis 2:4a? If 2:3b serves as an inclusion, then what possibilities would that exclude for the function of 2:4a?

3. Explain the significance of your conclusion to the history of how the two Creation accounts have been edited and *by whom*? This is like a mystery story: You should now have sufficient evidence to decide who the editor was who combined these two Creation stories. Why do the contradictions between the two accounts make your findings about the role of Genesis 2:4a more of a problem? Could the editor/redactor whom you have uncovered have done anything about these contradictions or tensions? (It might also help to know that the first Creation account was probably written around 550 B.C.E., whereas the second account was written around 950 B.C.E., that is, about 400 years earlier.)

A Literary/Critical Study of the Creation Stories

The First Story of Creation—Genesis 1:1—2:4a

1. Read Genesis 1:1—2:4a two times.[7]

2. On your first reading it should be apparent that this is a carefully structured account with a pronounced rhythm. Try to uncover the literary structures of this story of Creation. The following questions should provide clues for the structures operative in Genesis 1:1—2:4a. After you have thought about these clues, you will then be asked to sketch the patterns of this first section of the Hebrew Bible. When you do literary criticism there are basically three stages: (1) You determine those data that play a significant role in the structure (this is pure trial and error); (2) you arrange these data in a pattern (best done in a visual diagram); (3) you ask the important question, What does this pattern mean?

3. First, let us determine significant literary features. Numbers in the first Creation story are clearly going to be important building blocks for its overall literary structure: During a span of *seven* days there are *six* days of creating and *eight* crea-

---

[7]We shall now use the name most often given this account; it is called the Priestly Account (abbreviated P). The next chapter will provide more information about this source.

tive activities. We have to look now for the numerical patterns according to which these days and activities have been arranged: How many things or categories of things does God create on each day?[8]

In addition to the structural use of numbers, this story also organizes itself around its cosmology, that is, around its view of how the universe is structured. The ancient Near Eastern view of the cosmos divided everything into three locations: (1) Earth, (2) the Waters Around and Beneath the Earth, and (3) the Waters Above the Earth (the Heavens). All of this was experiential to the ancients: Digging a well and traveling across the seas seemed to prove the earth was surrounded by water circling the earth and by water below it; rainfall demonstrated the oceans of water above the earth.[9] The illustration pictured in this section is from an Egyptian New Kingdom (1570–1085 B.C.E.) papyrus and illustrates a tripartite universe similar to that which lies behind Genesis 1.[10] The sky goddess Nūt, decked out with stars, is being traversed by a boat bearing the Sun on its trip from east to west. (The two boats in the picture capture two stages in the Sun's trip: One boat represents the eastern part of the journey; the boat on the right is being received by Osiris, the god of the underworld, as the Sun sets in the west.) The sun boat sails on the "waters above" (the heavens). Below reclines the god Geb, who is bedecked with reeds and who represents the earth.

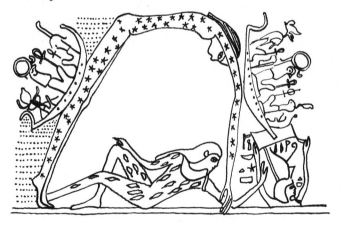

[8] The beginning verses (1, 2) are misleading and may cause problems in your structure. These verses should probably be translated as an introductory phrase, which really sets the stage for the first creative activity starting in verse 3. Thus, we render it,

> When God began creating the heavens and earth—the earth being *formless and void* with darkness upon the face of the deep and the spirit of God moving over the face of the waters—then God said . . . .

You see then that the author has explained the vague expression "formless and void" prior to actual creation in verse 3 in terms of the metaphors of (total) *darkness* and (limitless) *water.* The author then proceeds to elaborate each of these examples by first working on darkness and then on the waters.

[9] In this cosmic view, "heaven" is *not* the place of reward as in later Jewish, Christian, and Islamic theology.

[10] In the Egyptian model the three regions are the watery heavens, the earth, and the underworld, which often replaces the waters under and around the earth in Egyptian cosmology.

4.   Now let us put all of these data about six days, eight activities, and three locations together in a diagram in order to show how they structure the first Creation account. Remember that according to verses 1 and 2, God begins the first creative activity by "organizing" first total darkness and then the formless (that is, undifferentiated) waters.

**DIAGRAM OF THE LITERARY STRUCTURE
OF THE PRIESTLY CREATION STORY (Gen. 1:1–2:4a)**

DAY	CREATIVE ACTIVITY	COSMIC LOCATION[11]

[11] By "location" is meant that part of the tripartite universe (heavens, earth, and waters around and below the earth) where God is creating at that moment. This, then, refers to the location of God's creative attention. The reference to birds in Genesis 1:20 seems to link them with the seas. Remember that there can be no "cosmic location" assigned until it has been created.

5.   Once you have written out the diagram, you must try to see an overall pattern. Draw arrows and use whatever other visual devices you need to show the relationships between these parts. For example, is there a pattern in the arrangement of locations; there must be days in which God performs more than one activity; do these days appear in any order?

6.   Keep in mind that any competent writer will always use a structure for a purpose. Our ultimate goal is to discover what this long-dead writer (now called the **P Writer**) is trying to communicate. What meanings does your suggested pattern communicate? How do the structures convey that message?

Where do the structures of this first account focus our attention (verse numbers)? In other words, where are the most important parts of the story? (Remember that a passage may be significant either because of its placement *within* the structure or because of its placement *outside* the overall structure; for example, what role does the seventh day play in your overall pattern?)

How does the structure of the account focus our attention? List the ways. Why are these sections so important?

Based on where the author directs our attention, state what you think the author is saying. *In a complete sentence,* state the thesis of this author (P Writer).

7.   How is God described in this pattern? When God "creates" what verbs are used most frequently to describe this activity? How does this choice of words affect the description of God?

8.   Notice how important the creation of the human[12] is (verses 26–29). List several ways by which the author makes this section stand out from its background.

The strange phrase "Let us . . . ," where God speaks in the first person plural ("We . . . us"), is also found in Genesis 3:22 and 11:7. Is there any element common to all three of these passages? How do all three of these sections treat the relationship between humans and their deity? How is Genesis 1:26 different in this respect? What does a comparison of these three passages say about the *ideal* relationship with God?

9.   Look at the peculiar phrase "in our image, after our likeness" in verses 26–27. This is strange because the Israelites were forbidden to make "images of God," and so this phrase "image of God" would appear quite startling to the ancient reader. If it is so outrageous, then the P Writer must want to make an important point, for he appears willing to risk the reader's misunderstanding (and even hostility).

In what sense do you think we are created "in the image of God"?

---

[12] I have translated the Hebrew word *'adam* in verses 26, 27 by "human" or "human-kind" rather than the RSV's "man" because the Hebrew does not refer to the male gender as does the English word "man."

Why does verse 27 stand out? How has the author focused our attention on this verse? One hint: Of all the verses in the first Creation story this verse alone contains poetry. (At this point, be sure to read the section on Hebrew Poetry in Appendix E. Subsequent questions will presuppose that you have read this treatment of Hebrew poetry.)

We can keep the Hebrew word order in this verse (a **tricolon**, i.e., divided into three clauses or cola) by writing it out as follows (I have linked English words with a hyphen that are one word in Hebrew so that each **colon** or clause has the same number of words or word groups as the original Hebrew, i.e., four):

1.   AND-CREATED GOD THE-HUMAN IN-HIS-IMAGE

2.   IN-THE-IMAGE-OF GOD CREATED-HE HIM

3.   MALE AND-FEMALE CREATED-HE THEM

Now what kind of parallelism do we have in this verse?

Mark each of the four terms in line 1 above with the letters a, b, c, d. Notice how and in what order these terms recur in colon 2.

Which phrase is being stressed by this placement?

See how colon 3 echoes colon 2. How does poetic parallelism in colon 3 help explain the meaning of that troubling phrase "in his image"?

10.   Let's put all this confusing information together. According to the literary structure of verse 27, in what sense is the human created "in the image of God"?

11.   Now we have to find out what this ancient author understood by *human sexuality* ("male and female"). It is very important to keep in mind that our inquiry is *literary,* not biological! That is, we are not trying to discover the sixth-century B.C.E. biological knowledge about human sexuality; we are seeking to uncover clues *from the text alone* of the function of human sexuality in this literary Creation account.

Does sexuality in the P Writer account deal primarily with reproduction? Explain your answer carefully.

How does the author understand the male and female roles? That is, does the author relegate certain distinct role expectations to each sex?

In verses 27–29 ("You" in verse 29 is plural) the author keeps fluctuating between the singular and plural ("him/them, human/male and female"). Try to take this into account in your theory about how Genesis 1:1–2:4a understands male and female. Does the P Writer also fluctuate between singular and plural in talking about God?

In what senses could God be spoken of in the plural? Notice that whenever the P Writer uses the plural in this section for either God or the human, a *social* or *interactive* dimension is introduced in which the relationship between characters is highlighted. How does this aspect help us understand the parallelism between God as "we/us" and humans as "they"?

12.   Is the stress in the P Writer account on God or on the human? Explain your answer.

There is a sort of inclusion in the presentation of God: The passage begins with God alone and ends with God alone (seventh day). How does this help answer the question about the focus of the P Writer's account of Creation?

Historical-Cultural Criticism of Genesis 1:1—2:4a

1.   Let's take a moment to see where we are. We have already employed most of the literary tools that we learned in previous chapters of this text. Our reading of Genesis 1–11 has suggested that this segment is composed of several literary sources (source criticism); this was particularly evident in our reading of the two Creation accounts.

2.   When we asked about the type of literature we were reading in these first 11 chapters of Genesis and where in that society was that particular type or genre performed or recited, we were using *form criticism*.

3.   But the exercise on the function of Genesis 2:4a should demonstrate that there is also evidence of editing or redaction. Somebody (and you should already suspect who!) has linked these sources together, although we have yet to see what the editorial purpose was or, rather, the overall pattern according to which the sources have been combined. This involves *redaction criticism*.

4.   The use of these tools has already helped us reach an idea of the meaning(s) of the Priestly Creation story. For now, let us leave the author's literary world and talk a little about the historical and cultural world of the author of Genesis.

Most scholars (but not all) agree that the first author of Genesis was a priest who lived in exile in Babylon around 550 B.C.E.[13] The author's world had been virtually destroyed. The Davidic monarchy and the temple of Solomon had come to an end in 586 B.C.E. when the Babylonians destroyed Jerusalem. The ruling priests were brought to Babylon as captives. (You can read about this in 2 Kings 25.)

The priests were tempted to despair, for many felt that their God could not be worshipped apart from the temple in Jerusalem, which then lay in ruins. God could hardly be addressed in an alien land! (Read Psalm 137, which was written at this time.) A sense of their anguish can be felt in the Book of Lamentations, which "laments" these events.

Does this historical information help you further understand Genesis 1:1—2:4a? How would the portrayal of God in this Creation story meet the exiles' needs? Explain your answer.

---

[13] More about this Priestly Writer—called the *P source*—in the next chapter.

God's "speaking" appears very important in this first Creation story. Why would this be important to those readers we have just described? Why would this account, with its stress on God's "speaking," be a better beginning for an exilic readership than the second account of Creation, which they already knew?

5.   It is particularly helpful to contrast this account with a contemporary Babylonian story about creation of which the Priestly Writer must have been aware.

Read the Enuma Elish in Appendix B. Please answer the study questions found there to guide you through this complicated Babylonian myth. Both Genesis and the Enuma Elish arose in similar circumstances. The Babylonian Creation story was written around 1100 B.C.E., ironically during the reign of King Nebuchadnezzar I, whose namesake was to destroy Jerusalem 500 years later. In 1200 the Assyrians had conquered Babylon and removed the statue of Babylon's chief deity, Marduk, to Assyria. This political and religious catastrophe was not avenged until the reign of Nebuchadnezzar 100 years later when Assyria was defeated and the statue returned. This event was celebrated by the writing of the Enuma Elish, which attempted to explain how Marduk, who was considered throughout Mesopotamia to be an insignificant deity, could rise to such power. And so, like the Priestly Creation story, the Enuma Elish was a work of political propaganda composed after a religious calamity. Both works foster views about their respective creator gods, which were at variance with the norm.

6.   List the *similarities* between the two works.[14]

---

[14] Note that both begin with water as the symbol of the "formlessness" from which order was created. This probably reflects their common Mesopotamian background where the flood from the Tigris and Euphrates, which yearly destroyed cities, was a common metaphor for chaos. The second Creation story (2:4b ff.), on the other hand, begins with parched earth made fruitful with rain—more typical of a Palestinian origin. The Enuma Elish ends with the building of Marduk's palace. This motif is also present in the P Writer, for in Exodus 39–40 this person talks about the construction of God's temple in the wilderness in language similar to Genesis 1; see Exodus 40:16, 33. And so the P Writer also went from Creation to the building of a temple. P was also probably looking forward to the rebuilding of the temple in Jerusalem, which had been destroyed in 586 B.C.E.

7.   List the *differences* between the two works. Especially detail the differences in their respective portrayals of the Creator and of humankind.

For the first time, the people of Israel begin to express a specific idea of monotheism: not only is Yahweh their God but he is the *only* God.

8.   Read another work written at the same time, one also written for the exiles in Babylon: Isaiah 44:24–45:7.[15] This section has been set off by an inclusion in both 44:24 and 45:7: "I Yahweh [or the Lord] am doing all [these] things," which shows that this is a natural unit. (Also, despite the translation given in the RSV, the verbs in this section are *not* past tense: "who makes . . . who stretches out" rather than "who made . . . who stretched out." This is important for understanding the passage's view about Creation.)

Because an inclusion not only sets apart a section, much like paragraphs in a book, but also highlights the major theme in that section, we must discover exactly what Yahweh is "making/doing" (44:24 and 45:7) that is so important. First of all, note that the second element in the inclusion (45:7) adds a new term—"these." To what does the demonstrative pronoun "these" refer?

List some of the things that Yahweh is described as doing.

[15] This selection has been taken from a section of the Book of Isaiah, chapters 40–55, written around 540 B.C.E. by an anonymous prophet two centuries after the original prophet Isaiah of Jerusalem (ca. 735–701 B.C.E.). It is often called *Deutero-Isaiah,* or Second Isaiah. It was probably composed by an exile living in Babylon who was trying to reassure fellow exiles that Yahweh is still powerful and, in fact, is about to deliver them in a Second Exodus from their captivity through the means of King Cyrus, the Persian who was about to conquer Babylon and release the exiles.

These activities of Yahweh listed above seem to fall into two categories. Some refer to Yahweh's *cosmic* works in creating the universe, whereas others describe Yahweh's *historical* efforts on behalf of his people. Divide all the works of God in this section into these two groupings.

This section of Deutero-Isaiah is written in poetry; you can detect the parallelism in such verses as 45:1-3. Now study carefully the parallelism in 44:27, 28. This line parallels some of Yahweh's activities.[16] What does this line (44:27, 28) say about the relationship between the two categories of activities (cosmic and historical) distinguished above?

Recall that the verbs referring to Creation in this passage are in the present, ongoing tense (not the past tense as in the RSV). How does this grammatical fact clarify the author's relationship between Yahweh as *cosmic* creator and Yahweh as *historical* deliverer?

Often religious people today conceive of divine creation as what God *did* (past tense) way back in the past to start or initiate this universe. How does this view of cosmic creation compare with that of Deutero-Isaiah?

[16] The "drying up of the deep" in Isaiah 44:27 refers to an ancient Near Eastern Creation motif. Compare with Genesis 1:9.

Let's put all these data together now. At first it might seem a strange coincidence that both the Priestly Writer (P) and Deutero-Isaiah would emphasize Creation at this same critical juncture in Israelite history—the exile in Babylon. Draw on your newly acquired ideas about the relationship between Creation and salvation as seen in Isaiah 44:24–45:7 to explain the role of Creation in these two writers. In other words, why would a theology of Creation have been relevant to this exiled, depressed readership?

Genesis 2:4b–3:24

Literary-Critical Study

1.   This second narrative has been called the *Yahwist* (**J** Writer after the German spelling "Jahweh"), for the writer prefers to call the deity by the proper Hebrew name, Yahweh,[17] which your Bible always translates as Lord. (Notice that the first Creation story called the deity "God.") Because the narrative contains a considerable amount of dialogue, it can easily be considered as a play.[18] Divide the story into scenes. A change of actors, location, or literary form (narrative or dialogue) will determine a scene.

For each scene write out the following information: *location* (especially in relation to the tree in the center of the garden), *actors* on stage, literary form (narrative, monologue, dialogue), and the *relationship* between the actors (that is, unity, equality, discord, submission).

[17] Because of the sacredness of the divine name Yahweh, Judaism prefers to read the word "Lord" wherever "Yahweh" occurs in the Hebrew Bible. The translation in the RSV follows this practice; thus, wherever the RSV uses the word "Lord" this renders the original Hebrew name Yahweh.

[18] Recall the three steps in doing literary criticism: (1) Isolate significant data; (2) arrange them in a pattern or structure, (3) find the meaning conveyed by that pattern. The questions follow these steps. In the case of Genesis 2:4b–3:24, the significant data are the use of dramatic scenes to express relationships among the actors; we shall next try to arrange these scenes in a pattern; last, we shall examine their meaning.

Arrange the scenes into a structure or pattern. Is there a relationship between the various scenes? Can you indicate this in the way you arrange the scenes? Which scene is stressed by this arrangement? Relate this structure to what you think the entire Creation story is about.

Locale plays an important role in the organization of the narrative. Is there motion from one location to another? Is there also a pattern here that supports your diagram above? (Remember your given location is the tree "in the center of the garden." Everything is located relative to that tree.)

The story is also concerned with character relationships. Almost every scene has something to say about the relationship between the various component elements in the created cosmos. (The serpent represents the animal world and is not Satan.) Talk a little about the relationship between the actors in each of the scenes and how it changes. Does this help you understand the meaning of the overall story?

Read the punishment scene (Genesis 3:14-19). How are the punishments of each of the guilty parties related to the crime? Do the punishments relate to changing character relationships noticed above? Try to illustrate your answer in terms of humankind's (*'adam*) relationship throughout the story to the soil/ground (*'adamah*) in Genesis 2:7, 9; 3:17-19.

2.   What does the J Creation story say about the relationship between male and female? (Be sure to justify your response from the text and compare it with the P account.) Throughout history many have argued that this account considered women to be inferior for the following reasons: (1) The male was created first, and woman was only created to meet man's needs; (2) To call something by name (Genesis 2:19) is to exercise control over it; because the male seems to name the woman (2:23), then he would have dominion over her; (3) Woman was created from the male's side; therefore woman is "derived" from man and thus secondary. I want you to take each of these three arguments and test them against the text: Does a careful reading of the text support these three arguments? (*Clues:* (1) Remember that *'adam* beginning in Genesis 2:7 generally means "humankind" not "male" and does not denote a proper name (Adam); (2) The proper words for "male and female" occur for the first time in Genesis 2:23.)

Is the wording of the human's "naming" in Genesis 2:23b exactly the same as in Genesis 2:19?[19] What effect does your answer have for the J Writer's concept of the relationship between male and female?

---

[19] Notice the grammatical use of the passive voice "is called" in Genesis 2:23. Often in Hebrew the passive voice is employed to denote the agency of God: "God will call."

3.   Now formulate the main thesis of this Creation story. Secondly, contrast its concerns with those of the Priestly Writer.

Redaction Criticism

1.   We have already discovered that the Priestly Writer (P) knew about the second Creation account (J) before writing this account; P even introduced it (Genesis 2:4a). Because P's introduction in this verse also told us that P was aware of the second Creation story (which had probably been written 400 years earlier), why would P feel that one had to preface the older version (2:4b—3:24) with a Creation story of one's own (1:1—2:4a)? The P Writer even wrote contradictions into this account although P could have thoroughly harmonized the two. Why?

You already have an idea what the first account means and what the second account means. What further meaning results from the editing of both accounts together?

In what sense are the views of Creation in P and J (especially of the human) directly opposite? Characterize each one around the twin motifs of *blessing* and *curse*. Can the reading of the two together, as consciously intended by P, establish a composite view of Creation with a built-in tension? Explain your responses.

The Cain and Abel Story (Genesis 4:1–16)

1.   Read the Cain and Abel story (Genesis 4:1–16).

List all the *words* and *images* in this story that recall Genesis 3 and thus resume its story line.

What is the significance of this "parallelism"? Relate it to the "tug-o'-war" (blessing and curse) that has been created by the Priestly redactor (editor) by the joining of the two Creation narratives.

How is the motif of the soil/ground (*'adamah*) continued in this episode?

How is the "direction-from-the-center" motif of Genesis 2:4b–3:24 continued in the Cain and Abel story? What significance does this have?

2.   Read the two genealogies: Genesis 4:17–24 (Cainite) and Genesis 4:25, 26 (Sethite).

How do these two genealogies serve P's theme of the tension between blessing and curse that the P editor established in the two Creation accounts? Explain your answer carefully.

The Flood: Genesis 5:1—9:28

Redaction Criticism

1.   First let us examine the *redaction critical* question. In other words, we want to gain an insight into how this story has been woven by the editor (P) into the fabric of Genesis 1–11. This will provide insight into how the editor wants us to understand the Flood narrative.

2.   Look at the genealogy in Genesis 5:1–32. This genealogy follows a very peculiar structure, or pattern. Write out the pattern followed by each name entry.

Why do you think the repetitive phrase ". . . and he died" is unusual for a genealogy? (Think for a moment about the purpose of genealogies.) What role do you think this chapter plays in conveying the thesis of the P editor that we have seen up to this point?

Now look at the last entry (5:32) for Noah. How does this entry deviate from the preceding? Where in the Noah story is the standard genealogical pattern that is found in the rest of the chapter completed? (Cite chapter and verse.) What does this say about the redaction of the Flood story?

This entry for Noah is structurally important for our editor: It relates Noah both forward to Abraham and backwards to Adam. You will see a similarly patterned genealogy in Genesis 11:10–26. These two sections place Noah at the halfway point between Adam and Abraham (ten generations on either side). Look at Genesis 5:29. How does Noah's father, Lamech, understand the importance of Noah's birth? To what earlier event does this verse refer?

Literary/Critical Study of the Flood Account

1.   Some commentaries do not think that Genesis 6:1–8 belongs to the Flood story. (In fact, by calling it a "Flood story" we limit the essence of the account to the later narrative about the ark.) The questions that follow will determine both why the P editor included these verses and hint at the literary role they play. Read Genesis 6:1–4. Which of our two written sources (P or J) wrote this myth? Why did the sophisticated P editor, who so esteemed the uniqueness of God (see P's account of Creation), include such a primitive story?[20] What purpose could these verses play in the theme that the P editor has established?

Clue: Recall how the P Writer of the first Creation story understood the creative act—what verb did the writer especially prefer? Now, how would the outrageous events in Genesis 6:1–4 symbolize a threat to that order? In what sense would P perceive the myth in 6:1–4 as an "uncreation story"?

---

[20] From an historical-cultural point of view, this story is an example of a common type of myth in the ancient world in which deities have intercourse with humans, giving birth to demigods (such as the Greek Heracles or the Babylonian Gilgamesh).

2.   Genesis 6:5-8 clearly suggests that Genesis 6:1-4 is to be read alongside the Flood story (as a symbol of the uncreation to be washed away). Notice ways in which these verses in chapter 6 harken back *both* to the story of Noah's birth in Genesis 5:28-32, which is the frame to the entire flood narrative, *and* to both Creation stories (P and J).

Genesis 6:6 is very important. These verses contain a play on words that recalls Genesis 5:29 (and Genesis 3:14-19):

GENESIS 6:6	GENESIS 5:29	
". . . was sorry" (**nḥm**)	". . . bring relief" (**nḥm**)	
". . . it grieved him" (**ᶜṣb**)	". . . toil" (**ᶜṣb**)[21]	FN 21

How does Genesis 6:6 temper the enthusiasm expressed at the birth of Noah?

How does Genesis 6:9, 10 recall the genealogy in chapter 5 and what significance does this have for deciding whether 6:1-8 is an integral part of the "Flood story"?

4.   The reason for the Flood is found in a pun on the Hebrew root šḥt (pronounced "shahat") in verses 11-13, which can mean "be corrupt" or "to corrupt," that is, "to destroy." Notice the careful structure in these verses:

A   the earth became corrupt (šḥt) before God (11a)

B   the earth was filled with violence (11b)

C   all flesh had become corrupt (šḥt) (12b)

C′   the end of all flesh is coming (13a)

B′   The earth was filled with violence (13a)

A′   I am about to "corrupt" (šḥt) the earth (13b)

---

[21] This word also plays an important role in the punishment scene in Genesis 3:14-19 where it occurs in verses 16 ("pain") and 17 ("toil").

Puns in English are most often used as *codes* for humor; in Hebrew, how-ever, they are quite serious. If words actually sound alike, then they must denote things that are really similar. How does this play on the Hebrew root **ŠHṬ** serve to fix the moral responsibility for the destruction caused by the Flood? According to this pun, who is to blame for the destruction of the subsequent Flood? Be sure to explain your answer carefully.

Read the more ancient Babylonian Flood account in Appendix C (Tablet XI, lines 9–196). The reason for the Babylonian Flood is found in a poorly preserved myth. The Mesopotamian myth clearly was the source for the Genesis Flood narra-tive. List *similarities* between the Babylonian and the biblical deluge accounts.

According to each myth, what is the exact cause of the Flood that all but destroys humankind? How does this difference distinguish the two stories?

5.   The literary structure for the rest of the Flood narrative is somewhat com-plex, so I shall give a structural outline of the story as presented by B. Anderson. I want you to reread the narrative using this outline. Try to find common phrases or words that link the paired sections (for example, section 3 and 8, 4 and 7). Ac-cording to this pattern, where is the focus of the story and how does this affect the meaning of the narrative?

THE ARK NARRATIVE[22]

FRAMEWORK: Genealogy 5:32

        Prologue: 6:1–4 "Prologue to Disaster"
                    6:5–8 "Regret [**NHM** ^C**ṢB**] of Yahweh" (compare 5:29)
      Transition: 6:9, 10 (Style of the genealogy, 5:1ff.)

          1.   *Violence in God's Creation* (6:11, 12) [**ŠḤT**]
               [Human **ŠḤT** leads to God's **ŠḤT** in 6:13]

            2.   *First Divine Address: Resolution to Destroy*
                (6:13–22: "announcement-command as in Genesis 1")

              3.   *Second Divine Address: Enter the Ark*
                  (7:1–10: "command-execution")

                4.   *Beginning of the Flood* (7:11–16)

                  5.   *Rising Flood Waters* (7:17–24)

GOD REMEMBERS NOAH! (8:1–5)

                6.   *The Receding Flood* (8:1–5)
                    "God allows new beginning"

              7.   *The Drying of the Earth* (8:6–14)

            8.   *Third Divine Address: Leave Ark* (8:15–19)

         9.   *God's Resolution to Preserve Order* (8:20–22)

       10.   *Fourth Divine Address: Covenant Blessing* (9:1–17)

      Transition: 9:18, 19 (Recapitulation)
      Epilogue: 9:20–27 ("Drunkenness of Noah")

FRAMEWORK: Genealogy 9:28, 29

1.   Show similarities between this Flood story and the first Creation account.

      How do these links help us understand the significance of the Flood in the P edition of Genesis 1-11?

---

[22] B. Anderson, *Journal of Biblical Literature*, 97 (1978): 23.

2.   Is the final mood of the Flood story optimistic or pessimistic? Does the story reassure readers or warn them of imminent disaster? Explain your answer.

3.   What role does the strange story about Noah's drunkenness (9:20–27) play in P's thesis about two struggling directions for creation (blessing and curse)?

In what ways is this strange episode similar to that of the Cain and Abel story? (*Clue:* Notice the relationship of the characters in the stories and the sequence of each narrative with regard to the preceding story.)

4.   Let us use historical criticism for a moment. How would this Flood story in Genesis 5:32–9:29 have been perceived by P's original exilic audience? Would they have been reassured? If so, how? Before you answer, reconstruct in your mind the political and religious situation of these Babylonian exiles. (Re-read Psalm 137 or the Book of Lamentations.)

Recall that our literary/critical study of the Flood narrative found the pivotal point in Genesis 8:1–5. How would this midpoint have been read by Israelite captives in Babylon?

The Tower of Babel (Genesis 11:1–9)

Literary-Critical Study

Read the following biblical passage (Genesis 11:1–9) and interpret it using literary criticism. Keep in mind the three steps involved in literary criticism. I have included in parentheses various Hebrew words that are translated by the preceding English—these might be of some assistance as building blocks that set up the narrative's structure. Also be sure to take into consideration your earlier work on Genesis 1–12 and especially Genesis 1–3. Be clear and brief! Following the passage itself I have included some study questions that should help you focus upon the structure and meaning of this Tower of Babel story.

1. Now all the earth had one language and similar words. 2. And as men migrated from the east, they found a plain in the land of Shinar and settled there (**sham**). 3. And they said to one another, "Come, let-us-make-bricks (**nilbenah**), and burn them thoroughly." And they had brick for stone and bitumen for mortar. 4. Then they said, "Come let us build ourselves a city and a tower with its top in the heavens (**shamayim**), and let us make a name (**shem**) for ourselves, lest we be scattered abroad upon the face of the whole earth."

5. And Yahweh came down to see the city and the tower, which the sons of men had built. 6. And Yahweh said, "Behold, they are one people, and they have all one language; and this is only the beginning of what they will do; and nothing that they propose to do will now be impossible for them.

7. Come, let us go down, and there (**sham**) confuse (**nabelah**) their language, that they may not understand one another's speech." 8. So Yahweh scattered them abroad from-there (**mishsham**) over the face of all the earth, and they left off building the city.

9. Therefore its name (**shemah**) was called Babel, because there (**sham**) Yahweh babbled the language of all the earth; and from there (**mishsham**) Yahweh scattered them abroad over the face of all the earth.

1. This is a very carefully organized passage with every element fitting together perfectly. In order to reveal its structure, look for recurrent patterns. Underline all the words and phrases that are repeated in the story.

Connect all these repeated expressions with lines; this should match up all the repetitions. Is there any order revealed in the way the phrases are repeated?

Does this exercise reveal the pivotal point of the passage? Into how many parts can this story be divided? Explain your answer.

Besides repetitions, are there any clues that support this division? For example, divide the story into parts according to the following criteria: (1) main actors; (2) according to the direction of any motion (horizontal and vertical planes). In all these cases, where is/are the main division(s) in the story?

2.   After you have reached these theories about the organization of the piece, relate literary structure to meaning.

Try to find connections between this story and earlier stories in Genesis 1–11. Be specific (for example, look at verse 2; which earlier story does this recall?).

How exactly would the Priestly editor read the efforts of the human builders? Are they examples of advances in human technology accomplished by cooperation or do their efforts at "tower building" recall the theme of "uncreation"? In the mind of P, how would this story recall Genesis 6:1–4? Be specific!

3.   Do you see any way in which the Hebrew words in the text above help communicate the meaning of the story? Try to retell the entire story by using these key words.

Redaction Criticism

1.   Let's examine the editor's (that is, P's) use of the genealogies. Look now at chapter 10 of Genesis. Knowing what you do about the Tower of Babel story, why do you think that chapter 10 seems to be out of logical sequence? Why would a more natural chapter order have been: 11, 10? (Be specific!)

If the original order had been Genesis 11, 10, why would the editor (**P**) have positioned chapter 10 out of its more natural order following the Tower of Babel episode? Try to formulate an answer by: (1) recalling the "blessing and curse" dynamic that the P editor seems to have constructed up to this point; (2) Try getting a feel (in terms of P's thesis) for the effect of both orders. In other words, why would the P editor have objected to ending the introduction (Genesis 1–11) with the more natural order of chapter 11, then chapter 10?

As things now stand, our editor has given two accounts of the spread of humankind over the face of the earth. The genealogy in Genesis 11:10ff. would exemplify the spread resulting from the judgment of Yahweh at the tower (11:8). Can you suggest what the spread of humankind witnessed in chapter 10 (in its present order) might illustrate? Link it with a divine command in Genesis 9, which this genealogy might now be seen as illustrating. How do these two explanations now develop the editor's overall thesis?

AN OVERVIEW OF THE ENTIRE BOOK OF GENESIS

We shall now see the Primeval History (Genesis 1–11), which was mentioned at the beginning of this chapter, in the context of the rest of the Book of Genesis. Because some readers might have the suspicion that the emphasis on *literary* features has been at the expense of the *theological,* the approach to the remainder of Genesis will focus on the close relationship between the literary and the theological features of the book. As Genesis becomes literarily more complex in its treatment of both characterization and narrative, so also its portrayal of the interaction between humans and Yahweh becomes more intricate.[23]

Read the rest of the Book of Genesis; do not become preoccupied with names and details; just bear in mind the main thread of the fate of the three Patriarchs (Abraham, Isaac, and Jacob) and their families (especially Joseph). Be sure that you are particularly familiar with the passages referred to in the questions below.

1.   How does the phrase "These are the generations/descendants/history (*toledoth*) of . . ." (Genesis 2:4, 6:9, 11:27, 25:19, and 37:2) divide up the Book of Genesis into literary units?

Look at the narrative passage introduced by each of these headings below, and give the name of the figure who is the central character in each of these narratives.[24]

GENERATION OF . . .   MAIN CHARACTER OF NARRATIVE

2:4

6:9

11:27

25:19

37:2

Which Patriarch does not have a narrative cycle about himself?

[23] Most of the material in this section has been taken from Robert Cohn's article, "Narrative Structure and Canonical Perspective in Genesis," in *Journal for the Study of the Old Testament,* 25 (1983): 3–16.

[24] We shall call each narrative complex centered around an individual a *cycle.*

Narrative Complexity of the Cycles

1.   Recall the episodes in Genesis 1–11. Would you describe these individual stories (Adam and Eve, Cain and Abel, Noah, Tower of Babel) as independent from a literary point of view? In other words, to what extent does each story, in order to be intelligible, require what precedes or what follows it?

2.   Now let us look at the narrative complexity of the Abraham Cycle. Like the Primeval History, the Abraham Cycle is composed of different episodes (Pharaoh and Sarah, Sacrifice of Isaac, Rescue of Lot, Sodom and Gomorrah). Compare the literary independence of these stories with those of Genesis 1–11. Are most of the Abraham stories linked together?

How does the fact that in the Abraham Cycle we are dealing with a *single* individual compare with the situation in Genesis 1–11?

What issue(s) or problem(s) seem to thread their way through almost all of the Abraham Cycle? Compare this literary situation with the Primeval History.

3.   Study the narrative structure and organization of the Jacob Cycle.

Compare the length of the episodes in the Jacob Cycle with those of the Primeval History and the Abraham Cycle.

Can the stories in the Jacob Cycle be read independently? For example, does the Jacob and Laban story (Genesis 29–31) make sense apart from what preceded it?

How does Laban's cheating of Jacob tie in with earlier stories in the Jacob Cycle?

4.   There is a play on two Hebrew words (*bekorah, berakah*) throughout the Jacob Cycle. These words both have several meanings around which the story is organized.

BERAKAH   blessing of Isaac (Genesis 27)

Jacob's gift for Esau (Genesis 33:11)

BEKORAH   birthright (Genesis 25:31)

first-born daughter (Genesis 29:26)

Try to retell the story of Jacob using these two words—each with its two meanings. What does this tell us about the narrative complexity of the Jacob Cycle?

5.   How does the story of Joseph compare with the literary structure of the preceding three cycles? Is it composed of a series of episodes or stories like the earlier cycles? Make your response as detailed as possible.

Many people think that the bizarre Tamar story in Genesis 38 interrupts the Joseph story. Let us examine the literary relationship of Genesis 38 to chapters 37 and 39.

Compare the roles of Judah in Genesis 37 and Genesis 38. Do you find any examples of irony?

How does "clothing" function in the two chapters?

Compare the motif of *sexuality* in the portrayal of Judah in chapter 38 and of Joseph in chapter 39. How would this comparison fit in with the overall Joseph story?

What does this tell us about the literary complexity of the Joseph story?

Character Portrayal in the Narrative Cycles

1.   Contrast character portrayal in Genesis 1–11 and in the Abraham Cycle. Are the figures in Genesis 1–11 "flesh and blood" people with whom you could identify?

    Look at the *conflicts* in the two cycles. Against whom do the people in Genesis 1–11 fight? How are the conflicts in the Abraham Cycle different? With which type of contest can you more readily identify?

    Compare the *moral* interaction of people in each cycle. Can you identify with the moral choices and temptations faced by Adam and Eve? Cain and Abel? The builders of the Tower of Babel? Are the moral choices faced by Abraham different? If so, explain.

    As examples, look at the moral decisions of Abraham in Genesis 12:10–20 and Genesis 22. Is Abraham right or wrong? How are these choices different from the one made by Eve in Genesis 3?

2.   Describe the character of Jacob.

Is there any character development in the Jacob Cycle, that is, is the earliest portrayal of Jacob identical with the Jacob who is reconciled with his brother in Genesis 32, 33?

How does this development compare with any development of a character in Genesis 1-11 or of Abraham?

3.   Describe the character of Joseph in the Joseph story.

Is there any character development in the Joseph story? If so, whose character(s) mature throughout the narrative?

Portrayal of God in the Narrative Cycles

1.   Describe and illustrate the description of God in Genesis 1–11, and contrast it with the deity's portrayal in the Abraham Cycle.

    In which cycle is God more intrusive into the narrative? (In other words, contrast the ways that God intervenes in the narratives; is this intervention more abrupt and "miraculous" in one?) Explain your answer.

    In which of the two cycles are humans given freer rein to make their own decisions?

    In which of the cycles is God described in more *anthropomorphic*[25] terms? Be sure to illustrate your response from the text.

---

[25] "Anthropomorphic" means "after the fashion of a human"; to describe God in anthropomorphic terms is to ascribe to God such human characteristics as a body, human emotions, etc.

2.   How is the way that God communicates with Jacob different from the divine communication to Abraham or to the characters of Genesis 1–11? Compare the *frequency* of God's appearances in Genesis 1–11 to that in the Abraham and Jacob Cycles.

Notice that the two main theophanies or divine appearances in the Jacob Cycle (Genesis 28 and 32) serve a structural purpose; they provide a type of "inclusion." First, explain how they serve as an inclusion. Second, what significance would this literary feature have for the way God is portrayed in the Jacob Cycle?

3.   Let us now look at the theology of the Joseph story. Compare the frequency of the mention of God in this cycle to the preceding ones.

Does God appear to, or talk directly with, Joseph?

Look at some of the passages in which Joseph mentions God's activity: Genesis 45:5-8, 41:16, 40:8. Who *actually* is described as performing the activity? Through whom does God work in each of these cases? What significance does this have for the presentation of God in the Joseph Cycle?

God is mentioned in conjunction with *dreams* in both the Joseph and Jacob stories. How does the role of God in dreams differ in each case? How does this help us understand the different theologies of these two narratives?

4.   Contrast the involvement of God in the Joseph story with God's involvement in Genesis 1-11, in the Abraham Cycle, and in the Jacob Cycle.

Is it correct to state that God plays no real role in the Joseph story? Is the story really nonreligious: Foreigner makes good by his own shrewdness? Explain your response.

5.   All of these Narrative Cycles can be compared to the ways in which they deal with moral *retribution*. Each cycle depicts different ways in which people receive punishment for wrongdoings. Moreover, punishment comes through different agents in the various narratives. Contrast the way that retribution is handled in Genesis 1-11 to the way it is handled in the Patriarchal Cycles.

Narrative Art and Theology in Genesis

Now we shall integrate our findings on narrative complexity, character portrayal, and theology in the Book of Genesis.

1.   You should have noticed by now an almost inverse relationship: Throughout Genesis, as literary complexity increased, God's *explicit* role decreased. Thus, the simple stories of the Primeval History presented an active God directly intervening in human affairs; but by the time of the intricate Joseph story, the human is the main actor, and God is definitely in the background. Carefully describe the theology[26] of the Joseph story in the Book of Genesis. Is the relationship of divine and human more sophisticated in the Joseph story or is this cycle really *non*religious? Explain your response.

2.   Show how the literary structure of the Book of Genesis is related to the religious theme of the relationship between God and humans in the Book of Genesis.

---

[26] This text does not presuppose any particular religious belief on the part of its readers; however, even for a nonbeliever it is clear that the Bible is a *religious* work, that is, it talks about God and humans. A literary critic can then study how that religious or theological message is conveyed.

Consider ways in which rhetorical/literary criticism is a *necessary* tool for understanding the theology of the Bible.

FURTHER READINGS

Bernhard W. Anderson, "From Analysis to Synthesis: The Interpretation of Genesis 1–11," *Journal of Biblical Literature,* 97 (1978): 23-29.

B. Anderson, "A Stylistic Study of the Priestly Creation Story," in *Canon and Authority: Essays in Old Testament Religion and Theology,* G. W. Coats and B. O. Long, eds. (Philadelphia: Fortress, 1977), pp. 148-162.

Robert Cohn, "Narrative Structure and Canonical Perspective in Genesis," *Journal for the Study of the Old Testament*, 25 (1983): 3-16.

J. P. Fokkelman, *Narrative Art in Genesis* (Amsterdam: Van Gorcum, 1975). This excellent study analyzes large sections of the Book of Genesis using literary criticism. I am highly indebted to the author's study of the Tower of Babel story (pp. 11-45).

Kenneth R. R. Gros Louis, "Genesis 3–11," in *Literary Interpretations of Biblical Narratives* Vol. 2, Gros Louis and J. Ackerman, eds. (Nashville: Abingdon, 1982), pp. 37-52.

P. D. Miller, Jr., *Genesis 1–11: Studies in Structure and Theme* (*Journal for the Study of the Old Testament Supplement Series,* 8; Sheffield, England: Journal for the Study of the Old Testament, 1978).

Phyllis Trible, *God and the Rhetoric of Sexuality* (Philadelphia: Fortress, 1978). See pp. 1-23 on Genesis 1 and on literary criticism in general. See pp. 72-139 on Genesis 2:4–3:24. These treatments of both Creation accounts offer a skilled and sensitive treatment of the creation of male and female in both P and J accounts.

Jerome T. Walsh, "Genesis 2:4b–3:24: A Syntactic Approach," *Journal of Biblical Literature,* 96 (1977): 161-177. This excellent article, which, among other things, divides the J Creation story into scenes, can be quite technical in places.

CHAPTER 4
THE THEME OF THE PENTATEUCH AND ITS ORIGINS

GOALS AND OBJECTIVES: This chapter builds on the information that the student acquired in Chapter 3; it also compares the reader's hypotheses about Genesis 1-11 with the results of scholarship over the last century. Chapter 4 can be divided into three main sections. It will first of all tie together all of the individual episodes of Genesis 1-11 and discuss the overall thesis of that introduction to the Torah/Pentateuch. Secondly, it will relate that thesis to the comprehensive thesis of the Torah, the first five books of the Hebrew Bible (literary criticism). Thirdly, this chapter traces the development of that final thesis through its various stages (tradition criticism), beginning with early oral recitals on through the documents J (the Yahwist), **E (the Elohist), D (the Deuteronomist),** *and the final exilic redaction of the Priestly Editor (source and redaction criticisms). This last section relates the emergence of these religious documents to the historical crises faced by the Israelite community; it thus serves to acquaint the student with the sweep of Israelite history from the premonarchical period to the dissolution of the Davidic Dynasty in 586 B.C.E. and Exile (historical-cultural criticism). This chapter's attempt at a synthesis is difficult, for the earlier scholarly consensus about the topics covered in this chapter (the Exodus, Conquest, the Pentateuchal Sources, etc.) has begun to crumble. Chapter 4 presents a responsible view of where matters now stand, but the student is strongly recommended to search through the* Further Readings *at the end of the chapter for exposure to a wider range of contemporary scholarly opinions about these important issues.*

We shall finally build on all the bewildering information you assembled in the previous chapter. This chapter has three goals. First, we shall tie our study of the different episodes in Genesis 1-11 together by showing how the Priestly Editor has used these component parts to convey his theme. Second, we shall expand beyond this 11-chapter introduction to see how this theme carries into the rest of the Torah or Pentateuch. (After all, the themes in an introduction should certainly manifest themselves in the main work.) Third, we shall depart from our literary study of the first five books of the Hebrew Bible and chart the history of their formation. Here we shall see how each of the sources we have already discussed (the Yahwist, the Priestly Editor, the Elohist, and the Deuteronomist)[1] came about and in response to what historical promptings.[2]

THE THEME OF GENESIS 1-11

David Clines, in his study of the Pentateuch, sees a choice between two themes in the first 11 chapters of Genesis. The reader will have difficulty choosing one over the other.

[1] Humans tend to destroy what God has made good. Even when God forgives human sin and mitigates the punishment, sin continues to spread, to the point where the world suffers uncreation. And even when God makes a fresh start, turning his back on uncreation forever, humankind's tendency to sin immediately becomes manifest.

[2] No matter how drastic human sin becomes, destroying what God has made good and bringing the world to the brink of uncreation, God's grace never fails to deliver humankind from the consequences of its sin. Even when humankind responds to a fresh start with the old pattern of sin, God's commitment to the world stands firm, and sinful humankind experiences the favor of God as well as righteous judgment.[3]

The Creation Stories Set the Theme

Both of the above possibilities make clear why the Priestly Editor prefaced his own Creation account (1:1–2:4a) to the well-known Yahwist story (2:4b–3:24). The traditional version focused upon the origin of human sin through arrogance and its resulting punishment; the likely exilic situation of the Priestly Writer did not call for an emphasis on sin and its punishment, which the people were already experiencing at that very moment.

In 586 B.C.E. the people of Judah had lost their temple in Jerusalem, the Davidic dynasty had been exterminated, their land had become a province of the neo-Babylonian Empire, their civil and religious bureaucracy had been deported to Babylon, and a large number of people had fled to Egypt. These five events amounted to more than a national tragedy, for each of these was considered a religious impossibility because of a divine promise. The Yahwistic religion itself was being challenged! To the exiles in Babylon the religion of their conquerors with its worship of the chief Babylonian deity Marduk (see the Enuma Elish) certainly must have seemed tempting; for the god Marduk, who had mastered the goddess Tiamat, appeared as a powerful creator with control over heaven and earth. The exiled people of Israel did not need to begin their story of national origins with a tale of evil and punishment.

And so the P Writer began with a version of Creation in order to sketch a world that was "good . . . good . . . good . . . very good." This world was the object

---

[1] These latter two sources have not yet been dealt with, but will be touched upon in the third section of this chapter.

[2] This latter section will be highly problematic, for any historical reconstruction based mainly on literary sources must remain such; but in this case, my version of the history of these sources must remain even more highly theoretical because scholars are now proposing major revisions of the model that I present in this section, although no such revision has yet won over the majority of scholars.

[3] *The Theme of the Pentateuch* (Journal for the Study of the Old Testament Supplement 10; 1978), p. 76.

of repeated blessing. The deity was utterly in control, and he created by mere word of his mouth with no opposition whatsoever.[4] At the root of P's world was not the chaos and confusion apparent to a defeated people, but a divine order without taint. God placed humans at the pinnacle of his pyramid and made them as male and female, plurality within a unity, even a reflection of himself (Genesis 1:27). The Babylonians considered humans to be fundamentally evil; in the Enuma Elish they were made of clay and the blood of an evil god (Kingu); they were created as slaves of the gods. The Mesopotamian pessimistic view of humanity stands in sharp (and probably intended) contrast to P's vision. According to this priest exiled in Babylon, humans were intended by their deity to be in his very image and to stand at the summit of his carefully orchestrated world.

Despite the exalted status of humans in P's creation account, the editor focuses on the transcendence of God: His account begins with God ("In the beginning God . . .") and ends with God on the seventh day. This literary inclusion is reinforced by P's favorite verb in the first chapter of Genesis, namely, "separate"; for the deity creates by "separating" everything into its properly assigned sphere, and heaven remains "separate" from the earth.[5] This emphasis on God was due not only to the priestly background of the editor, but also to the situation of the exiles who had to have their attention refocused on the deity and their confidence in his control reconfirmed.

When the reader now turns to the more traditional J story of Genesis 2:4b–3:24, this older narrative appears in a new light. Although these two chapters express through myth the origins of sin and human discord, it is clear that this alienation is not the order intended (or tolerated) by Yahweh. Whenever humans snatch at equality with the divinity ("you shall be like god . . ."), the results are disharmony between the man and the woman, even though they had been created specifically for mutual assistance. In the beginning Yahweh had placed everything in a harmonious relationship: Humans were in control of nature (symbolized by the naming of the animals), the man and woman were mutual helpers, and all were subject to the deity who provided for them. The Yahwist described sin as a breakdown in that hierarchy. Animals (the serpent) try to dominate humans, the male and female turn on each other in recrimination, and both refuse submission to divine authority. All that the punishment scene in chapter 3 does is to solidify what humans have already accomplished.

When the two Creation accounts are now read together by a sixth-century exilic audience, these three chapters concede the possibility of disharmony, death, and chaos. But these are not radically part of Creation (as they were in Mesopotamian thought); they were humanly engineered aberrations. The events of 586 B.C.E. did not show that God had abandoned power to chaos (always a possibility in Babylonian myth), but that once again human beings were allowed to intrude on Yahweh's intended order. Even as Yahweh remained in control despite the scene at the center of the Garden of Eden, so Yahweh was still in charge even in exilic Babylon.

The P Editor, by adding his own Creation account, has established a twofold dynamic between the *divine intention* ("It was good") and the *human rebellious response.* In a real sense human efforts are toward "uncreation," for their disharmony in chapter 3 strikes at the root of divine order. Nevertheless, God's reaction to rebellion is not to carry out the threatened punishment "You shall die" (Genesis 2:17),

---

[4] Contrast P's deity with Babylonian Marduk, who had to struggle for his life against Tiamat.

[5] Notice that in the phrase "heaven and earth" used by the P Writer, "heaven" always precedes "earth"; the order is reversed in the following J account as the reader immediately notices in Genesis 2:4b.

but to reestablish an order to allow the survival of his creation. Thus we already have the main theme that we can now trace through the rest of Genesis 1–11.

From Cain to Noah: The Development of the Theme

As your own work indicated, many words and phrases have been carried over from chapters 2 and 3 into the following story of fratricide; the P Editor wants us to see the Cain and Abel episode as an example of the spread of sin. Sin not only spreads on the horizontal plane (to the east of Eden), but it intensifies to the point of fratricide (the murder of one's brother).

This growth of sin can be appreciated in the continuation of the motif of the *soil/ground* (*'adamah*) that had been the source of human life (Genesis 2:9). Adam had been formed from the soil/ground (*'adamah*), but he was cursed to return there in death after a life of frustration cultivating the soil. In the Cain and Abel story the ground is once more defiled by a curse as it receives the blood of a brother murdered by a tiller of the soil (Genesis 4:10–12). God's punishment further alienates humans from the source of their life, for the cultivator of the soil[6] is now doomed to wander as a nomad (the opposite of a farmer) across its face (Genesis 4:14).[7]

Here we also have the motif of the *mitigation of punishment,* for God does not execute Cain; God allows natural consequences to flow from murder, but he also takes extraordinary steps to safeguard the guilty Cain from the fate Cain inflicted on his brother, Abel (Genesis 4:15). Humans may rush headlong toward death and the breakdown of harmony (first husband against wife, now brother against brother), but Yahweh acts to reestablish life.

The two genealogies that follow reinforce this movement. The generation of Cain grows in violence (*the spread of sin*) until it reaches Lamech (Genesis 4:23–24), who is 77 times more violent than Cain. The genealogy of Seth, however, documents the simultaneous *spread of grace,* for with Enosh true religion begins (people call upon Yahweh by name).

The genealogy of chapter 5 serves two functions. First, it forms the framework around the Ark Narrative, which is the very heart of the journey from Creation to Abraham (Genesis 12). Second, the unusual repetition of the phrase "and he died" forms a stark refrain announcing the spread of death in the midst of a genealogy that documents the spread of life.[8]

The announcement of the birth of Noah (Genesis 5:28–29) aptly reflects the theme around which the P Editor has organized Genesis 1–11. Lamech, the epitome of ruthlessness, is also the father of Noah. Noah is not only the halfway point between Creation and the Patriarch Abraham, but he also represents the hope to reestablish what has been lost by humankind in Eden. Notice how many of the important words from Genesis 3 (including *'adamah*) have been carried into Genesis 5:29. Noah can reverse the curse of the first couple (Adam and Eve). In the midst of this chapter of recurring death is still found hope.

---

[6] Many scholars detect here a judgment against various professions, like the fight between the ranchers and the farmers in the Old West. The fact that the violent Cain becomes the forefather of technology and metallurgy (Genesis 4:19–22) may suggest an antitechnology bias on the part of the author at some stage of the telling of this story.

[7] It is important here to make what seems a subtle distinction: God does not really intervene to invent an arbitrary punishment. Cain's removal from the soil (Genesis 4:14) is a logical *consequence* of his desecration of it (Genesis 4:10–11). The same is true of the dynamics of the punishment in Genesis 3.

[8] The phrase "and he died" in chapter 5 is unusual, for by their very nature most genealogies stress the continuity of life rather than the discontinuity of death.

The Noah's Ark Narrative begins with that strange myth preserved by the Yahwist in Genesis 6:1–4. Although this is a common myth in the ancient world, we should examine its literary function in the context of P's reuse of the story. Remember, according to our editor's own version of Creation (Genesis 1), Creation was actually an act of "separation": Elements were separated into their proper spheres. God remains aloof and separate from what he creates. The P Writer probably retells this story about intercourse between heavenly beings and the women of earth to illustrate that creation itself was threatened by this sexual union between the heaven and the earth. These verses then set the stage for the Deluge (the Flood), which is more than a meteorological event—it is uncreation. If Creation separated the waters above (heaven) from the waters below (earth), then the Flood is joining (uncreation) what had originally been separated (creation).

Genesis 6:6–7 dashes any hope suggested by the naming of Noah in Genesis 5:29. As you saw in the previous chapter, these verses in chapter 6 take up the important vocabulary from Genesis 5:29 (Hebrew **nḥm** and **ᶜsb**) and state that God will now undo Creation.[9] The reason for this uncreation is conveyed in verses 11–13, which play on a variety of meanings for the Hebrew root **ŠHT**, which here means "corrupt" (verses 11 and 12) and "destroy" (verses 13, 17). These verses are important for they fix the blame for the Flood and thereby distinguish Genesis from its older Babylonian model preserved in the cuneiform Atrahasis. In Atrahasis, humans are destroyed by Enlil because they have become so prolific that their noise disturbs his rest (recall Tiamat's similar objections to the rowdy younger gods). Enlil's reaction cannot help but strike us as a bit pathological. In Genesis, however, the real cause of the Flood is *not* Yahweh but humans. Humankind has become so corrupt (**ŠHT**) that God resolves on destruction (**ŠHT**). The use of the same Hebrew root in both cases is more than an innocent pun; it argues that the destruction is inseparably connected with and logically flows from human corruption. God does not really punish humans; God merely allows events to take their own natural course toward dissolution.

The Flood that follows is clearly intended as an uncreation, the direct opposite of events in Genesis 1. The waters above (the rain) join together with the waters below (the Flood), overcoming the land (*'adamah* in Genesis 7:4) that had been separated apart from them in Genesis 1. The words of Genesis 7:21–24 form almost a mirror-image of P's initial story of Creation.

However, as in the cases of the first couple (Adam and Eve) and of Cain, God will not allow evil to prevail. At this very moment of darkness, God remembers (Genesis 8:1) and stops uncreation. What follows is a replay of P's Creation account in Genesis 1. Once again the wind blows across the waters and living creatures are told to go forth, be fruitful and multiply upon the earth (8:17). But true to the dominant theme, our editor is not content to bring us back to our point of departure. Things are not simply back whence they started. For in Genesis 9, God swears an oath (makes a covenant) that he will never again allow uncreation to destroy Creation (Genesis 9:9–11). God's grace always overwhelms human sin.

The story of the Flood would be of particular interest to P's exilic audience. Ironically, Babylonian literature itself frequently likened Babylon's historical destruction under the Assyrian king Sennacherib to the mythical deluge. The reader-exile could clearly see the Flood of Genesis as a symbol of the utter destruction of all his or her beliefs. And yet when uncreation was at its very moment of victory, God *remembered*! God again re-created the threatened order. There could even be a more important message of hope in this story. Some scholars see the ark itself as

---

[9] Compare the vocabulary in Genesis 6:7 with Genesis 1.

a symbol of the temple. The P Writer is very intent on supplying a chronological framework for the Ark Narrative, so that the Flood abates and Noah emerges on New Year's Day (8:13)—the very day on which the Israelites celebrated the dedication of the Solomonic temple that the Babylonians destroyed in 586 B.C.E. Possibly then the ark reassures the people that they will again find safety from chaos within a temple (to be rebuilt).

In the bizarre tale about Noah's drunkenness (Genesis 9:20–27) we again have a story whose original meaning is unclear, but which the editor here reuses for a new literary function.[10] This story then reaffirms the twofold dynamic *spread of sin-spread of grace.* Despite God's intervention to stop the human fall into watery chaos and despite the divine oath never to allow uncreation to win over Creation, humans again fall into the pattern of sin. Just as Adam's son Cain had reinitiated the spread of sin, so has Noah's offspring.

From Noah to Abraham

The Tower of Babel story has clearly been integrated into the primeval history of Genesis 1–11. In its eastward migration (Genesis 11:2), humankind continues its march away from the center of the garden.[11] As in the garden, human harmony (one language and cooperation) yields to chaos (confusion of tongues and dispersal) because of arrogance.

The story has been skillfully crafted along two geometrical planes: the *horizontal* (migration from the east to one spot) and the *vertical* (the tower goes up and God comes down). This spatial orientation recalls P's cosmos established in Genesis 1. The humans assemble in order to bridge the separation between the heaven and the earth (Genesis 11:4). To the Priestly Editor, this represents another assault on Creation itself.[12]

The literary structure of the passage clearly diagrams the opposition. The story is structured into two opposing parts by several factors (horizontal vs. vertical, human actors vs. the divine actor, word plays). These parts portray the face-off between the human and the divine: "Let us . . ." (11:3) versus "Let us . . ." (11:7). The theme is also reflected in clever word plays. The humans want to make a name (*shem*) by assembling there (*sham*) to assault the heavens (*shemayim*); they begin by making bricks (*nilbenah*), but end up being confused (*nabelah*). Those who had assembled there (*sham*) are now dispersed from there (*mishsham*): The reversal of letters marks a reversal in plans.

Because chapter 10 frequently alludes both to the dispersal of humankind and to multiple languages—features not really accounted for until Genesis 11:1–9—its position seems baffling. Possibly this chapter at one time followed the Tower of Babel incident, but here we can probably see the interest of the P Editor in maintaining a polar theme; for, if chapter 10 followed Babel, the order might appear

---

[10] It has been somewhat clumsily inserted here, for you notice that the offending son was Ham, yet his son Canaan was cursed (Genesis 9:25). At one point the story was probably a folk explanation why the Israelites were able to displace the stronger Canaanites in the land of Palestine: The original inhabitants of Canaan had been cursed because of a misdeed of their forefather and namesake.

[11] The center symbolizes harmony; the banishment to the east represents alienation and sin.

[12] This is essentially the same evil as represented in Genesis 6:1–4.

more logical, but the effect would be to amplify the role of sin's spread. The introduction (Genesis 1–11) would then end on a lengthy note of human sin and a long description of its resulting dispersal. This would tip P's careful polar balance. But if he moves chapter 10 before chapter 11, verses 1–9, he can cleverly give two accounts for the spread of humankind over the face of the earth. Chapter 10 now comes under the influence of the divine command in Genesis 9:7 ". . . be fruitful and multiply." The spread of humanity can now be seen as *curse* (11:9) and *blessing* (Genesis 10).

Throughout Genesis 1–11, P has sketched a drama in which divine initiative toward good has been challenged by human rebellion leading toward the very overthrow of Creation. Every act of human sin has been followed by a divine response mitigating punishment and reestablishing order. This dynamic then forces the question: What now? What hope does human society have after its dispersal in Genesis 11? The P Writer intends the answer to be Abraham (Genesis 12ff.), the Patriarch of the Israelite people.

We are finally ready to evaluate one of the first exercises you completed in Chapter 3 of this text. It seems that there is both a break *and* a link between Genesis, chapters 1–11 and 12ff, between the introduction and the main body. Genesis 1–11 differs from what follows both in scope (human history vs. a single family) and mood (sweeping *divine* interventions vs. focus on *human* decisions). The stage shifts from a vague world setting to the Fertile Crescent.

But there are also clear ties between the sections. The most striking is the continuation of the motif of the *'adamah* (soil/ground), to which we have referred on several occasions. In Genesis 12:3 Abraham is promised that "by you all the families of the earth shall bless themselves." The phrase "families of the earth" is not uncommon, except that elsewhere the normal Hebrew word for earth is not *'adamah* as it is here in Genesis 12:3. So the author seems to have intentionally used the less common word *'adamah* in this expression in order to evoke the motif from Genesis 1–11. The presence of the word *'adamah* in a context of curse and blessing further supports this suggestion.

The barrenness of Sarai (11:30) hints at an issue that will play a major role in the rest of the Book of Genesis. It already suggests the crisis of faith: How can a patriarch with no legitimate children be the father of a people as promised by Yahweh in Genesis 12:2?

This complex relationship of Genesis 1–11 and 12ff is significant. Abraham represents God's response to the worldwide spread of sin in Genesis 11. The curse of humankind and human alienation from the life of the soil receives a divine response in 12:1–3. In Abraham as the father of the Israelite people all the earth can receive blessing instead of curse. The future of humankind now depends on its relationship to these particular people, whose history we are about to learn. Perhaps the people exiled in Babylon had been tempted to dismiss their God as a local Palestinian deity who had been bested by the cosmic Marduk; the P Editor has now placed this Yahwistic promise in Genesis 12:1–3 in the context of the theme of divine initiative for good against the human drive toward disharmony. The history of their forefathers has been given a universal significance by its being edited into the cosmic history of Genesis 1–11. In Abraham the struggle between blessing and curse finally focuses on Abraham as humankind's hope for ultimate blessing.

And by you all the families of the earth (*'adamah*) shall bless themselves. (Genesis 12:3)

THE THEME OF THE PENTATEUCH:
THE THREEFOLD PROMISE

The early history of the Israelite people is arranged around a threefold promise made to the Patriarchs Abraham,[13] Isaac, and Jacob. Already in Genesis 12 we encounter the three components of that promise, which will form the thread through the first *six* books of the Hebrew Bible. Yahweh promised Abram, as he was first called, (1) *descendants* ("a great nation"), (2) a *special relationship* with the deity (covenant, blessing), and (3) the *Land of Canaan* (Genesis 12:7). These three are not only found in the J source of chapter 12 but also in such P passages as Genesis 17: (1) "I will make you exceedingly fruitful" (17:5–6), (2) "and I will establish my covenant between me and you and your descendants" (17:7), (3) "and I will give to you . . . all the land of Canaan" (17:8).[14]

From a literary point of view, the entire first six books of the Hebrew Bible (from Genesis to Joshua) form a *thematic* unit, for it is only at the end of this six-book collection that all three elements of the divine pledge are realized.[15] Only with the conquest of Joshua is the promise of the Land of Canaan finally achieved.

All three elements of the patriarchal promise (*progeny, special relationship, Canaan*) are handled in exactly the same way: God promises, but human obstacles stand in the way of the accomplishment of the promise; however, God overcomes these obstacles to realize each of the three constituents in the divine pledge. Furthermore, although all three elements are mentioned throughout the Hexateuch (first six books), various groupings of books *concentrate* their treatment on a single element (its obstacles and their overcoming). And so, the Book of Genesis focuses on the pledge that from Abraham would come a mighty nation (*progeny*); Exodus and Leviticus concentrate on the Covenant transacted on Mount Sinai[16] (*special relationship*); Numbers, Deuteronomy, and Joshua are especially concerned with the occupation of the promised land (*Canaan*).

Now let us examine how each of the three aspects of the patriarchal promise is treated in these books.

Progeny: Genesis 12–50

Yahweh has promised that from Abraham would stem a mighty nation, but there are clear obstacles that threatened this divine pledge. First of all, Sarah,[17] his wife, is sterile — a complication already suggested in Genesis 11:30. This theme of the sterility of an ancestress (Rebekah and Rachel) will also be a factor in the case of the Patriarchs Isaac and Jacob. Not only is Sarah barren but she is also advanced in years: Abraham and Sarah don't appear to be models of fertility. Abraham has a child, Ishmael, through a slave concubine named Hagar, but the promised line must come through his legitimate wife (Genesis 16–17).

[13] Abraham was also called *Abram* when God first called him.

[14] Notice all three of these in the other source, the Elohist (Genesis 28), which we will discuss later in this chapter.

[15] And not at the end of the *five*-book Pentateuch. If you sense that there is something strange here, you are right. The theme of the Promise to the Patriarch *and* its Fulfillment needs the first *six* books of the present Bible—a Hexateuch, for only in the present Book of Joshua do we have a record of the possession of the Land of Canaan promised to Abraham in Genesis; but for important reasons yet to be discussed, Jews accepted as the heart of Judaism a five-book grouping, the Pentateuch. As we shall see, however, these first six books, the so-called Hexateuch, had quite different editorial histories. But more about this later in the chapter.

[16] Also called Mt. Horeb in some biblical sources.

[17] Originally called Sarai.

The strange episode in Genesis 12:10-20, in which the gallant Abraham tries to safeguard his own life by passing off Sarah as his sister, also serves to heighten suspense about God's pledge.[18] For placing the ancestress of Israel in jeopardy of marriage to an outsider threatens the realization of God's promise of progeny.

In Genesis 17 the 90-year-old Sarah finally becomes pregnant by the 100-year-old Abraham.[19] Sarah's response to the news is laughter, and so the boy is fittingly called Isaac, which means in Hebrew "he laughs." Chapter 22, the Sacrifice of Isaac, is a last episode that challenges Abraham's promise to be the father of a nation. Abraham is told to offer up his *only*—a factor stressed in the chapter—son. The Patriarch is in a clear bind: If he ignores God's challenge, he will be unfit; if he carries it out and sacrifices his only chance for offspring,[20] then the divine promise becomes impossible to fulfill. (Read the chapter to see how Abraham gets out of his dilemma.)

The Book of Genesis further chronicles the history of this family and its internal squabbles. Despite the unlikelihood of its continuance through exile and brother attempting to kill brother, by chapter 50 the family grows from the sterile and aged Abraham and Sarah to a large people in exile in the land of Egypt. This motif actually poses the problem with which the Book of Exodus begins: The people have grown too numerous for the Egyptians (Exodus 1:7).

Special Relationship: The Books of Exodus and Leviticus

Exodus and Leviticus are primarily concerned with that special agreement concluded by the Israelite leader Moses on Mount Sinai (the **Sinai Covenant**). Throughout much of the Hebrew Bible this Mosaic covenant will embody the essence of Israel's special relationship to her deity. Once again God's promise stands over against human obstacles to its accomplishment.

When persecuted by the Egyptian Pharaoh, the people of Israel[21] cry to Yahweh for deliverance; Yahweh sends them Moses to deliver them from Egypt and to return them to the promised land of Canaan. The story of the Exodus from Egypt begins with the account of the plagues that convinced the Egyptians to let the people go and of the Israelites' subsequent flight across the sea.

For the rest of the Bible, the Exodus is to remain a model of God's power to free his people from slavery and captivity. After the Babylonian captivity of 586 B.C.E., the prophet who wrote Isaiah 40-55 will even speak of a New Exodus from captivity (this time in Babylon).[22]

The main resistance to a particular linkage with Yahweh surfaces in the desert after the Israelites have left Egypt. When the hardships of the nomadic desert

---

[18] A similar story is told of Isaac's wife, Rebekah, in Genesis 26 and for the same literary effect.

[19] The mention of the ages certainly stresses that the promised conception is totally due to divine intervention.

[20] Remember Sarah is now about 103 years old.

[21] This word no longer is used as another name for Jacob, but of his offspring who have now become a nation.

[22] We know very little about any historical basis behind the account of the Exodus from Egypt; there are no Egyptian records to elucidate the event, and the biblical version is both composed of differing sources and heavily colored with mythological language. For example, the story of the sea splitting in half and the drowning of the Egyptian chariots is considerably influenced by myths about the creator god battling the watery god of chaos (for example, Baal against Yamm [ANET, pp. 129-131] and Marduk against Tiamat). In most ancient Near Eastern versions of the myth, the victorious deity celebrates by creating. Perhaps in the Israelite story, this language suggests that Yahweh by overcoming his enemies is creating a people for himself.

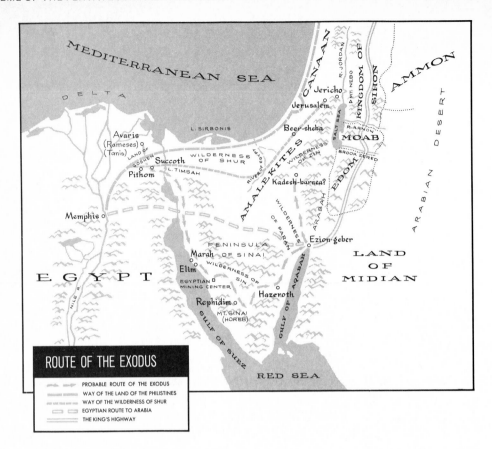

life oppress the Israelites, they murmur (complain) and wish that they were slaves back in Egypt rather than free but starving people of Yahweh. This "murmuring" motif (read Exodus 16:8 and 17:7) strikes at the very root of God's overtures to his people: "Your murmurings are not against us [Moses] but against Yahweh." Despite God's feeding of the people with the breadlike manna, the people still murmur against God (17:7). But God overcomes their reluctance and they arrive at the foot of Mount Sinai where their covenant[23] with Yahweh will be concluded (Exodus 19).

The description of the covenant-making and of its content begins in Exodus 20. This agreement includes the familiar Ten Commandments (Exodus 20:2–17); however, according to the Hebrew Bible the stipulations of this contract were far more extensive than that and extended through the following Book of Leviticus. Many liturgical and cultic regulations are included.[24]

During the making of this covenant, Moses serves as the intermediary between Yahweh and the people. In Exodus 32, Moses appoints Aaron as his representative while he meets with the deity on Mt. Sinai. However, in his extended absence the people grow restless and construct an idol in the form of a golden calf. Although this story is quite complex and has been influenced by later biblical history (the story of King Jeroboam in 1 Kings 12) and by cultic struggles between later rival groups of priests who traced their lineage either to Moses or to Aaron, here it illustrates the familiar dynamic of a human rebuff to a divine initiative: No sooner has Yahweh entered into a privileged relationship with Israel than they reject him.

[23] More about this legal concept in Chapter 6.

[24] We shall discuss this later in this chapter, but it seems that the entire body of Israelite civil and liturgical law has been collected in this place as if *all* law stemmed from Sinai and derived its authority by association with Moses.

Finally, after the punishment of the idolaters, the contract between God and the Israelites is concluded by the end of the Book of Leviticus (see Leviticus 26:46). Thus, despite human obstacles, God has realized the second element of his promise, the *special relationship*.

The Promised Land: Numbers, Deuteronomy, Joshua

The remaining three books in our original Hexateuch deal with Israel's journey from Mt. Sinai to the Land of Canaan, which had been promised to Abraham in Genesis 12.[25] The first ten chapters in the Book of Numbers are an elaborate census of the tribes of Israel in order to determine their strength for the battle to conquer the promised land. The long list of numbers in this census has provided the title for the book ever since its early Greek translation. Finally, in Numbers 10:29, the Israelites begin the long-awaited move from Mt. Sinai toward southern Palestine.

Given the short distance involved, it probably comes as a surprise that this journey will eventually take 40 years and that the Israelites shall ultimately enter via the roundabout east border on the Jordan River near Shittim. What happened? You should by now be prepared for the possibility of *human frustration* for God's plans.

They arrive at Kadesh-barnea on the southern edge of Palestine (Numbers 13), but Moses wisely sends out spies to reconnoiter the land they are about to invade. The spies return with the good news/bad news: The land is so fertile (the good news) that it takes two people to carry one bunch of grapes, *but* the inhabitants are so fierce (the bad news) that the Hebrew spies felt like grasshoppers next to them. The people lose confidence in Yahweh's ability to deliver on his promise and *murmur* against his bringing them out of Egypt in the first place (Numbers 14:1–4). Although they are reluctantly goaded into a half-hearted invasion anyway, their faithlessness has been decisive: They are soundly defeated at Hormah (Numbers 14:45).

Their lack of trust in Yahweh's ability to deliver on his promise of the land results in the punishment that not one of the generation that left Egypt will be permitted to enter the Land of Canaan. And so they are condemned to wander around the desert for 40 years (the age of a generation) before they are allowed another chance to invade the promised land (Numbers 14:26–35).

The wandering nation next tries to enter Canaan from the east, but there are still other obstacles to the divine promise. Read the story of Balaam in Numbers 22–24. As the Israelites attempt to pass through the land of Moab east of the Dead Sea, the Moabite king, Balak, hires a professional magician from Mesopotamia to put a curse on them (Numbers 22:11) so that the Israelites could be destroyed. The Mesopotamians had such a reputation in these matters that the Israelites appeared doomed.

Once again, however, God intervenes to counter human certainty. The humorous[26] story about Balaam's ass in Numbers 22:21–35 shows that a normally dumb donkey can be wiser than a professional Mesopotamian seer. To the consternation of his employer, Balaam is directed by God to deliver a blessing not a curse (Numbers 24:3–9, 15–19).

---

[25] You can sense the geography involved by checking Map of the Conquest on p. 000.

[26] Because we have already seen that biblical literature functions just like all human literature, please don't be surprised to find humor in the Bible. You should have been prepared for this possibility by your reading of the Book of Jonah.

The Division of the Land

The people finally arrive at the banks of the Jordan River, which forms the eastern boundary of Palestine. At Shittim, opposite Jericho, they prepare to cross over when they rebel against Yahweh, who is about to deliver on his final promise. Numbers 25:1–9 seems a small episode but it left quite an impression on later biblical literature. At the moment when the threefold patriarchal promise is about to be realized, a large number of the people switch allegiance to the agricultural deity Baal. They have not quite left the desert for the settled life of the field when many of them change gods for an apparently more suitable Canaanite fertility god, Baal of Peor.[27]

[27] The prophet Hosea will develop this theme extensively in his book.

God punishes the guilty but—as usual—does not renege on the promise. In the Book of Deuteronomy, Moses, who, remember, has not been allowed to enter the promised land, gives his farewell address to the people. This speech, which is virtually the entire book, leaves the Israelites with final legal instructions on how they should conduct themselves once they have entered Canaan and occupied it (see Deuteronomy 4:1–8). Hence, the name of the book in Greek really means the "second law." At the end of the book Moses is shown the promised land from a mountain and then dies (Deuteronomy 34). The Book of Joshua is an idealized[28] account of the conquest of the land by Moses' successor Joshua. This book presents a picture of an army organized of all the tribes first conquering the center, then the south, and finally the north of the Land of Canaan (see map of conquest). The land is then partitioned among the tribes. At the end of the book (Joshua 24) the people agree to abide by their special relationship (covenant) with Yahweh, who at last has delivered all his promises (progeny, special relationship, the land) made to Abraham in Genesis 12.

If the first six books of the Bible (Genesis to Joshua) are held together by this threefold promise with its divine triumph over all human obstacles, then let us see how Genesis 1–11 introduces this theme. The element of *progeny* is suggested by the recurrent command to "be fruitful and multiply," which highlights P's creation account in Genesis 1 and his re-creation account in Genesis 8–9. Like Abraham and Sarah, humanity itself begins with one couple and ends by populating the earth. The motif of *relationship* is introduced by the startling claim of the Priestly Writer that humankind was created in "the image and likeness of God." God is willing to initiate such a relationship, but considers it arrogance (the *hubris* of Greek tragedy) when humans attempt to snatch it for themselves (Genesis 3:5; Genesis 6:1–4; Genesis 11:1–9). We have already seen how the theme of the *land* (Hebrew *'adamah*) has been treated in Genesis 1–11. Thus, Genesis 1–11 introduces both the content of the threefold promise as well as the way it is presented (divine initiative, human frustration, eventual triumph of God's intent).

THE HISTORY OF THE WRITING OF THE PENTATEUCH/HEXATEUCH

Some loose ends still need to be tied in this section of the chapter. First of all, what about all this confusion regarding a Hexateuch (Genesis through Joshua) versus a Pentateuch (Genesis through Deuteronomy)? If from a literary point of view it takes the first six books (Hexateuch) of the present Bible to resolve the patriarchal promise satisfactorily, then when and why were the first five books (Pentateuch/Torah) bracketed off as the religious norm for Judaism—even though from a *thematic* point of view this leaves the promise of the land unresolved so that this authoritative (that is, *canonical*) Torah now ends on the strange note of Moses' death?[29] (This would be analogous to a New Testament Gospel that ended with the Crucifixion and no account of the Resurrection of Jesus other than the promise.)

[28] We suspect that this account has been made somewhat idealized because (1) it does not agree with a short biblical summary found in Judges 1 in which the tribes do not wage war as a unit and in which they are virtually incapable of taking any urban centers that were reported earlier as captured by Joshua; and because (2) archaeological evidence of city destruction does not agree in many cases with the claims of the Book of Joshua. For example, Jericho and Ai had long been in ruins when Joshua came before them.

[29] As we shall see there is also a source-critical problem, for the Pentateuch is composed of parts from two entirely different written collections: (1) JEP and (2) the Deuteronomist.

Secondly, we have been referring to such written sources or documents as the **Priestly Writer**, the Yahwist, the Elohist, and the Deuteronomist. It is time that we knew a little more about their history and background, even though in doing so we are heading into one of the most hotly contested areas in contemporary biblical research.

This section, then, will chart the "tradition history" of the writing of the normative (technically called "canonical") Pentateuch from its earliest oral recitals, through the contributions of each of the written sources, through their successive redaction, or editing, all the way up to the bracketing off of the final five-book Pentateuch. This treatment provides an example of *tradition criticism,* in which various traditions are traced through their various stages until they achieve canonical written status in the Bible as we have it today.

Because this survey will bring together sources as well as historical-cultural criticisms, it will also provide a helpful overview of the history of Israel and Judah during much of the biblical era. This textbook has delayed talking about biblical history in a cohesive manner until the reader has been prepared to see its relevance to the texts that have already been analyzed.

Problems to Be Solved

At the outset, keep in mind some literary (and thereby *religious*) problems that I hope this historical survey will at least address if not answer. The dilemma can be formulated in several ways. You are already familiar with the first formulation: How could believers have taken the first five books as canonical for their religion,[30] even though this meant that the constant theme of the *promised land* must now remain unfulfilled?[31] Reading the present Pentateuch is much like waiting for the other shoe to drop. The Pentateuch now ends on the stark note of the death of Moses.

Another problem deals with laws. There are virtually no laws or legislation reported elsewhere in the Hebrew Bible. The rulers or kings in the royal chronicles of 1 Kings, 2 Kings, and 1 Chronicles, 2 Chronicles are not portrayed as lawgivers. At some point all the different laws from various time periods were collected and read into the Pentateuch. Moses even promulgates such anachronistic laws as those regulating the monarchy in Deuteronomy 17:14–20. When and under what influence did Moses emerge as the lawgiver *par excellence*? Our study of the history of the writing of this five-book collection will suggest answers for all these questions.

Although the Yahwist (J source), probably written around 950 B.C.E., is the first written document about Israel's origins that has come down to us, there was an important period prior to the emergence of the J source during the early monarchy. We shall first of all examine the early period prior to the Yahwist; this covers the period of the Israelite tribes from the conquest or occupation of the Land of Canaan, through the tribal associations, to the formation of the monarchy under King Saul and King David (from around 1200 to 1000 B.C.E.). The beliefs of this beginning stage are probably preserved in ancient historical creeds. (An outline of the history that follows can be found in the chronological charts in Appendix F.)

[30] Remember, the sixth book, the Book of Joshua, is obviously still in the Hebrew Bible; all we are saying is that the preceding five books at some point constituted an independent collection and were given a very special role in Judaism.

[31] Furthermore, who combined portions from two literary works to construct this Pentateuch, although the combining of the Book of Deuteronomy with the JEP works of Genesis, Exodus, Leviticus, and Numbers separated it from its own Deuteronomist collection (Deuteronomy, Joshua, Judges, Samuel, and Kings)?

Early Oral Recitals of Israel's Story

Even though the present Pentateuch is a written document, the end-product of a long period of redaction, some scholars claim to discover within its writing relics of earlier *oral* accounts of Israel's history, which have been frozen in writing like a mastadon in Siberia's ice. These creeds or confessions bear evidence of being far older than the present written context in which they have been entombed. Many of them were connected with Israel's religious cult, and a liturgical cult is noted for its ability to conserve archaic texts.[32] These oral accounts of the people's birth were probably recited at religious festivals and served to unite the worshippers into a community based upon an appreciation of their common origin celebrated in the recital.

Many of the passages treated below have clearly been edited by later authors, particularly by the Deuteronomist in the seventh century B.C.E. Current scholarship debates whether these creedal statements represent late *summaries* of biblical history (and hence are worthless as sources for Israel's early understanding) or whether they reveal the kernel of Israel's earliest traditions about its origins, although now clothed in later language. In the latter view defended earlier in the twentieth century by Gerhard von Rad and Martin Noth, these early confessions mark the germ or nucleus from which the entire Pentateuch gradually emerged. This textbook, although aware of the contemporary controversy, treats these "historical credos" as representatives of Israel's earliest traditions. The Deuteronomist, in whose late works many of these creedal confessions are found, displays a markedly conservative orientation; he (we can only assume it was a male) has probably preserved these early statements, especially at home in the north of Jerusalem, as part of his restorative program, which was aimed at recalling Jerusalem back to its early roots.

Read the following short, but probably ancient, historical recitals: 1 Samuel 12:8; Deuteronomy 6:20–25, 26:5–9; Joshua 24:2–13; Psalm 78; Psalm 105; Psalm 106. Notice that they can be broken into two categories depending on where they end their account. Below, arrange them into two groups (A and B) depending on the scope of their history (especially their ending point).

GROUP A   GROUP B

---

[32] Note the archaic language preserved in the Christian *Our Father*: "Our Father who *art* in heaven, *hallowed be thy* name . . . ."

Next compare the historical scope (that is, the extent of the history covered, where it begins and ends its treatment) of both groups to the historical scope of the Hexateuch (Genesis through Joshua), and to the Pentateuch (Genesis through Deuteronomy). Does either group (A or B) correspond with the period of history covered in either the Hexateuch or Pentateuch?

Recall our treatment of the major events in the Pentateuch earlier in Chapter 4. What major event is conspicuously *not* mentioned in either group of historical recitals?

Which later written collection (Hexateuch or Pentateuch) represents a more natural growth from the early oral versions of Israel's origins?

From the Occupation of Canaan to the Yahwist (J)

According to Martin Noth, the early creedal recitals discussed above had already been expanded into an historical epic by the period before the emergence of the monarchy in the eleventh century. Noth placed this hypothetical early epic, called *G* (from the German word *Grundlage*—"basis"), centuries before the J and E sources, which were supposedly derived from it. The scope of such an ancient epic (G) is debatable. Although some scholars disagree, the source G probably differed from the later Yahwist's version in that it lacked a Creation story at its beginning.[33] Thus this early epic really followed the outline of the earlier creedal recitals: Patriarchs→ Exodus→ Wandering in the Desert→ Occupation of the Promised Land.

Considerable dispute centers on the role of traditions about the Sinai Covenant in such an epic. Many scholars call attention to the conspicuous absence of Sinai in the early creedal confessions; some explain this by arguing that Sinai repre-

---

[33] The theology of creation is so intimately related to the later monarchy, because both deal with the maintenance of cosmic and social order, that its insertion probably first took place in J under the Davidic monarchy.

sents a separate tradition that was only later added to the older recitals.[34] However, Bernard Anderson attributes the silence of the earliest recitals about Sinai to the fact that Sinai was not one of Yahweh's mighty deeds on behalf of his people, but rather represented the people's response to Yahweh's activity. Similarly, the Christian Eucharist is not mentioned in any of the Christian creeds (Apostolic, Nicene, Constantinople) because the Eucharist represents the community's grateful response to the events recalled in the creeds.

Let us examine the history of this early period beginning with the occupation of Canaan and the formation of some type of tribal confederation. This will provide the historical stage against which to examine Israel's earliest religious beliefs.

Israelite Occupation of Canaan

The historical reconstruction of the Israelite occupation of the Land of Canaan remains quite controversial. The Book of Joshua suggests that an organized army under Joshua systematically overcame the native Canaanites (Joshua 1–12) and then distributed the conquered territory among the 12 tribes that comprised Joshua's force (Joshua 13–22). The first chapter of the Book of Judges suggests a more modest picture: The Israelites were able to hold only the sparsely populated hill country while the densely populated plains and urban centers remained firmly under Canaanite control. As we shall see, this latter scenario is better supported by the meager archaeological evidence that has been uncovered. Perhaps the Israelite subsistence in the rugged hill country that runs north and south was made possible by the new technologies of terrace farming and waterproof plaster that allowed them to coat cisterns that could store rainwater. These developments permitted new settlements away from the natural springs controlled by the Canaanites along the Mediterranean coastal plains.

There are three main theories about the occupation of the Land of Canaan. The first is the *conquest theory*. This view most agrees with the picture in Joshua 1–12 and regards the occupation basically as an outside invasion of Canaan. This model uses the biblical account as well as some archaeological data supporting the destruction of a few urban centers such as Hazor and Lachish around the late thirteenth century B.C.E. (These cities were reported as conquered by Joshua.) However, in general, neither the biblical nor the archaeological data require this model. For the Bible itself contradicts the unified conquest presented in Joshua 1–12 (compare Judges 1); the conquest account in Joshua 1–12 also seems to have been borrowed from the tradition of a limited group in central Canaan (probably from the Tribe of Benjamin) and then secondarily expanded to become the global "Israelite" tradition. Secondly, recent excavations do not support the view of an invasion of Canaan and the disruption of its culture. For example, Jericho, Joshua's most famous conquest, had already been in ruins for centuries by the end of the thirteenth century B.C.E. Archaeology cannot establish that what thirteenth-century destruction did take place resulted from an external Israelite invasion. It is more plausible that Egyptian armies wrought such destruction in attempts to reestablish control over Canaan. Such urban devastation fits equally well with the Social Revolution Model described below. Nor can natural catastrophe (for example, fire) be ruled out as the cause of such destruction.[35]

---

[34] According to Gerhard von Rad, inclusion of the Sinai stories was due to the Yahwist, whereas Martin Noth thought it had already taken place in G.

[35] Many major American cities in the nineteenth century experienced major fires that destroyed their centers. Archaeological evidence of this mass destruction should never be elevated to proof of a foreign invasion of the United States in the last century.

The second view concerning the occupation of the Land of Canaan is the *immigration theory*. This model sees the occupation of Palestine as a result of a lengthy period of peaceful infiltration. People migrated into Canaan over a long time and from several different directions. These drifters who infiltrated the land are usually imagined as nomads or seminomads moving their sheep to better grazing areas in the hill country (transhumance). It was only under King David that these people acquired political control over their neighbors. This theory stresses those biblical accounts that portray a long period of peaceful coexistence between Israelites and Canaanites. (Many of these stories are preserved in the Book of Genesis: see Genesis 38.) The Immigration Model asserts that later Israel was a mosaic composed of separate traditions brought in by people entering Canaan with widely different backgrounds. These traditions only gradually became amalgamated into a whole "Israelite" tradition.

The final theory that seeks to explain the Israelite occupation of Canaan is the *Social Revolution Model*. Recent theories developed by G. E. Mendenhall and N. Gottwald borrow from sociological studies and suggest that the Israelite takeover of Canaan resulted from a mainly internal social upheaval which replaced the tyrannical Canaanite monarchies. Such a revolution took place gradually and was made up of disenchanted social groups of widely different backgrounds. Some were *peasant* escapees from the brutal Canaanite feudal system on the plains near the Mediterranean. As farmers withdrew from this oppressive system, they would flee to the hills where they were safer from the Canaanite city-states that depended on the chariot for their military superiority. Others fighting the Canaanite city-states were probably drifters and social outcasts called ᶜapiru or ᶜabiru in contemporary records. Many of these fought as guerrillas against the dominant political system.

Supposedly this phase of the breakdown of the Canaanite bronze-age feudal system is documented in letters from Palestine found in Amarna, Egypt (ANET, pp. 483–490). These were written around the thirteenth century B.C.E. to the Egyptian Pharaoh, who was legally the overlord (suzerain) of all these diverse city-states. The correspondence, an urgent plea for help, talks about bands of guerrillas called ᶜapiru (the Hebrews?) who are plaguing the established Canaanite cities of Palestine. These letters do not describe these bands as outside invaders but as local brigands.

According to this latter theory, the hills were full of disorganized and disenfranchised peasant and ᶜapiru revolutionaries. These would have been joined by small groups of Semites who constantly drifted into Canaan from Egypt, among which would have been Moses' group. Moses' band, which fled Egypt in the Exodus, would have been numerically quite small;[36] it would have been just one example of the countless Semitic groups that moved to and from Egypt during this period. However, there was something different about this group of refugees from Egypt. Like their fellow Semites in the mountains of Palestine, they too had fled political and economic tyranny. The religious experience of this group at Mount Sinai would provide the catalyst for the bonding of all these diverse social elements.

At Sinai, Yahweh had replaced all other gods and political systems: He alone was Lord and the Israelites owed allegiance to no one else. As we shall see in Chapter 6 of this text, this belief was early expressed in the legal format of the international vassal treaty in which the Sinai Covenant was worded. The new group then brought into the hill country a new religious concept of radical freedom quite at odds with the Canaanite city-state schema in which religion was mediated by the

---

[36] Much smaller than the figures given in the Book of Numbers, which tries to read the larger governmental structure under the later monarchy into the Exodus event. This was done for theological motives, much like modern preachers might try to place their twentieth-century Christian congregations spiritually at the foot of the Cross on Calvary.

king who derived his kingship from the gods (especially Baal). According to Sinai, there is no one between Yahweh as suzerain and the people. This small band entered the mountains and provided the ideology around which all these guerrilla bands united. And so the true story of the conquest of the land would combine local natives with a (smaller) group of fellow Semites from outside (Moses' band). Accordingly, the treaty in Joshua 24 might well represent the ceremony whereby the natives adopted the religion of the newcomers.

The Tribal League

One of the most controversial questions in modern biblical research is: What type of union/league/confederation did these early Israelite tribes form? Any early (around 1200 B.C.E.) association must have been quite primitive. The tribes seem to have remained politically independent, unified only around a common portable shrine, namely, the Ark of the Covenant, brought in by the group once led by Moses. The number of tribes appears to have been flexible, although in later tradition it was linked carefully to the number 12: Whenever one tribe died out, then one of the remaining tribes would be split into two new tribes to maintain the number 12.

Scholars have tried to understand this union by resorting to ancient models. Martin Noth suggested that this early tribal system could best be understood on the model of the Greek and pre-Roman Italian city-states. These completely independent states formed a religious union (called an *amphictyony*) around a common religious shrine. These cities were usually in multiples of 6 or 12, so that the shrine could be maintained by each city for one or two months of the year. Normally these cities would only gather together at the shrine for common religious festivals; however, during times of common danger, they would form a temporary military coalition under a single leader for the duration of the threat.

Recently, scholars have brought objections against Noth's amphictyonic model taken from Greece. These objections include the following: (1) The Israelite tribes do not seem to have had *one* central shrine; perhaps each tribal group had its own Yahweh cult center at Gilgal, Shiloh, etc.; (2) most of the "judges" in the Book of Judges functioned as *individual* tribal war leaders rather than as amphictyonic leaders over all the tribes; (3) evidence that all the tribes ever operated as a unity (amphictyony) is disputed; (4) amphictyonies elsewhere in the Mediterranean seem to have allowed other religious commitments and therefore never insisted on the exclusivity demanded of the Israelite tribal league; and (5) other examples of amphictyonies were between city-states *not* tribes.

Some biblical scholars have preferred an ancient Near Eastern example, the Sumerian Kengir League, in which many of the early southern Mesopotamian cities united around the common shrine of the god Enlil at Nippur.

As long as we are not ruled by our models and remember that they are precisely that, they can be helpful. In one sense these examples help us understand the loose unity of the 12 tribes, whose recent union would later have been understood in terms of being the descendants of the 12 sons of a common ancestor, Jacob. There were Yahweh shrines, to which the portable Ark was conveyed, variously at Shiloh, at Shechem, and at Gilgal. Such a loose confederation (or amphictyony) would correspond to the origin of the tribal system as suggested above. A unity, which had resulted from a common flight from political oppression, would probably be suspicious of any strongly centralized system centered around a king, whose power would supposedly be god-given. According to the Book of Judges (which represents a later idealization), whenever the tribes as a whole were threatened or whenever they had a judicial matter of common concern, they would appoint common leaders (called *judges*) for a period of time. These periods of crises are documented in the Book of Judges. The tribal hostility toward monarchy is reflected in the story in Judges 9. Here Abimelech is appointed king, but the book's attitude about the institution of the monarchy is especially reflected in the parable in Judges 9:7–15. Read the parable and write down what you think it says about the characteristics of the monarchy. (Be specific!)

The unheroic fate of Abimelech (fatally wounded by a woman's millstone) also suggests antipathy toward the institution.

The weaknesses of this loose confederacy finally became apparent. First of all, it was cumbersome in times of real military threat. Read the ballad in Judges 5 where the tribes were threatened by a Canaanite attempt to split the tribal hill country at the Valley of Jezreel near the city of Megiddo; if they controlled this important valley, which stretched east to west, the Canaanites could isolate the northern group of tribes. The tribal troops were summoned, but many refused to respond and are cursed in the song (Judges 5:15b–17, 23).

This danger became even more severe because a new military power appeared around this time. About the same time that the Israelite presence appeared in the hills (1200 B.C.E.), the seacoast was invaded by groups probably related to the early Greeks mentioned in the *Iliad* and the *Odyssey*. These "Sea Peoples," as they were called in Egyptian literature, were named *Philistines* after one of their groups. (They gave their name to this geographical region—Palestine.) The Philistine military background and their control over ironworking technology gave them a military advantage, and they soon threatened even the mountain regions. This new danger highlighted the weakness of the tribal union when, in the Battle of Aphek (around 1050 B.C.E.), the Philistines not only defeated the tribes but even captured the Ark of the Covenant, the very symbol of the tribal confederation (1 Samuel 4).

The inability of the tribal league to enforce common moral principles is stressed in the strange story of Judges 19, in which the Tribe of Benjamin commits an outrage against a traveler. The league judiciary system is invoked by sending the 12 gruesome pieces to the 12 tribes (Judges 19:29). Nevertheless, the confederation cannot force the Tribe of Benjamin to punish the guilty parties, and so to cut out the potential contamination the tribes are forced to march against all of Benjamin and almost to eliminate that tribe (Judges 21:3).

At last the pressure to form a more tightly knit political unit becomes almost irresistible. The account of the reluctant formation of the first monarchy around 1020 B.C.E. is reported in the book of the last judge, Samuel. Although chapters 8–12 in 1 Samuel betray a very complex editorial history and an equally complicated view of the monarchy, the amphictyonic hostility toward kingship can be clearly detected in such passages as 1 Samuel 8:6–18 and 1 Samuel 12:19. Samuel, the representative of the old Mosaic tribal league, finally appoints the Benjaminite Saul as the first king, a choice basically dictated by Saul's military expertise, which was much in need during this threat by the Philistines.

At first Saul's kingship seemed to be a success. He defeated the Philistines; he restored the Mosaic priesthood of the old amphictyony, which then moved to Nob; he set up his royal capital at Gibeah. Archaeological excavations reveal that Saul's capital was really only a military garrison. However, in the end King Saul failed to establish a dynasty that outlasted him. The Bible cites several incidents that culminated in Samuel's rejection of Israel's first king. He was paranoid about his young aid, David; and as David's popularity grew, Saul sought to murder him. His frenzy to kill David even led to Saul's murder of the old amphictyonic priesthood at Nob because it had briefly sheltered the escapee David. To alienate the old priesthood further, Saul was pictured as usurping the priesthood of Samuel by offering sacrifice when that priest was delayed (1 Samuel 13:7b–15a).[37] Saul also is portrayed as resisting the amphictyonic religious custom of the "ban" in which all the booty after a military victory was sacrificed to Yahweh[38] because it was really he, not the army, who was considered to have won the battle (1 Samuel 15:10).

In any case, the last judge, Samuel, rejected Saul as king. His real failure lay in the fact that he was given a royal duty but not the means to achieve it. Although a king entrusted with the defense of his country, Saul was not allowed by the suspicious Samuel to exercise full royal power. He was doomed from the beginning. The monarchy had still not broken away from the old religion's fear of centralized power (perhaps because of its association with the Canaanite royal religious tradition that the Israelites had broken away from). A tragic figure, Saul is one of the few people in the Bible to commit suicide (1 Samuel 31:4).

Around 1000 B.C.E., Samuel anointed David king over Israel. Here at last was a success; David's family would rule over at least part of the country for the next 400 years until the Babylonian destruction of Jerusalem in 586 B.C.E. David succeeded whereas his predecessor, Saul, had failed because David accommodated himself to the conservative amphictyonic religion. At the same time, David moved toward a *theological basis* for his dynasty.

David recognized divisions in the old tribal system by having himself crowned king both in the north as well as in his own native south (Judah). Much like the old Austro-Hungarian monarchy of the last century, his was a dual monarchy. David then moved his power base outside the old tribal framework by capturing without bloodshed the Jebusite city of Jerusalem, which to that time had been claimed by no tribe (see Judges 1:21). He purposefully used his own personal troops in the assault and not tribal forces, so that David could legitimately claim the city as his own royal property. David made Jerusalem his royal capital; like the District of Columbia, which is outside the territorial claim of any American state, David's capital was outside the territorial claim of any of the jealous tribes. He moved the old Ark of the Covenant, which as the very symbol of the former tribal league had been disregarded by Saul, into the new capital. David then appointed a dual priesthood to officiate in his royal shrine. Abiathar was in the line of the conservative tribal league priests of Mosaic origin who had watched over the Ark at Shiloh; but David also appointed a mysterious priest named Zadok, who quite possibly was a native Canaanite priest from the population of captured Jerusalem. Such a clever choice would both respect the older Mosaic religion (Abiathar), while setting the stage for the incorporation of many Canaanite elements (Zadok) into the new royal religion.

---

[37] To be fair, it should be noted that kings in the ancient Near East customarily functioned as priests; Saul was really only claiming for himself what was the right of the contemporary monarch; perhaps Samuel regretted the king actually moving in the direction he had already feared.

[38] Remember the adage, "To the victor belong the spoils."

This view of Jerusalem from the south shows the Ophel, a spur of land in the center of the picture extending out from the present-day walls of the Old City. This was the site of David's Jerusalem. Behind the Ophel, on the other side of the walls, is the Moslem Dome of the Rock which marks the approximate location of Solomon's temple.

David's movement of the Ark into Jerusalem, commemorated in Psalm 132, accomplished two things: (1) It combined the old conservative religion with his new royal center and (2) his piety toward the old Mosaic religion was portrayed as being the counterpart of God's faithfulness toward him and his dynasty (Psalm 132:11–12). David then created two new traditions: a **Zion Tradition**, namely, that Yahweh dwelt in a very special way on Mount Zion in Jerusalem; and a **Davidic Covenant**, namely, the religious claim that David and his family had a special promise from God that they would always rule over Jerusalem (see 2 Samuel 7, and especially Psalm 89:31–36). David cast this divine pledge in the literary form of the Near Eastern **Royal Grant**, whereby a monarch would promise to bestow on a faithful vassal some gift; these grants focused on the sovereign's responsibilities toward the subject. By rooting his rule in a direct gift from Yahweh, David had freed the monarchy from its dependence on such figures of the old tribal system as Samuel; he had, however, set up the possibility of a tension between two entirely different covenant models: (1) the *Mosaic,* which stressed the people and their responsibility toward the deity, and (2) the *Davidic,* which emphasized the deity's one-sided and eternal pledge toward the Davidic dynasty.

Amazingly, David's kingdom went in one generation from being a loose group of tribes in the Palestinian hill country to a leading empire in the Near East. This was accomplished by skillful marriages, economic treaties, and actual conquests (and by a brief period of weakness in her neighbors to the north, Assyria and Damascus, and to the south, Egypt). David's capture of his new capital intact provided him with the skilled bureaucracy necessary for his emerging empire. However, David now needed a new story about the origins of Israel to go with his new empire. The king had to accommodate the older Yahwistic religion to the more cosmopolitan setting of his empire, which now included countless people of different religions. What was to be their religious status in the official royal cult? David, or possibly his son, Solomon, commissioned a new literary history of Israel that would create a role for David's kingdom, which of course had been ignored in the religious accounts of the old tribal league.[39] The result was the **Yahwist**'s work, the J Document or J Source.[40]

This document probably extended originally from Creation (Genesis 2:4b) to some version of David's rise to royal power in Jerusalem, although the J version of this latter account is *not* identical to David's rise to power found in the present Book of Samuel, which dates from the seventh-century Deuteronomistic historian.[41] David had extended the older story of origins from the Patriarchs to Creation itself; this was not by accident. Royalty in the ancient Near East was quite frequently associated with Creation and the creator deity (remember Marduk's coronation in the Enuma Elish). This conveyed the belief that the king was an element in the very order of things and not just someone engaged in politics. The J Writer's account, beginning on a universal stage with human Creation, also suited the broader scope of the Davidic imperial religion, which governed an empire of many diverse peoples and religions; the older story (G) had begun with the "nationalistic" Israelite patriarchs (recall Deuteronomy 26).

The key to the theology of the J document is found in Genesis 12:1–4 where Abraham first receives Yahweh's promise. First of all, recall that this passage resolves the sin and confusion of humankind by offering them blessings if they associate with Abraham and his successors (read *David*). Otherwise their curse will continue. This provides a sort of royal foreign policy for David's empire. (The same theology is found enshrined in Psalm 47.) Also notice that Yahweh's promise to Abraham is one-sided, that is, it is completely in the format of the royal grant, which was the model of the so-called Davidic Covenant found in places like 2 Samuel 7. Genesis 12 stresses Yahweh's promise more than Patriarchal responsibilities.

The promise of the land is detailed in Genesis 15:18,[42] where we find mention of the territory's borders. It is striking that these borders do not correspond to those of the old tribal amphictyony; however, these borders basically agree with those of the Davidic-Solomonic empire (1 Kings 4:21)—a territory ruled over only once in Israelite history and for only about a 50-year period. According to the J Writer, the promise of the land was not really fulfilled under Joshua (as it was for the tribal league) but only under David.

In sum, we should argue that the Yahwistic epic is a prosaizing, propaganda work of the United Monarchy, and specifically the program of Solomon to constitute an Oriental monarchy in the Canaanite pattern. The older epic, cut loose from the covenantal cultus of the tribal sanctuaries of the league, was shaped by the Yahwist for new institutions and new functions.[43]

[39] Recall the old oral recitals, many of which go back to the tribal period. These recitals do not mention a role for a monarchy.

[40] For a treatment by some recent scholars who would date the J source centuries later than David, see the survey article by Douglas Knight cited at the end of this chapter.

[41] As we shall see later, based on *theme* (Promise/Fulfillment) we theorize that J originally must have included a section on David's empire, which would complete the promises made to the Patriarchs; however, in the present Bible, J as a written source cannot be documented after the end of the Book of Numbers, although some would attribute Judges 1 to J. So J's hypothetical story of David has been lost.

[42] Notice in this chapter the *royal grant* format of God's "covenant making"; in other words, God binds himself, not Abraham.

[43] Frank M. Cross, "The Epic Traditions of Early Israel: Epic Narrative and the Reconstruction of Early Israelite Institutions," in Richard E. Friedman, ed., *The Poet and the Historian: Essays in Literary and Historical Biblical Criticism* (Harvard Semitic Series 26; Chico: CA: Scholars Press, 1983), p. 30.

A Northern Source: The Elohist (E)

The empire of David (ca. 1000–961 B.C.E.) and Solomon (ca. 961–922 B.C.E.) was short-lived. Solomon had assumed the typical role of the Near Eastern despot. The old portable tent of the tribal league was no longer suitable for an established monarchy, so he constructed the temple on Mount Zion, which adjoined his royal palace and, in one sense, served as a royal chapel. He tried to break up the older tribal system by dividing the area into administrative districts that disregarded tribal boundaries. He used forced labor to construct a line of forts around the kingdom. Solomon must have angered believers in Yahweh by his political marriages with nonbelieving wives, who then constructed shrines to their religions in Jerusalem.

Solomon also exiled the co-priest Abiathar to the northern village of Anathoth because he had conspired against the king when Solomon first assumed the throne. This meant that, from Solomon on, the main priestly family in Jerusalem was descended from Zadok and had no ties to the traditional Mosaic amphictyony. The demise of the empire was further hastened by the recovery of her powerful neighbors to the south (Egypt) and to the north (Damascus and Assyria).

When Solomon died (ca. 922 B.C.E.) his son Rehoboam (ca. 922–915 B.C.E.) was unable to assume the throne of a united kingdom. Rehoboam's arrogance led to the succession of the northern tribes under King Jeroboam. The carefully maintained dual monarchy of David now collapsed into two separate kingdoms. The old Davidic center remained at Jerusalem, which ruled over the Tribe of Judah—an area about the size of Rhode Island. The larger northern tribes were called *Israel,* which was never able to establish as stable a dynasty as had Judah. Israel's capital was later to be built at Samaria.

The ruins of the palace of King Ahab (ca. 869-850 B.C.E.) in Samaria. This capital city of Israel overlooking the important trade routes north of Jerusalem was first built by Ahab's father King Omri (ca. 876-869).

Israel and Judah — 850 B.C.E.

Israel seemed to maintain closer ties to the old Mosaic religion; after all, most of the older shrines of the Ark of the Covenant (Shiloh, Gilgal, and Shechem) had been in the north. The Mosaic priesthood, called *Levites,* remained in power in Israel and were assigned two shrines at Dan and Bethel, which had old patriarchal associations. The Mosaic religion was safeguarded by an institution called *prophecy,* whose role it was to approve or disapprove of kings according to their relation to the traditional faith.[44] (This role was similar to that of Samuel with King Saul.) And so Judah with its shrine in Jerusalem, and Israel with its shrines in Dan and Bethel, were to remain in conflict with each other for the next several hundred years. These

---

[44] See the example of the northern prophet Elijah in Chapter 7, which deals with prophecy.

kingdoms were also based on different religious emphases: Judah on the Davidic Covenant and Israel on the older, more traditional Mosaic Sinai religion.

Naturally, the northern kingdom of Israel could not use the Yahwist history as the official account of its origins because this latter account was closely linked with Davidic aspirations. Therefore, the north was responsible for the creation of the rival **Elohist Document** (E source), so called because of its Hebrew word for the deity *'elohim*. As you can imagine, this source had no story of Creation; it preferred to begin at the more traditional starting point used by the old oral creedal confessions: the story of the Patriarchs. (This is why we did not encounter the E source in our careful reading of Genesis 1–11.) The scope of E probably followed these ancient creeds quite carefully and went from the Patriarchs up to the Occupation of Canaan.[45]

The Elohist document stressed Moses, the Covenant, and human obligations toward the deity; in fact, much of what we know about the laws of Sinai and the Ten Commandments has been preserved for us in the E source. A striking contrast between the theologies of J and E can be seen by comparing the divine promises in Genesis 12:1–4 and Genesis 15 (J) with Genesis 22 (E). In the J account, Yahweh's promises are unconditional and one-sided: God promises to Abraham but does not exact anything from him in return. In Genesis 22, on the other hand, the promise (22:15–18) comes *after* Abraham has demonstrated his faithfulness and obedience.

Although the two kingdoms were often at military odds with each other, the northern kingdom of Israel continued side by side with the Davidic Judah to the south for the next 200 years. Israel was finally destroyed by its northern neighbor Assyria in 722 B.C.E. and was made a province of that vast empire. Those who preserved the E traditions probably fled south to Judah where they took refuge. (Recent archaeological excavations in Jerusalem show that Jerusalem was expanded at this time to accommodate the refugees.) Under the Davidic King Hezekiah (715–687 B.C.E.), the J and E documents were combined. The result was a JE amalgam of traditions, although the southern location would guarantee the dominance of J's Davidic element. Because the J document provided the framework for the JE combination, the E tradition has not survived in as complete a form as has J.

King Josiah's Revival: The Deuteronomist (D)

In 701 B.C.E. (during the time of the prophet Isaiah) Assyria turned its attention to the small southern state of Judah. King Sennacherib marched against Jerusalem, but for some unclear reason he was unable to take and destroy the city. He probably had to retreat prematurely in order to protect his own interests back in Assyria. King Hezekiah of Jerusalem and his followers interpreted their delivery as a miracle that could only bolster the official Zion and Davidic traditions: Not even the mightiest army in the world could prevail against Yahweh's holy mountain and dynasty.

Judah's enthusiasm was to be short-lived, for only a few years later she was forced to submit to the inevitable and to become a vassal of Assyria. Much of the treasure of Solomon's temple was sent as booty to Nineveh, the Assyrian capital. During the long reign of King Manasseh (687–642 B.C.E.) Assyrian religion made strong inroads into Yahwism; in fact, the god Assur was probably worshipped in the temple alongside Yahweh. It was during this dark era for traditional religion that an underground movement was developing. Refugees, perhaps from the north's de-

---

[45] E's version of the occupation of Canaan has not clearly survived in our present Hebrew Bible, for the Book of Joshua is attributed to the later Deuteronomistic Historian (see below). However, some scholars claim that the DH's Conquest story in Joshua 1–12 was derived from E.

struction in 722 B.C.E., were constructing the basis for eventual religious reform. Judah's sorry state could no longer sustain the triumphant version of its origins espoused in the earlier JE epic. These refugees, perhaps literary and religious descendants of Abiathar exiled by Solomon to Anathoth, attempted a symphony of northern and southern theologies. *From the north* they derived the idea of a religion centered on Moses, the Sinai Covenant's stress on personal obligations, and the old Levitical priesthood; *from the south* they borrowed the notion of the importance of Mount Zion/Jerusalem and a positive role for the Davidic monarchy (even though the powers of the king were severely restricted in Deuteronomy 17).

Their writings remained unofficial until the time of King Josiah (640–609 B.C.E.), who was regarded as one of the greatest kings in Judah since David. By the time of Josiah, Assyrian power in the area had begun to deteriorate, and Josiah moved north into the former territory of Israel to fill the political vacuum. When Assyria could no longer maintain its rule, the Davidic king cleansed the temple of its foreign contamination; in the temple were found writings that Josiah adopted as the basis for his reform of Yahwism (2 Kings 22). Undoubtedly these writings, composed by the secret reform group during the reign of King Manasseh, were the heart of the present Book of Deuteronomy (chapters 12–26).

The Book of Deuteronomy appears as if it were the last words of Moses before his death and before the crossing of his people into the promised land. In reality, it represents the reform program of the refugees, perhaps from Anathoth in the north. By placing all the stipulations of the reform in the mouth of Moses— even laws governing the monarchy—they are clearly extolling Moses as the center of true religion. The **Deuteronomist** also stresses the role of the Levitical priests who traced their lineage back to Moses (Deuteronomy 18:1–8). All laws have been placed in the mouth of Moses, who alone survives as the true lawgiver and as the sole source of authority. The Davidic king has been reduced to the enforcer of Mosaic precepts. However, the Book of Deuteronomy also recognizes the importance of David's Jerusalem, which emerges as the only place of true cult (Deuteronomy 12:1–31). King Josiah followed this recommendation and destroyed all the rival shrines, including Bethel to the north. He then brought all the unemployed priests to Jerusalem and provided for them.

The Deuteronomic scribal school responsible for this reform then rewrote Israelite history for two reasons: (1) to judge each monarch by how carefully he measured up to the ideals of the Book of Deuteronomy and (2) to have Israelite history culminate in the glorious reign of the reformer Josiah. A good king enjoyed prosperity and a long reign, whereas a monarch judged deficient could expect the ignominious death that was usually prophesied at his coronation (see 1 Kings 22:37). (This work continues the northern stress on the role of the prophet in maintaining Mosaic purity of religion.) The Deuteronomistic historians took old traditions and edited them around their purposes; this historical survey formed the **Deuteronomistic History** (DH) of Joshua, Judges, Samuel, and Kings.

The DH probably added Deuteronomy 1:1–4:40 and most of Deuteronomy 29–34 in order to recast the Book of Deuteronomy as the introduction to this new collection, which now extended from Deuteronomy to 2 Kings. The theology of this new corpus can be seen in a reading of Deuteronomy 1:1–4:40 and summed up in the conditional admonition:

> You must keep his statutes and commandments which I command you today, in order that you and your children after you may prosper, and that you may extend your days on the land which Yahweh, your God, is giving you forever. (Deuteronomy 4:40)

In this corpus, the breakaway northern monarch Jeroboam represents the arch-fiend because he split worship between Jerusalem and Bethel; conversely, Josiah is the model king and in some sense a reflection of Moses himself.

The relation of this Deuteronomistic corpus—Deuteronomy to 2 Kings—to the earlier combined document of JE should be clarified. The two works seem to have remained independent, even though Deuteronomy presupposes JE; there are no clear examples of the Deuteronomist in the JE collection from Genesis to Numbers, although some would see traces of J and E in DH. In any case, this *hypothetical* early edition of JE must have included its own version of the conquest of the land and the rise of David, for these themes were so integral to its story. At some point this redundancy was simplified by the deletion of the JE version of these events so that only the DH account of these traditions survived in the books of Joshua through 2 Kings. (Some scholars, however, suspect that the J version of the Conquest underlies Judges 1, which emphasizes the success of Judah in contrast to the failures of the northern tribes; they also maintain that Joshua 1–12 has been derived from the E version of the Conquest. Decision on these matters is almost impossible.)

This collection had to undergo a quick new edition when the reign of Josiah ended in his defeat and death in battle, and his family soon went into Babylonian captivity. In 609 B.C.E., Josiah was killed in battle fighting the Egyptian Pharaoh, Necho, near Megiddo. His untimely death in battle must have been a profound embarrassment to the Deuteronomistic theologians who believed that a good king could always expect a long and prosperous reign. From the time of Josiah's death the fate of Judah quickly disintegrated and she came under the power of the neo-Babylonian empire, which was replacing Assyria. When Judah sided with Egypt against Babylon, Jerusalem was conquered in 597 B.C.E. and her young king, Jehoiakin, was sent into Babylonian exile; in 586 B.C.E. his uncle, Zedekiah, was defeated by King Nebuchadnezzar of Babylon, who punished this renewed rebellion by blinding the king, destroying Jerusalem, and exiling the city's leading citizens. (This period provides the background for the prophecies of Jeremiah.)

The work of the authors of the Book of Deuteronomy and of the Deuteronomistic History was quite fortuitous. For unless the shift from the David-centered orientation of the earlier JE history—which stressed David's empire as the fulfillment of Yahweh's promise—to the Deuteronomist's stress on the prepolitical Moses had taken place, it is difficult to imagine how the religion could have survived the destruction of that dynasty in 586 B.C.E.

An exilic editor had to make changes in the Deuteronomistic History written during the upbeat reign of Josiah in order to explain these sudden unanticipated reversals. According to this revision, the nation was just now being punished for the earlier sins of the evil King Manasseh; the punishment had only been briefly delayed because of the piety of Manasseh's grandson, Josiah (2 Kings 21:10–15).[46]

Revival in Exile: The Priestly Writer

It is hard to date accurately the Priestly Writer (P) because so much of this author's cultic and religious material is really quite ancient. However, it appears as if the final editing of this archaic material was done during the Babylonian captivity (around

---

[46] There is new evidence, however, from manuscript discoveries along the Dead Sea at Qumran, that the Hebrew text of the DH continued to undergo changes and growth; in fact, there probably were several different editions of DH at any given moment until the text was finally stabilized by becoming canonical, or authoritative, in the community.

550 B.C.E.). Indeed, much of this material, especially P's stress on Creation, recalls his fellow exile and contemporary *Second Isaiah,* the author of Isaiah 40–55. It seems that his exilic editing was done in order to reassure the people that God had not lost control in 586 B.C.E. and that he would honor his promises. The nation would be restored to the land and a rebuilt temple would become their source of life. And so although it looks as if P is editing a story about Israel's *past* beginning with Creation, he really is proposing a view of the *future* with Israel's re-creation. (And so P's work is more *conative* than *referential.*)

In P's story of the Flood, Noah's ark saves the people from almost certain destruction, and on New Year's Day[47] it emerges from chaos to become the source of recreated life and of God's eternal covenant with all nature (Genesis 9:16); this is a symbol of the new temple proposed by P, which, as the center of true cult, will represent life emerging from the chaos of national destruction.

The P Writer collected legal material from all different periods, especially laws dealing with the cult, dietary restrictions, feast days, etc., and put them into the mouth of Moses, where they were promulgated on Mount Sinai. After the debacle of 586 B.C.E., only Moses' authority survived. The P Writer wanted to outline a world where *stability* would be assured against the onslaught of *chaos* by the maintenance of distinctive religious rules and by a Zadokite priesthood descended from Aaron (see Numbers 25:7–13 for an "eternal covenant" with the Aaronic priesthood).

As far as scholars can detect, the editorial work of P seems confined to the JE accounts; there is only slight (and disputed) evidence of P material in Deuteronomistic Joshua. However, once again, we should state that his work must have included some account of the occupation of the land, for this concept is central to his reassurance to the exiles that they will someday return. (However, in P's ideology, the land was probably not conquered by humans but was given by God.) Some time later, as we shall soon see, these two separate written collections were integrated: JEP, which P had edited to stress *stability* through the cult, and Deuteronomy with the Deuteronomistic History, which emphasized the risks in trying to maintain faithfulness to the Law. This final redaction would have been facilitated by the role of the Book of Deuteronomy, which presupposed JE and formed the basis for the ongoing Deuteronomistic History. Redundant versions of the Conquest and of David's rise to power (those in JEP) would have been dropped at this stage. The resulting combination would then include an historical sweep from Creation to the hopeful release of Jehoiakin from Babylonian prison (2 Kings 25:29).

According to P there are three significant moments in his editing of the earlier JE account: (1) Creation, (2) Moses' building of an elaborate sanctuary in the desert (Exodus 39–40), and (3) the distribution of the land to the Israelites.[48] P's optimistic[49] view of an orderly, systematic Creation, which highlights God's unchallenged power, must have appealed to his near-despairing audience. P's idea that the Sabbath, a major liturgical idea in postexilic times, was rooted in Creation itself (". . . and God rested on the seventh day") suggests that Israel's cult is not arbitrary but part of the fundamental world order that God has sworn to preserve (see covenant with Noah, p. 109). The building of the tabernacle in the desert renewed the hope of those in the "new desert" (the Babylonian captivity) that there

---

[47] Solomon's temple, destroyed in 586 B.C.E., had been dedicated on New Year's Day.

[48] Perhaps Joshua's division of the land in Joshua 19:51 is meant to recall God's *separation* at Creation in Genesis 1—this would reveal a giant inclusion in the work of the Priestly Writer. (However, such evidence of P in the present Book of Joshua remains quite controversial.)

[49] Remember the refrain "it was good."

would eventually be rebuilt a site for God to dwell in their midst. As we saw when we discussed the threefold promise to the Patriarchs, which the P Editor has made the organizing theme of his work, the land was an important motif for this priestly editor. Just as the desert tabernacle of Moses was in the center of the Israelite camp, so the new temple would be in the center of the land of Israel to which the exiles will return after their wandering.

Another priestly program for restoration was proposed by the Prophet Ezekiel, who had been one of the priests in the Jerusalem temple who had been deported to Babylon in 597 B.C.E. This first exile, a decade before Jerusalem's destruction, had been reserved for the higher ranks in society: artisans, priests, royal family, etc. (2 Kings 24:14). From 593 until around 571 B.C.E. this exiled priest observed the dissolution of his society from afar. Half of his prophetic book is devoted to announcing Israel's impending doom. However, as soon as Ezekiel has heard of Jerusalem's destruction (Ezekiel 33:21–22), he then prophesies restoration. This national resurrection is vividly described in his vision of a valley of dead, dried bones that are restored to life by the spirit of God, which blows over them (Ezekiel 37). This renewal will bring together the north (Israel) and the south (Judah) in reconciliation (Ezekiel 37:15–22). Ezekiel's detailed program for the future in chapters 40–48 reveals his priestly background and reflects many similarities to the theology of his contemporary Babylonian captive, namely, the Priestly Writer. Both priests linked the future of the land to the rites conducted in the rebuilt temple in Jerusalem by Aaronic (Zadokite) priests. Although Ezekiel was to assign a role to a Davidic "prince," the major power in the New Jerusalem was in the hands of the Zadokites. The status of royal Judah was also diminished so that strife between north and south would be alleviated.

Ezra's Reform: A Pentateuch

Up to this point we still have not answered our original dilemma: How were the two separate histories, JEP and D, combined? How was the stress on the occupation of the land as a program for Israel's future restoration shortened to the present five-book Pentateuch, which combines books from both collections? The work edited by the Priestly Writer in exile offered hope to his readership by showing the reliability of God's promises (despite all human obstacles), especially his promise of the land. When did the five-book collection (Pentateuch), ending on the unsettling note of Moses' death outside the land, become normative (canonical)? To put the problem in more literary terms: When was the Book of Deuteronomy—the linchpin of the Deuteronomistic History—separated from that corpus and linked with the preceding JEP material? (The Book of Deuteronomy becomes part of the Torah, while the remainder of the DH [Joshua through 2 Kings] now forms the beginning of the second division of the Hebrew Bible, the Prophets.)

The optimism of P and Ezekiel (shared by their fellow exile Second Isaiah) was not completely realized. Although in 540 B.C.E. Cyrus the Great of Persia allowed the exiles to return home after his conquest of Babylon, the restoration was quite modest. The land remained a diminished territory in the new Persian Empire.

The temple in Jerusalem was eventually rebuilt (520–515 B.C.E.) but proved to be divisive as groups fought over qualifications for membership in the new community and over its legitimate priests.[50] The people who had stayed behind in the

---

[50] This latter squabble was between successors of Zadok, who traced their lineage back to Aaron, and the old Levitical (Mosaic) priesthood, which had been represented in David's day by Abiathar.

ruined land resented the claim of those returning after 50 years to rule the restored community. The acrimony of Isaiah 56–66 reveals the social tensions.

For a stark example of this internal squabble centering on contradictory views about the restoration of the temple, read the following two contemporary prophetic works: Isaiah 66:1–3[51] and Haggai 1:1–11. The importance of the temple differed according to which group would officiate in it.

This inner-community strife is a major contributing factor in the eventual emergence of a new type of literature, **Apocalyptic**, in which the minority party in the struggle feels so alienated from its community and so pessimistic about the present society that it envisions God bringing the world to an end and beginning all over again with a New Creation.[52] This cosmic upheaval is usually described in language appropriated from the old cosmic Creation myths populated with Tiamat-like dragons and sea monsters (Leviathan).[53] Such borrowings were natural, for most of these Near Eastern myths portrayed Creation as a result of a battle between opposing forces, which perfectly fit the mind of the besieged members of the post-exilic community writing apocalyptic literature. The disenfranchised party felt so cut off from community religious and civil structures, that it is characteristically pessimistic about the ability of any human agency to reform. Apocalyptic literature typically stresses the solitary role of God, often conceived of as a divine warrior, who alone can reform by destroying and re-creating. Early apocalyptic writings in Isaiah 24–27, 56–66, and Zechariah 9–12 generally display the frustrations of the Levitical party that felt sidetracked by the Aaronic/Zadokite reformers represented by Ezekiel 40–48 (see Ezekiel 44:10–16), the Priestly Writer, and the prophets Haggai and Zechariah 1–8.

This postexilic period also produced a third historical work to join the earlier accounts of JEP and the DH. The product of the **Chronicler** (1 and 2 Chronicles) has been variously dated from 525 to 375 B.C.E., depending upon its relationship to the Book of Ezra-Nehemiah,[54] which is currently being debated in modern scholarship. The books 1 and 2 Chronicles chart the history of Israel from Adam down to the postexilic time of Ezra and Nehemiah. The early period, especially from Adam to Saul, is mainly represented by genealogies (1 Chronicles 1–9). The period of the monarchy is generally agreed to have been excerpted from some version of DH, whom the Chronicler seems to presuppose even in sections not borrowed from DH.

The Chronicler is mainly interested in the southern kingdom of Judah and ignores northern history. This historian concentrates on David's and Solomon's establishment of the temple cult in Jerusalem (1 Chronicles 10–2 Chronicles 9); Chronicles presents a polished view of these two kings in order to stress their suitability to build and staff the temple. The theology of the Chronicler affirms that the postexilic community in reestablishing both the temple on Zion and an order of Law has continued the truest traditions of the Davidic Dynasty. This historical work also attempts a reconciliation between elements in the community by outlining roles for both Aaronic/Zadokite priests and for Mosaic Levites, many of whom are described as singers and prophets in the temple (1 Chronicles 16:4–36).

---

[51] Chapters 56–66 of Isaiah are called *Trito-Isaiah*, or Third Isaiah, and were probably written around 520 B.C.E.

[52] Examples of apocalyptic literature within the Hebrew Bible are Trito-Isaiah (chapters 56–66), Zechariah (chapters 9–12), the Apocalypse of Isaiah (Isaiah 24–27), and the later Book of Daniel 7–12.

[53] See Isaiah 27:1, 65:17–25; Daniel 7:1–8.

[54] In Jewish tradition, Ezra-Nehemiah is regarded as one book.

As a result of religious deterioration in Judah over the next several generations, the Persian authorities finally decided to intervene. Judah was too important for their empire, for it straddled that narrow bottleneck between Mesopotamia and the rebellious province of Egypt. The exact date (around the middle of the fourth century B.C.E.) and sequence of activities are almost impossible to reconstruct from the Book of Ezra-Nehemiah. The book seems to interweave the reforms of Ezra and Nehemiah, beginning with the efforts of **Ezra** (Ezra 7–10), then Nehemiah (Nehemiah 1–7), Ezra again (Nehemiah 9–9), ending with Nehemiah (Nehemiah 10–13). Ezra's efforts are mostly religious: He brings the Law to Jerusalem and he insulates the community by driving out contaminating influences and intermarriages.[55] Nehemiah's efforts are more political: He provides for Jerusalem's physical safety by reconstructing her walls. Despite the book's efforts to bring the roles of the two writers together (see especially Nehemiah 8:9 and 12:26), most scholars believe that their efforts were separate and that they have been brought together by a redactor to stress the similarity of their reforms: Both have surrounded Jerusalem with a bulwark—Nehemiah's wall and Ezra's law. Slight evidence favors the earlier arrival of Nehemiah. Scholars have often attributed the chronological confusion in Ezra-Nehemiah to the problem of references to the reign of the Persian king Artaxerxes (Ezra 7:7; Nehemiah 2:1, 13:6). Was this Artaxerxes I (465–424 B.C.E.) or Artaxerxes II (404–358 B.C.E.)? Many say that Nehemiah arrived during the reign of Artaxerxes I, and Ezra arrived during the reign of the later Persian king. But this historical reconstruction remains too hypothetical. Rather than assuming confusion due to mistaken identities, perhaps we should focus on the theological plan of the redactor (redaction criticism) who wanted both to show similarities in the efforts of Ezra and Nehemiah (interspersing their reforms) and to stress the priestly reforms of Ezra (placing him first).

In any case, it seems that Persia dispatched two Jewish leaders, the civilian authority Nehemiah and the priest, Ezra. Ezra, acting as Persia's secretary of Jewish affairs, brought with him a version of the law (Torah) to which he had all of the people adhere (read Nehemiah 8). Many scholars believe that Ezra was responsible for bracketing off the first five books as Judaism's authoritative Torah. Deuteronomy 34 now forms the ending of this five-book collection. The Pentateuch then would have been the law read to the people at the Water Gate in Nehemiah 8.[56]

This simple accomplishment of regrouping the first books of the Hebrew Bible would have a profound effect on how Israel's story of her origins was now read.[57] By ending with the death of Moses on the other side of the Jordan River, Ezra would provide for a Judaism that could expect an indefinite future without control of the promised land. Their attention was now focused on the *hope* of the realization of this promise. Ezra had accommodated Judaism to the reality of its new depoliticized status in the Persian Empire: Unlike during the time of David's

---

[55] Perhaps this atmosphere explains the Book of Jonah discussed earlier. Jonah's author would in this case argue against a narrow nationalistic idea of religion, which he saw in the reforms of Ezra.

[56] In this hypothetical reconstruction Ezra would have accomplished the following: (1) He would have joined JEP and the Deuteronomistic work (Deuteronomy through 2 Kings); (2) Ezra would have deleted the redundant versions of the Conquest of Joshua and of David's rise to power, which were probably found in the original JEP; (3) Ezra bracketed off the five books of Genesis through Deuteronomy as the normative center of Jewish faith.

[57] Stories of origins are more than historical (referential) accounts. They form the self-identity of the community itself, and so they actually function as *conative* communication. They define the group that uses them.

Development of the Torah/Pentateuch

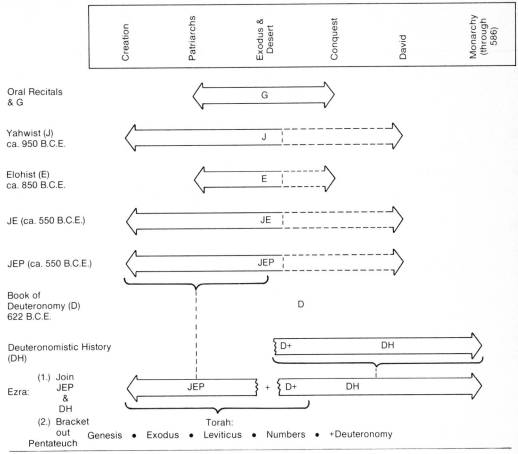

Unfinished (dotted) arrows show material that probably existed but which has no longer been preserved in the post-Ezra Hebrew Bible.

empire, Judah could now only *hope* for return to its land. For the next several millennia Judaism was to survive as a religion in **diaspora**, spread throughout the world. Ezra had also depoliticized the religion by completing the realignment of its focus from David, who now remains on the other side of the fence created by this bracketing, to the premonarchical lawgiver Moses.

FURTHER READINGS

The Theme of the Pentateuch

David J. A. Clines, *The Theme of the Pentateuch* (*Journal for the Study of the Old Testament Supplement* Series 10; Sheffield, England: JSOT, 1978). Much of the analysis of the thesis of the Pentateuch is indebted to this study.

Oral Recitals and Creedal Confessions

Bernhard Anderson, *Understanding the Old Testament*, 4th ed. (Englewood Cliffs, NJ: Prentice-Hall, 1986), pp. 101–103, 153–158.

Douglas A. Knight, "The Pentateuch," in *The Hebrew Bible and Its Modern Interpreters* (Chico, CA: Scholars Press, 1985), pp. 263-296. Knight's chapter provides an excellent review of contemporary scholarship on the formation of the Pentateuch, oral recitals, and the J, E, D, and P sources and their relationship to the overall Pentateuch.

Thomas L. Thompson, "Historical Reconstructions of the Narratives," in John H. Hayes and J. Maxwell Miller, eds., *Israelite and Judean History* (*Old Testament Library*; Philadelphia: Fortress Press, 1977), pp. 162-166. This article is quite skeptical about our ability to use the Historical Credos as a source of early, premonarchical beliefs.

The Israelite Tribal League and the Formation of the Monarchy

Bernhard W. Anderson, *Understanding the Old Testament*, 4th ed. (Englewood Cliffs, NJ: Prentice-Hall, 1986), pp. 142-150, 201-210.

Henry E. Chambers, "Ancient Amphictyonies, Sic et Non," in *Scripture in Context II: More Essays on the Comparative Method* (Winona Lake, IN: Eisenbrauns, 1983), pp. 39-59.

Norman K. Gottwald, *The Hebrew Bible: A Socio-Literary Introduction* (Philadelphia: Fortress Press, 1985), pp. 260-288. This section considers the theories about the occupation of Canaan as well as the structure of the early tribalization.

J. Maxwell Miller, "Israelite History," in *The Hebrew Bible and Its Modern Interpreters* (Chico, CA: Scholars Press, 1985), pp. 1-30. Miller's article contains an excellent bibliography of current works on Israelite historiography and on such issues as the origins of Israel, the monarchy, and the dating of the Books of Ezra and Nehemiah.

The Development of the Pentateuch and Its Sources

Peter R. Ackroyd, "The Historical Literature," in *The Hebrew Bible and Its Modern Interpreters* (Chico, CA: Scholars Press, 1985), pp. 297-323. This survey is especially helpful for its review of current writings on the Deuteronomistic History.

Douglas A. Knight, "The Pentateuch," in *The Hebrew Bible and Its Modern Interpreters* (Chico, CA: Scholars Press, 1985), pp. 263-296.

James A. Sanders, *Torah and Canon* (Philadelphia: Fortress Press, 1972).

CHAPTER 5
THE BOOK OF THE COVENANT
(Exodus 20:22–23:33)

GOALS AND OBJECTIVES: In Chapter 4 we saw the importance of laws in the Israelite story of her origins. The Elohist, the author of the Book of Deuteronomy, and the Priestly Writer included vast sections of law—all placed in the mouth of Moses, the model lawgiver in the Hebrew Bible. So overpowering a presence are these laws, that it has become customary to translate the Hebrew word for the first division of the Bible, Torah, *as The Law.[1] Because this legal tradition plays such an important role, we should look at it a little more carefully in Chapters 5 and 6, both against its* common Near Eastern background and its *individuality. We shall also examine many of the social and religious factors that affected Israelite legal understanding. In Chapter 6 we shall concentrate on the broad impact of the legal concept of "covenant" upon the Hebrew Bible.*

Chapter 5 will not only use most of the critical techniques that we have acquired in this text but it will also relate the important concept of "law" to Israelite religion. We shall first of all isolate some of the literary sources that comprise the Book of the Covenant (source criticism), and then we shall investigate the literary form and points of origin in Israelite society of these sources (form criticism). In studying the biblical editor's arrangement of these sources we use redaction criticism. *This chapter will also relate "law" both to the rest of the ancient Near East and to the special understanding of Israel herself (*historical-cultural criticism*). We trace the development and changes in law from Israel's borrowing of laws from the ancient world all the way to Israel's integration of these laws in accordance with her own religious concepts; this tracing of a tradition through various stages and adaptations constitutes* tradition criticism.

Carefully read the ancient Israelite law book in Exodus 20:22–23:33. This selection is probably from the Elohist, although as you shall see much of it is far older than the 850 B.C.E. date usually assigned that northern writer. Its introduction and conclusion, which set it apart from its Sinai context, suggest that it appears in the Book of Exodus as a self-enclosed literary unit. This section has been called the *Book of the Covenant* (BOC) or *Covenant Code* because of the supposed reference to it in Exodus 24:7.

---

[1] A better translation of "torah" is "teaching." The biblical Torah is made up of narrative *and* law.

SOURCE CRITICISM

Before we look at the Book of the Covenant itself, we should consider how the editor has arranged it (its broader literary context) and to what purposes. We shall begin by reading the entire section (Exodus 20:1–23:33) and then we shall isolate the component sources that comprise it. Remember that source criticism precedes redaction criticism, for we have to determine what materials (sources) had been available to the final editor (redactor).

1.   There are independent sections even within the BOC. Let us first separate them and then try to find if the editor has arranged them according to an editorial (that is, a redactional) pattern. Next we shall try to determine the editor's purposes based upon such an editorial structure.[2]

Exodus 23:20–33 is a later addition to the Book of the Covenant. Can you give some evidence that supports this assessment? How does this section fit in with the laws that precede it in Exodus 20:22–23:19? Is this latter section a "legal" text?

Which historical stage of Israel's life is this passage most interested in?

How does the historical period mentioned in Exodus 23:20–33 differ from that presupposed for all of the BOC?

---

[2] This procedure is quite similar to the stages we followed in literary criticism.

Exodus 21:1–22:17 also represents an independent section. List some reasons why this passage stands out from the legal section that precedes it (20:22–26) and that which follows (22:18–23:19). *Clue:* How are the laws in 21:1–22:17 worded/formulated differently from those that precede it or follow it?

Read Exodus 20:1–21. What event is being described here? Why does this section stand apart from the Book of the Covenant (20:22–23:33) that follows?

Could you skip over the Book of the Covenant to resume reading in Exodus 24:1 without losing the Sinai story line?

2. The results of our source-critical investigation seem to have isolated the following sources that make up the final BOC:

20:1-21//   20:22-26//   21:1–22:17//   22:18–23:19//   23:20-33//

3. We shall wait until we have completed our form-critical study of some of these sections before we can return to pursue the final redactional-critical phase of our study: Why has the editor arranged these independent sections in this manner?

FORM-CRITICAL STUDY

Let us make use now of the tool of *form criticism* to which we were introduced in Chapter 2. Recall that this criticism is sensitive to fixed literary patterns that are recurrent in particular social speech contexts.

1. Study the following two examples of laws from the Book of the Covenant (BOC) and try to describe the differences in the ways these two are worded or formulated:

> A: You shall not make gods of silver to be with me, nor shall you make for yourselves gods of gold. (20:23)

> B: If a thief is caught breaking in and is killed by a blow, there is to be no blood-vengeance for him, but there shall be blood-vengeance for him if it was after dawn. (22:2)

Can you find other examples of formulations like A and B in the BOC? List three examples for each category.

A.   B.

There are some laws that appear to be *mixed*; that is, they are worded differently from the pure instances of A or B. But with careful attention it should become clear that they too fit into one of our two categories. Analyze Exodus 22:13–15 and 23:4–5 and assign them to group A or B. Be sure to justify your decision.

2. Read the following selections from Hammurabi's Babylonian laws (written around 1800 B.C.E.):

> [14.] If a freeman has stolen the young child of another freeman, he shall be put to death.

> [21.] If a freeman has broken through the wall of a house, in front of that hole they should hang him and expose him.

> [117.] If a freeman has been forced by debt to sell his wife, his son or daughter (for service), or if he has had to turn himself over to service, for three years they shall work in the house of their buyer or of their obligee; their freedom shall be established on the fourth year.

[120.] If a freeman has deposited his grain in the storage of another and if a loss has then taken place in the silo, or if the owner of the storage shed has openned the storeroom and taken some grain, or if he has contested the total amount of grain which was deposited in his house, then the owner of the storage shed will swear an oath of innocence before the god. Then the owner of the storage shed shall hand over to the owner of the grain double the grain which he had received.

[195.] If a child has struck his father, they shall cut off his hand.

[196.] If a freeman has destroyed the eye of another freeman, they shall destroy his eye.

[197.] If he has broken the bone of a freeman, they shall break his bone.

[209.] If somebody has struck the daughter of a freeman and has caused her to miscarry the fruit of her womb, then he shall pay 10 shekels of silver for the fruit of her womb.

[210.] If this woman dies, they shall kill his daughter

[251.] If the ox of a freeman often gores and if the district authorities have informed him of the ox's habit of goring, but the owner has not covered his horns nor secured the ox, then if the ox gores a freeman to death, the owner shall hand over one half mina of silver.

[257.] If a shepherd has been negligent and he has let mange into the sheep-pen, then the shepherd will assume responsibility for the mange which he has let into the pen; he will pay back in kind and pay them to their owner.

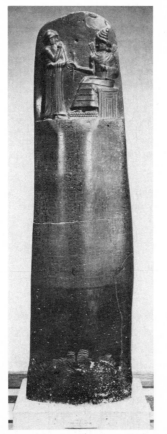

This eight-foot-high black monolith is inscribed with the law code of the Babylonian King Hammurabi (18th century B.C.E.). At the top the king (left) is portrayed before the sun god Shamash (right), the Babylonian god of justice (note the run rays on his shoulders).

3.   Which of the two literary forms in Exodus (A or B) best resembles the form found in these Babylonian laws?

Look at those laws in the Book of the Covenant that best approximate the form found in Hammurabi's Code. Find as many examples as possible in the BOC where laws not only agree in literary *form* but also in *content* with the samples from Hammurabi's laws. In other words, find laws in the Exodus BOC that correspond (form and content) with laws in the Mesopotamian selection.

Which of the two types (A or B) best corresponds with the format of the Decalogue or Ten Commandments (Exodus 20:1–17)?

Which of the two types or forms of laws in the Exodus section (A or B) seems to be the older? Explain your answer.

4.   Form criticism not only catalogues passages according to literary forms (genres or types) but it also speculates about the specific social context in which each type would have been used. You know from your own experience that much of your life is governed by laws and regulations; some of these come from local,

state, or federal government, and others from school and family. Hearing just a portion of a law would enable the listener to recognize its social context; for example, contrast "Be sure you are home by midnight on week nights!" with "Driving in excess of 55 mph is a motor vehicle violation punishable by . . . ." Try to assign each of the two literary forms of laws that you have isolated in the BOC (A and B) to a specific *social context. Suggestion:* You should first read extensive examples of each particular literary form and then list the types of activities governed by each. Do the activities associated with a particular category (A or B) tend to be similar in any ways? What area of society is concerned with such activities? You might then be able to think of the social context that is most appropriate to the interest of each form. Would one of these two groups of laws most likely be *civil law* enforced by the state? Or *family law* supervised by a family head? Or *religious law* governed by the priestly body? etc.

5.   Notice the tensions and contradictions within the Book of the Covenant. Some laws are humane and show concern for the vulnerable and the downtrodden; others condone harsh treatment of slaves and consider women as little more than property. List five or six examples of *harsh laws* and of *humane laws* in two respective columns.[3]

HARSH LAWS   HUMANE LAWS

Observe the reasons or motivations given for the humane laws ("because/ for . . .") in Exodus 22:21 and 23:9. List three other examples of such motivations.

[3] At times you have to allow for cultural differences: Exodus 21:17 might seem harsh to any of us who has said "damn" to his or her parent; but in the ancient Near East a curse was an effective, magical means of bringing about what was wished for. To curse a parent was considered no less malicious than poisoning the parent's food.

Of the two literary forms that you have isolated (A or B), which is more likely to be explained with one of these "motivation clauses"?

Study these "motivation clauses"; to what do most of them appeal? What is the dominant motivating force in these laws?

Can you tell where within Israelite society such clauses might have originated? (From your earlier answer, recall the social context where the forms of laws most associated with these clauses probably originated.)

What role does Israel's history play in these motivational clauses?

6.   Now let us describe the role of the *cult* (that is, public religion and ceremonies) in Israelite law.

Is one of the two literary forms you have studied more involved with cultic (worship and ceremonies) matters than the other? That is, which of the two (A or B) is most concerned with specifically cultic matters such as sacrifices and feast days? Support your answer with examples.

How does this compare with the Babylonian laws you have read? What role did Babylonian religion seem to play in their laws? (The examples cited above are generally representative.)[4]

Which laws—the harsh or the humane—are more likely to be associated with cult and worship? Support your answer with examples.

Now draw a conclusion about the role of the cult in Israelite law.

What factors seem to have made Israelite laws more humane?

7.   Read the international treaty between the Hittite king Mursilis (the suzerain) and his Amorite vassal Duppi-Tessub in Appendix D in the back of this book.[5] This is called an international **suzerainty** or *vassal treaty* because it was between nations that were not equals: The greater nation was the suzerain; the puppet state was the vassal. Notice under the heading "Future Relations of the Two Countries" that

---

[4] I refer to the actual stipulations of Babylonian law, not to the prologue of the Hammurabi Code, which is explicitly religious.

[5] Hatti-land was in the center of modern-day Turkey in Asia Minor; Amurru was farther south and encompassed present-day northern Lebanon and Syria.

many of the requirements are stated in "I/you" form:[6] "So honor the oath [of loyalty] to the king and the king's kin!" Write out some other examples from this treaty of similar formulations:

How do these examples compare with the Decalogue in Exodus 20:1–17 as far as content is concerned?

8.   Many of the treaty stipulations are in the familiar conditional style: "If you do this, then . . . ." Are these regulations identical stylistically to those conditional laws found in the Code of Hammurabi? Explain your answer carefully.

REDACTION CRITICISM

The preceding form-critical investigation should have isolated two different forms of law in the Book of the Covenant; moreover, it should have suggested a different origin (social context) for each type. One type of law is more peculiarly Israelite, in that it alone refers to Israel's own history and cult experience and it alone contains laws that differ significantly from those found elsewhere in ancient Near Eastern law books. Now let us return to the scheme showing the arrangement of the component sources:

20:1-21//   20:22-26//   21:1–22:17//   22:18–23:19//   23:20-33//

---

[6] Recall that the grammatical form of the imperative ("Do this!") is really in the second grammatical person, although unexpressed ("[You] do this!").

We can now ask the redactional-critical question: Why has the editor arranged these passages—all from different literary sources—in this fashion? Is there an editorial purpose discernible in their arrangement?

1.   Can you find laws in the BOC whose content do not seem relevant to the situation of a group of refugees in the Sinai Desert? List a few of these.

2.   It seems as if the editor here wants to take laws from different sources, social contexts, and time periods and place them all in the context of the Sinai revelation to Moses. How does the editor by the very arrangement of these segments make Sinai and its revelations the context for *all* law in Israel?

3.   Read Deuteronomy 4:20–27, which warns about obedience and the occupation of the Land of Canaan. Describe how the editor of the BOC has arranged the various sources to make clear the consequences if Israel does *not* follow the laws outlined in the BOC.

4.   Where has the editor positioned that block of law which was common to the ancient Near East (for example, to Hammurabi's Code)? Where has he placed laws which were more peculiarly Israelite?

Based on this arrangement, what statement does the redactor make about the relationship between the two types (A and B) of law?

Recall which of the two groups (A or B) tended to have the more humane laws. Which tendency (harsh/humane) dominates in our editor's arrangement of the sources?

5.   Write down some observations about the role of law in the religion of the Hebrew Bible: How has Israelite law, much of which was common to the ancient Near East, been incorporated into Israel's own particular traditions, such as the promise to the Patriarchs discussed in Chapter 4?

FURTHER READINGS

Bernhard W. Anderson, *Understanding the Old Testament,* 4th ed. (Englewood Cliffs, NJ: Prentice-Hall, 1986), pp. 95–109.

Norman K. Gottwald, *The Hebrew Bible: A Socio-Literary Introduction* (Philadelphia: Fortress Press, 1985), pp. 181–190.

Paul D. Hanson, "The Theological Significance of Contradiction within the Book of the Covenant," in *Canon and Authority,* George W. Coats and Burke O. Long, eds. (Philadelphia: Fortress Press, 1977), pp. 110–131. Much of the treatment of the Book of the Covenant in this present chapter is indebted to Hanson's article.

CHAPTER 6
LAW AND COVENANT
IN ANCIENT ISRAEL

APODICTIC AND CASUISTIC LAW

In our treatment of the Book of the Covenant in the previous chapter, we saw that most of the laws there could be divided into two types according to literary form. Some laws were stated as condition plus consequence: "If so-and-so does this, then . . . ." This type of law is called *casuistic* law, a word derived from the phrase "case" law. In this latter pattern, the penalty for violation is always explicit (fine, imprisonment, death, etc.). The other pattern found in Exodus is more direct; it states what one should or should not do (without mentioning exact consequences): "You shall . . ." or "You shall not . . . ." This is called *apodictic* law, and it is also the form used in the Decalogue in Exodus 20:1-17.

Form criticism is not only interested in distinct literary patterns but also in the social (in this case, legal) context that lies behind each pattern. It should be obvious that casuistic law characterizes the entire Law Code of the Babylonian King Hammurabi, which is about a millennium older than the Elohist. Indeed, almost all ancient Near Eastern Law, from Sumer to Assyria, is expressed in this precise form (just browse through ANET, pp. 159-198). Also, an examination of the content (what is being legislated) in those casuistic laws in the Book of the Covenant will reveal that as far as content they are quite similar to laws found in Babylon. These laws as a whole govern wholly *civil* matters dealing with property, personal injury, slavery, etc. It seems fair to conclude that this type of law, many stipulations of which seem quite harsh by our contemporary standards, generally represents a common Near Eastern heritage and forms the oldest component of the Exodus Book of the Covenant.

The social and legal context behind apodictic laws has never been as obvious. Because—until recently—no one had discovered comparable legislation elsewhere in the Near East, scholars thought that apodictic laws must be unique to Israel. Indeed, much of the content of such regulations seems to be peculiar to Israel's religious consciousness (see the Decalogue, for example). In the previous chapter we also

discovered that apodictic laws tended to differ from casuistic laws both in their content (more humane) and in their close association with Israel's unique religious/ cultic experience (recall the motivation clauses). Some thought that the more personal, second-person formulation of this type of legislation ("You shall . . . /shall not . . .") was especially suitable for a religion that stressed personal ties between its people and their God. Now, however, scholars claim to have discovered the Near Eastern background behind apodictic law; this discovery does much to aid our appreciation of various aspects of Israelite religion.

Although the antiquity of the concept of "covenant" remains a hotly disputed topic in current biblical studies, the form of Israel's apodictic law suggests the ancient Near Eastern vassal treaties (Hittite and Assyrian) such as those found in ANET, pp. 203–206, 531–541.[1] If this discovery is true, this means that Israel pat-

---

[1] Some scholars argue that this apodictic pattern could also have been influenced by the similar literary form of the wise maxim (see Proverbs 24:14–21). We do not have to decide one over the other, namely, vassal treaty vs. wisdom background, because Israel's legal tradition was heavily influenced by wise people and scholars who tried to explain it to the masses (recall the use of the "motivation clause").

terned her relationship to Yahweh after the legal standing of a vassal to his suzerain. Israel at (early?) stages in her religion saw her covenant with Yahweh as a vassal treaty.

This hypothesis, and it should be recognized as such, would also clarify Israel's constant suspicion about kingship. For if Israel saw her relationship to Yahweh as vassal to suzerain, then a fundamental corollary of that would be that she recognize no other lord between Israel and Yahweh. This theology would really represent a radical freedom at odds with the Near Eastern norms for kings. Because kings in antiquity demanded absolute obedience from their people, the Israelite king could be perceived as a challenge to the absolute suzerainty of Yahweh over his vassal people.

THE NEAR EASTERN TREATY AND ISRAEL'S COVENANT

In this section we shall study the constituent features of the Near Eastern vassal treaty, such as the one between Mursilis and Dubbi-Tessub, and how these features are found in Israel's formulation of her covenant with Yahweh.[2] We shall next uncover evidence of such treaty influence in sections of the Hebrew Bible, especially the prophets, even where the Hebrew word for "covenant"—**BERIT**—is fairly rare.

Six elements were usually found in ancient Near Eastern vassal treaties:[3]

1.   A *preamble* introducing the two treaty parties.

2.   An *historical prologue* that details the past relationships between the contracting parties.

3.   The actual *stipulations* describing the two parties.

    a.   The first stipulation was usually a general demand for the vassal's total loyalty.

4.   A clause describing the *publication* of the treaty and its public recital.

5.   A *list of the gods* of both parties who witnessed the treaty and would watch over it.

6.   A list of *curses and blessings* for those who either kept or disregarded the treaty.

Read the treaty between Mursilis and Dubbi-Tessub in Appendix D and notice the presence of most of these elements. The provision for the publication of the treaty is found in a copy of the treaty between Suppiluliumas and Kurtiwaza

---

[2] As we will soon sense, this word *covenant* (**BERIT** in Hebrew) is ambiguous; the same Hebrew word is used both for the Sinai Covenant, which recalls the *vassal treaty,* and for the Davidic Covenant (2 Samuel 7), which was probably modeled after a different Near Eastern literary form, the *royal grant.*

[3] As we might expect, the matter is considerably more complicated than will be presented here. Because the treaty form was used for millennia in diverse geographical locations, there were considerable variations in form. It is also difficult to judge when this pattern influenced Israelite theology; although its clearest form may be in the Book of Deuteronomy, evidence of early influence exists.

(ANET, p. 205). Many of these same features can be found in the Decalogue (Ten Commandments) in Exodus 20:1–17. Below in column A write out the features of the vassal treaty; in column B write out passages from the Decalogue that best correspond:

COLUMN A   COLUMN B

1.

2.

3.

4.

5.

6.

As we see, the evidence for the treaty pattern in Exodus 20 is not perfect. Although in a monotheistic religion it would be awkward to include a reference to witness deities, we also miss a clear reference to blessings and curses. (Some scholars claim that Exodus 20:5—"I am a jealous God"—is a remnant from the treaty curses, but this seems unlikely.) A clearer dependence on the treaty is found in the seventh-century B.C.E. Book of Deuteronomy, which as a whole seems to be more closely patterned after that international model.[4]

MOSES' FIRST DISCOURSE—the history of God's dealings with Israel (Deuteronomy 1:1—4:43)

MOSES' SECOND DISCOURSE (Deuteronomy 4:44—28:69)

> Introduction (Deuteronomy 4:44–49)
> Covenant and Commandments

> The Ten Commandments (Deuteronomy 5:1–33)
> Exhortation to keep them for the sake of God's grace in history and
>   of future blessings and curses (Deuteronomy 6:1—11:32)
> The Laws (Deuteronomy 12:1—26:19)

A COVENANT CEREMONY AT SHECHEM (Deuteronomy 27:1–26)

> Provision for publication of Book

BLESSINGS AND CURSES (Deuteronomy 28:1–69)[5]

There are even subtle references to Israel's vassal/covenant treaty with Yahweh in biblical contexts that do not use the Hebrew word **BERIT**, or "covenant." Such allusions are particularly important in the prophets who seem heavily imbued with the theology of Sinai even when they avoid using the word covenant.

The Hebrew prophets frequently used the words: **ḤESED** ("steadfast love"), **DA^CAT** ("knowledge"[6]), and **'AHABAH** ("love"[7]). Besides their broader usages, these words can also have technical legal meanings, which in some contexts seem rooted in the relationship between God and people conceived of as a treaty (covenantal) bond.

In many ancient Near Eastern letters exchanged between the suzerain and his vassal, a relationship that presupposes a treaty, the vassal is required to "love" and "know/recognize" his master. In the vassal treaty of Esarhaddon of Assyria, the vassal is obliged "to love the crown prince designate . . . as you do your own lives" (ANET, p. 537). The Hittite king (called "the Sun") instructs his vassal Huqqanas, "And you, Huqqanas, know only the Sun regarding lordship. Moreover, do not know another lord! Know the Sun alone." Look at the following excerpts from ancient Near Eastern correspondence (Mari in the nineteenth century and Amarna in the fourteenth century B.C.E.).

> Many are the people who love me in the city, few are rebels.

> Behold the city! Half of it loves the sons of Abdi-Ashirta, half of it loves my lord.

> Apart from Yasmah-Addu, the king our Lord, we do not know another king.

---

[4] The following outline of the Book of Deuteronomy according to the vassal treaty is taken from D. R. Hillers, *Covenant: The History of a Biblical Idea* (Baltimore: Johns Hopkins Press, 1969), p. 150.

[5] Many of these curses are almost identical to those in such contemporary Assyrian treaties as found in ANET, pp. 534–541.

[6] In the sense of "to know God."

[7] In the sense of "to love God."

In the Book of Deuteronomy, where we encounter the phrase "love God" so frequently (Deuteronomy 6:5, for example), this love involves more than sentimental attachment; it is clearly the same as "to serve" (indeed, the Deuteronomic phrase "heart and soul" is frequent in Near Eastern treaty situations):

> And if you will obey my commandments which I command you this day, to love Yahweh your God, and to serve him with all your heart and with all your soul. . . . (Deuteronomy 11:13)

The Hebrew word **HESED**, often translated as "steadfast love" (see the refrain in Psalm 118), in the right context can be another technical "treaty" word. It can indicate the loyalty that should exist between two people bound by an agreement/treaty. In 1 Samuel 18:3, David (soon to be king) makes a "covenant" (**BERIT**) with Jonathan, the son of his deadly rival King Saul: Jonathan would warn David about his father's plots against David, who in turn would protect Jonathan when he ascended the throne (1 Samuel 20:11–17). For David's part in the sworn covenant, the future monarch is to maintain "loyalty" (**HESED**) toward Jonathan: 1 Samuel 20:15. **HESED** seems especially to characterize the attitude of the suzerain ("the greater party") toward his vassal ("the lesser party").

With this background to the words "love," "know," and "steadfast love," we can now appreciate the covenant/treaty references in the prophet Hosea:

> For I [Yahweh] desire steadfast love and not sacrifice, the knowledge of God, rather than burnt offerings. (Hosea 6:6)

In the ancient Near East when a vassal did not keep his treaty, then the suzerain would immediately bring (legal) charges against the vassal for violation of his sworn oath. The suzerain would call upon the witness deities to punish the guilty party. In the prophets there are many cases in which the prophet announces that Yahweh has a legal case (Hebrew **RÎB**) against his people. Undoubtedly the legal background behind Yahweh's charges is the treaty (Sinai Covenant), which the people are accused of disregarding: Yahweh's legal messenger (the prophet) is suing (**RÎB**) the people for abrogating contractual obligations to their suzerain spelled out in the Sinai Contract (Covenant).

The treaty background in the prophets becomes even more certain when we compare the threats of the prophets (for example, Jeremiah 5:6) with treaty curses. The prophets do not creatively invent possible divine action; their warnings are derived from the traditional curses found in these Near Eastern vassal treaties.

Frequently those who are summoned by the prophets to witness these judicial proceedings (**RÎB**) resemble many of the deities summoned as divine witnesses in Near Eastern treaties (sun, moon, mountains, etc.). Examples of just such a legal summons can be found in Isaiah 1:2–3, 10–20; Jeremiah 2:4–12; Psalm 50; and Deuteronomy 32.

Hear what Yahweh says:
Arise, plead your case (**RÎB**) before the mountains,
and let the hills hear your voice.
Hear, you mountains, the controversy (**RÎB**) of Yahweh,
And you enduring foundations of the earth;
for Yahweh has a controversy (**RÎB**) with his people,
and he will contend with Israel . . . .
and what does Yahweh require of you
but to do justice and to love **HESED**
and to walk humbly with your God.
(Micah 6:1–2, 8; read the rest of Micah.)

1.   Now read Hosea 4:1–3 and explain *in detail* the treaty references in this passage.[8]

2.   Read Jeremiah 2:1–37.

The entire chapter is a dialogue reporting speech between several parties. First, mark off the speeches of each party and designate who is speaking.

Interpret the conversation in terms of a legal dispute (**RÎB**) between a suzerain and his vassal.

Who do you think first brought charges of infidelity, the suzerain or the vassal? Justify your answer from the text.

Where in the text is there a reference to the agreement (covenant) which is now the basis of the dispute?

What are the main *counter*-charges that Yahweh brings against Israel?

[8] The word "kindness" in Hosea 4:1 translates the Hebrew **ḤESED**.

Relate these charges that the suzerain (Yahweh) brings against his vassel (Israel) to the actual stipulations of the Decalogue (Exodus 20).

FURTHER READINGS

Bernhard W. Anderson, *Understanding the Old Testament,* 4th ed. (Englewood Cliffs, NJ: Prentice-Hall, 1986), pp. 96–109.

Delbert R. Hillers, *Covenant: The History of a Biblical Idea* (Baltimore: Johns Hopkins Press, 1969). This is a very clearly written presentation of "covenant" in the Hebrew Bible.

J. J. M. Roberts, "The Ancient Near Eastern Environment," in *The Hebrew Bible and Its Modern Interpreters,* Douglas Knight and Gene Tucker, Eds. (Chico, CA: Scholars Press, 1985), pp. 93–94. This short reference to the current status of discussion about covenant in the Hebrew Bible cautions us against the current pendulum swing against accepting the concept of "covenant" as an old concept in the Bible.

THE PROPHETS

CHAPTER 7
INVESTIGATION OF ISRAELITE PROPHECY

GOALS AND OBJECTIVES: Chapters 7 and 8 deal with prophecy, which is found in the second part of the Hebrew Bible. Chapter 7 guides the student through a close reading of several small but significant passages. These selections should help the reader acquire an elementary idea of Israelite prophecy. Deuteronomy 18 and 34 not only introduce the Deuteronomic theology on prophecy but also sound a warning about different biblical views on the prophet's authority. The Elijah story is not just the Deuteronomistic account of one northern Israelite prophet but is almost an essay on the very nature and authority of the prophet. The reading of Amos will acquaint the student with the complex redactional process (redaction criticism) evidenced by almost all of the prophetic books, which not only contain the oracles of Israel's seers but also witness to centuries of religious adaptation and literary reediting.

As we recall from our earlier treatment of the formation of the Hebrew Bible, these Scriptures were divided early (by 132 B.C.E.) into three parts: the Law (*Torah*), the Prophets (*Nebi'im*), and the Writings (*Ketubim*). The Torah—the Pentateuch or first five books of the Bible—was the first section to acquire authority in the community that was to become canonical (around the fourth century B.C.E.). Next (about two centuries later), the exilic community recognized the Prophets as canonical.

In this threefold division, the Prophets encompass more books than those we would normally regard as prophetic. This section includes many of the historical books written by the Deuteronomistic Historian: Joshua, Judges, Samuel, Kings.[1] Our reading of the Elijah story in this chapter shows how important the prophet was to this historian. In fact, the entire Deuteronomistic History is arranged around prophecies and their fulfillments (2 Kings 17:13–14).

However, the Prophets also includes such regular "prophetic" books as Isaiah, Jeremiah, and Ezekiel—called the *Major Prophets* because of their sheer

---

[1] These latter two books were further segmented into 1 and 2 Samuel, and 1 and 2 Kings because their length made them too large to fit on one scroll; but Samuel and Kings are each only one literary work. In the New Testament similar "publication restraints" forced the single work of Luke to be placed onto two scrolls: Luke's Gospel and his Acts of the Apostles.

size; and the smaller books of the 12 *Minor Prophets*: Hosea, Joel, Amos, Obadiah, Jonah, Micah, Nahum, Habakkuk, Zephaniah, Haggai, Zechariah, and Malachi. It is with these latter types—the prophetic books proper—that this chapter is particularly interested.

METHOD OF INQUIRY

This chapter and the next will deal with prophecy in ancient Israel. Once again we shall devote the first chapter of our treatment to a close reading of several important passages that allow the reader to formulate theories about various forms of Israelite prophecy. Chapter 8 will incorporate these findings into a short treatment of prophecy in contemporary biblical research.

We shall read Deuteronomy 18:9–22, Deuteronomy 34:10–12, 1 Kings 17–19, and the Book of Amos. From these seminal passages we can gain an understanding of the prophet in Israel. The reader, however, should be aware of an almost unavoidable flaw in our inquiry. Almost all of these passages are either the product of, or have been edited by, one group. The *Deuteronomistic Historian* (remember our treatment in Chapter 4) plays an important part in our understanding of the Hebrew prophet, for almost all of the passages in the Bible that talk *about* the prophet (1 and 2 Samuel; 1 and 2 Kings) are the product of this group's editing[2]; furthermore, there is even evidence that this group also edited the regular prophetic books (for example, Jeremiah), which had been regarded as the "words of the prophets themselves." Thus, very little has come down to us except through the "filter" of the Deuteronomistic group.

Too often this viewpoint blinds us to the important fact that Old Testament prophecy was *not* a monolithic institution. "Prophecy" describes many quite different—and even contradictory—phenomena in the Hebrew Scriptures.[3] Be sure to keep this warning in mind as we now proceed to read passages which in the main reflect the Deuteronomistic Historian's (DH) viewpoint. Deuteronomy 34:10-12, however, should warn us that this was not the *only* understanding.

Before we begin with our inductive approach to define prophecy in its many forms, you should write down your present understanding of the Israelite prophet. Below, describe what you think the prophet was: (1) What was his or her[4] mission? (2) With whom did he or she work? (3) What types of activity did he or she engage in? Naturally, you should expect that this understanding will mature over the next two chapters, but this preliminary sketch can be valuable.

Deuteronomy 18:9-22

Read Deuteronomy 16:18—18:22 in order to view the literary context for Deuteronomy 18:9-22. As you recall from Chapter 4, the Book of Deuteronomy as a whole portrays itself as the last instruction of Moses before he died and before his people crossed the Jordan River into the Promised Land. Notice that this particular section of the Book of Deuteronomy contains guidelines for the conduct of the most important public officials who will rule over the people after Joshua's conquest: judges (Deuteronomy 16:18—17:13), the king (Deuteronomy 17:14-20), and the Levitical priests (Deuteronomy 18:1-8).

Deuteronomy 18:9-14 then turns its attention to the "agent of communication" between the people and Yahweh. These verses seem to rule out almost every standard means of communication used in the ancient Near East: diviners, soothsayers, augurs, sorcerers, charmers, spiritualists, wizards, and those who consult the dead. The obvious question becomes: How then can Israel communicate with her God? The answer follows in verses 15-22. The prophet shall fulfill this role.

---

[2] Most of the stories preserved by the Deuteronomistic History are considerably older than the date of their editing—as is the case with the Elijah stories, but we can never be totally sure how free any passage is from the redaction of this school.

[3] We shall consider several of these different prophets in the following chapter.

[4] I often use the masculine pronoun to refer to the "prophet"; in actuality, women also were described in the Hebrew Scriptures as prophets. And so the woman who authenticated the very Book of Deuteronomy in 2 Kings 22:14 was a prophet; and the prophet Isaiah was married to a "prophetess"; Deborah of Judges 4:4 was also called a prophet. However, the classical prophets in the Scriptures were male.

1.   Deuteronomy 18:15 is an important verse for the understanding of this important passage. First of all, to whom does the "like me" refer?

The verb in Deuteronomy 18:15 has been interpreted in Jewish tradition in two quite different ways. Does "The Lord your God *will raise up* for you a prophet" refer to a single future event? In this case, it would best be translated "*At the end of time* the Lord will raise up a single prophet. . . ." This understanding of the verb led many to expect a single future prophet—often Elijah—whose appearance would mark the end of the age.[5] Another reading of 18:15 understands the verb to refer to a continual series of prophets: "I will *continually* raise up *a series of* prophets for you." In this reading the passage refers to a series of prophets, to the recurring office of prophet. Which reading do you think was intended? (Be sure to consider the larger context of 18:15.) Explain your answer.

2.   According to Deuteronomy 18:15–22 what is the source of the prophet's authority?

To the Deuteronomist, what is the significance of the fact that the prophet is spoken of as "like me"? (You might want to review some of the main beliefs of the Deuteronomist discussed in Chapter 4.) What does this comparison contribute to the credibility and authority of the prophet?

---

[5] Perhaps this reading lies behind the comment in the Book of Malachi 4:5. This expectation played an important role in the early Christian Church's understanding of Jesus in the New Testament.

3.   The diviners of the ancient Near East would often use such means as a sheep's liver, the pattern of oil on water, dreams, etc., as ways to discern the will of their deity. Their god would communicate his or her message by imprinting it on the folds of a sheep liver or on the swirling motion of oil dropped in a basin of water. There, supposedly, the trained diviner could detect the message and interpret it to the people. What is the main instrument of communication in the case of the Israelite prophet? How does the Israelite deity communicate to the people?

4.   Look at the criteria for deciding the authenticity of the prophet (verses 21–22). Some of this might well stem from a later editing of the Book of Deuteronomy, but what weakness does this point out in prophecy? How helpful or practical are these criteria for deciding the *true* from the *false* prophet?

5.   Now describe the nature of the prophet, his authority, and role in Israelite society as deduced from this passage.

Deuteronomy 34:10–12

1.   First, let us see how these verses fit in with their surroundings. Which of the last several verses (8–12) in Deuteronomy 34 provide the best ending for the Book of Deuteronomy? You should look for the verse that not only ends Deuteronomy but that also makes the transition to the Book of Joshua, which follows Deuteronomy and whose main character succeeded Moses.

Reconstruct the editorial stages of Deuteronomy 34:9–10. Where do you think the book originally ended? Were there any additions to this original text? Explain your answers.

2.   Now examine Deuteronomy 34:10–12. Compare these verses with the earlier Deuteronomy 18:9–22. Mark the verbal similarities between these two sections.

Does the author of Deuteronomy 34:10–12 agree or disagree with the view of prophecy found in Deuteronomy 18:18–22? Be sure to explain your answer.

3.   Compare the views about the nature of prophecy found in these two passages. Which view do you think belongs to the original writer of the Book of Deuteronomy?

4.   Many scholars think that Malachi 4:4 (Heb. 3:22) is not just a verse in the late prophetic Book of Malachi, but was the final warning placed by the editor of the entire collection of prophetic writings (books of Isaiah to Malachi). And so, when

these earlier readers had finished reading all of the prophets they would especially keep in mind the final thought of Malachi 4:4, which would then close off all the prophetic writings. If this is true, with which passage (Deuteronomy 18:9–22 or Deuteronomy 34:10–12) would this final editor of the prophetic collection have felt most akin? Explain your answer. (Would the verse in Malachi 4:5 help you decide the kinship of the Malachi passage?)

1 Kings 17–19

The story about Elijah in 1 Kings 17–19 is more than the account of an important ninth-century B.C.E. northern Israelite prophet. The account edited by the Deuteronomistic Historian in the seventh century B.C.E. probably served as a model for this important writer's concept of prophecy itself. In this light we shall examine these three chapters that have been taken from a more extensive Elijah saga (including 1 Kings 21; 2 Kings 1; 2 Kings 2); however, these three chapters, as you can see from the following outline, form an independent literary unit.

OUTLINE OF 1 KINGS 17–19

A.   Elijah in Trans-Jordan (17:2–7)

    B.   Elijah outside of Israel to the north (17:8–24)

        C.   Yahweh's command and Elijah's return to Israel (18:1–2a)

            D.   Ahab and Obadiah on the road to meet Elijah (18:2b–6)

                E.   Elijah and Obadiah (18:7–15)

                    F.   Elijah and Ahab (18:16–20)

                        G.   Elijah on Mount Carmel (18:21–40)

                    F′.   Elijah and Ahab (18:41–42)

                E′.   Elijah and his servant (18:43–45a)

            D′.   Elijah and Ahab on the road to Jezreel (18:45b–46)

        C′.   Jezebel's threat and Elijah's flight from Israel (19:1–3a)

    B′.   Elijah outside of Israel to the south (19:3b–18)

A′.   Elijah in Trans-Jordan (19:19–21)

These 13 sections of 1 Kings also show an appropriate division into Elijah in private (A, B, C and A′, B′, C′) and the central sections in which Elijah is portrayed in a public confrontation with his monarch Ahab (D, E, F, G, F′, E′, D′). Note some of the following correspondences:

B and B′

Miraculous provisioning of Elijah with a jar and cake. In B, Elijah's life is saved by a Sidonian woman; in B′, Elijah must flee a Sidonian Queen (Jezebel). In 17:22 a life is saved by a "voice"; in B′, Elijah is restored by the "voice of the Lord" (1 Kings 19:12).

D and D′

These sections highlight the contrast between the faithful Obadiah and Elijah and the faithless Ahab. In D, one fed the prophets, the other sought to kill them.

1 Kings: Chapter 17

1.   Notice how this chapter is set apart by an inclusion in verses 1 and 24 by the use of "word": "my word" and "word of the Lord" (Yahweh). The motifs or word(s) chosen for inclusion are seldom unimportant. This motif "word" can help us chart the role, power, and authority of the Israelite prophet. All of the questions that follow aim at focusing attention on the complex interaction of the prophet with both his sovereign Yahweh and with the recipients of his message. The power and efficacy of his message also touch on the important issue of the prophet's authority. Mark all the instances of "word" or "to speak/to say" in 1 Kings 17.

2.   The bold word that Elijah addressed to the king in 1 Kings 17:1 immediately poses the question about the *source*,[6] *power,* and *authority* of this individual's message, which is another way of asking what was going through Ahab's mind, "How dare he [Elijah] speak to me like this? And why should I, the King, pay him any heed?" Recall the two uses of "word" in the chapter (verses 1, 24) that established the inclusion; how does the shift from "my word" to "word of the Lord" address the question about one *source* of this message? Explain the importance of your answer for the phenomenon of prophecy.

---

[6] In what follows I use the terms "source" and "interrelationship": The two are related. "Source" refers to the origin of the word which the prophet bears, but as you will soon discover, the Israelite prophet received a word both "from above" and "from below"; he is truly an *intermediary* for several "groups." And so the "source" of his message also involves all of his social relationships and interactions.

3.   Now let us investigate what 1 Kings 17 says about the *power* and *authority* of this word. Throughout the chapter, four people are addressed by a "word": Ahab, Elijah, the Sidonian woman, and even Yahweh. On the chart below, indicate (1) by whom the word is brought to each of these four; (2) his or her response to that word; and (3) the results of his or her response (that is, what happens because of this response?).

CHARACTER	BEARER OF WORD	RESPONSE	RESULTS
Elijah			
Ahab			
Sidonian woman			
Yahweh			

A subordinate motif throughout chapters 17–19 is food–famine/life–death. Show how this motif fits in with the response of Elijah and the Sidonian woman to the word.

Notice that even Yahweh is responsive to the word (of Elijah) in verse 22! How does the actual wording of Yahweh's response in verse 22 differ from the response of Elijah and the Sidonian woman in verses 5 and 15?

4.   Of the four (Ahab, Elijah, the Sidonian woman, Yahweh), whose response to the word remains in doubt?

5.   Look at the placement of the main figures below; using arrows, diagram Elijah's relationship to each of the main characters in the chapter. In other words, if Elijah delivered a message to the king but did not receive one, then you would sketch a one-directional arrow from Elijah to King Ahab.

ELIJAH   YAHWEH   SIDONIAN WOMAN   AHAB

6.   Using all of these data, try to describe the interrelationships, power, and authority of the prophet in Israelite society as depicted in this story about the prophet Elijah. Also, try to interrelate these three elements: How does the source of the prophet's message affect the prophet's power and authority? How does the power of the word borne by the prophet relate to the authority that the listener recognizes in it?

1 Kings, Chapter 18

1.   Look at the first real scene in the chapter (18:2b–6). How does the author contrast Obadiah[7] with King Ahab?[8]

How does this scene use spatial imagery (far, close, high, low, etc.) to dramatize this contrast? (In fact, this imagery is developed through the rest of this chapter and in 1 Kings 19.)

2.   Notice the irony in the following scene (verses 7–16). The king made each foreign monarch take an oath by his god that Elijah was not hiding on his soil (verse 10). In what kingdom had Elijah actually been hiding? Who was the king of that territory and who would have been the deity by which he swore his oath to Ahab? (See 1 Kings 16:31–33!) Who had commanded that Elijah take refuge in that district?

How is this irony, which exploits the strength and weakness of various deities, developed throughout the rest of the chapter?

[7] In this chapter the meaning of the Hebrew names is probably important: Obadiah means "Servant of Yahweh" and Elijah means "Yahweh is my God."

[8] It might be helpful to note that the Hebrew of verse 5 reads "so that the animals are not cut off." Thus, the use of the verb "to cut off" gives an interesting clue to Ahab's personality, for his wife Jezebel is allowed to "cut off" the prophets (18:4) while Ahab's concerns are for the animals. It is part of the literary skill of the biblical author that he names the valley where Elijah hid in chapter 17 "Cut-off Gulch."

3.   As is evident from the ring-structure that characterizes chapters 17 through 19, the central scene in the chapter is Elijah's confrontation on Mount Carmel. Not only do these verses (21–40) demonstrate the historical conflict between Baal-worship and Yahweh, but they also illustrate an important function of the Israelite prophet. This scene could be organized around the different parties whom Elijah addresses. In the chart below, indicate the group/person with whom Elijah speaks (the *addressee*) and also describe that group's/person's *response* to Elijah:

ADDRESSEE   THE RESPONSE OF THE ADDRESSEE

4.   With which addressee is Elijah most concerned (based on the attention that Elijah devotes to speaking with him/them)? How would you describe the nature of Elijah's concerns regarding that addressee?

How does the alternation between addressees depicted in the chart above especially focus attention on the address in verses 30–35? (Examine the structure of the dialogues.) Why would this series of liturgical directives have such prominence in the entire chapter?[9] (Recall the addressee with whom Elijah is most interested and that individual's current religious situation.)

[9] Your findings here will also help you evaluate the relationship of the prophet to the liturgy—an issue discussed in the next chapter.

5.   This scene is also dominated by the motif of "answering." The true god is the one who can *answer* (18:24); and so we have a sharp contrast between silence and responsiveness.[10] Mark all of the occurrences of the word "answer" in this scene (1 Kings 18:21–40).

Contrast the two answers to the entreaties of the Baal prophets in verses 26 and 29. What implications does this have for the author's view of prophecy?

6.   The changing allegiance of the people of Israel plays an important role in chapter 18, as you have already detected. How does the initial stance/position of the people (verse 21) resemble that of the frenzied Baal prophets (verses 26–29)? What is the author suggesting by this correspondence? How else does the author indicate the people's first allegiance? (See verse 24.)

Take the phrase "draw near" in verses 21–40; mark its occurrence, and then show how this phrase charts the stages in the people's return to Yahweh after following Baal.

[10] The author delights in stressing that this contest between Yahweh and Baal was quite uneven: First, it was 450 to 1 (compare verse 22), and, second, Baal was particularly worshipped as the god of rain—water was his specialty!

7.   The remaking of the altar (verses 31ff.) recalls the ceremony in Genesis 35. Write out some of the correspondences between these two passages and suggest the significance.

8.   Where in Chapter 18 is Elijah first called a "prophet"? Pulling together all of the information that you have garnered, what additional information has this chapter added to your picture of the Israelite prophet?

1 Kings, Chapter 19

General Observations on Literary Structure

The most important scene in 1 Kings 19 is obviously Elijah's encounter with Yahweh at Mount Horeb[11] (19:9-19), which is set off by the inclusion "there" and "from there," thus highlighting Elijah's trip to and from the *sacred space* of Israelite tradition. This central scene is itself subdivided into three subsections by the threefold occurrence of the phrase "and behold" in verses 9b, 11b, and 13b. "Behold" also sets up a concentric structure, for scenes 1 (verses 9-11a) and 3 (13b-18) both describe conversations between Yahweh and Elijah, whereas scene 2 (verses 11b-13a) depicts the theophany itself.

The Meaning of 1 Kings 19

1.   The identification of Elijah's mountain as Horeb obviously invites a comparison with Moses, who received the Law on Mount Horeb—also called Sinai. But there are further recollections of the Mosaic theophany that stands at the heart of Israelite religion. Read Exodus 32, 33:12-23, and 34:28. Write down some of the similarities between Yahweh's appearances to Moses in Exodus and to Elijah in 1 Kings 19.

---

[11] Horeb is also called Sinai.

2.   Compare and contrast the two theophanies in 1 Kings 18:26–39 and 1 Kings 19:11–13. What is similar in both? Describe the differences.[12]

What portrayal of Yahweh emerges from the consideration of *both* appearances?

How would the mode of Yahweh's appearance in the Mount Horeb theophany be particularly suitable for a story about the nature of prophecy itself?

3.   What exactly are Elijah's complaints before Yahweh?

How does Yahweh in 1 Kings respond (in both his theophany and his dialogues) to the complaints of the despondent Elijah? How does Elijah's task to commission a successor fit in with his earlier complaint?

---

[12] Even the Hebrew of the important phrase in 19:12 is striking; "a still small voice" (RSV) must mean something like "the thin sound of silence."

4.   Now let us look for a moment at Elijah's stance during this theophany. Several times before Elijah has stated that he *alone* among the prophets had survived (18:22, 19:10, 19:14). Is this really true? What about the prophets preserved in the cave (18:4, 18:13); why are they not included? Can you think of any reasons why Elijah is more of a prophet than those hidden away in a cave?[13]

Notice the irony! How has Elijah's position in 1 Kings 19:9ff. now become like the earlier prophets saved by Obadiah in chapter 18? Contrast Elijah's statement in 18:22 with his pronouncement in 19:10, 14. What crucial word is missing?

How exactly does this irony help us better understand the proper place for the prophet in Israelite society? How does Yahweh's command to Elijah in 19:11 serve as a command to each Israelite prophet?

5.   Now for the most important question of our entire treatment of 1 Kings 17–19. Try to reconstruct the author's view of the Israelite prophet. Be sure to incorporate into your sketch such issues as the relationship between the prophet and

---

[13] Recall that the correct stance of the prophet has been portrayed as "standing before Yahweh" (17:1, 18:15)—which is probably the image of the prophet as messenger attendant on the monarch in his royal court.

the word[14]; the relationship with the Sinai Covenant and Moses; those parties in Isralite society with whom the prophet interacts; orientation with past, present, and future[15]; the prophet's authority; and the continuity of the prophet's role.

Let us check your view of the prophet. Recall the treatment of the Book of Jonah in Chapter 2. This satire represents Jonah as an antiprophet—in a sense, Jonah is the exact *opposite* of what a prophet should be. How does this ironic description of Jonah's prophecy fit in with the description above deduced from your reading of the Elijah saga (1 Kings 17–19)?

The Book of Amos

It is clear that the Book of Amos is different from the prophetic texts that we have read up to this point. Instead of reading about a prophet, we now seem to encounter a collection of the prophet's actual words.

As you skim through the Book of Amos you will quickly note a feature of almost all prophetic books that can frustrate the reader: These books seem to lack organization. The Book of Genesis was easy reading compared to Amos: the former book had a plot and traced the adventures of one individual's family through several generations; Amos, however, seems to be a loosely organized potpourri of sayings. Some of the prophetic pronouncements seem so narrowly focused and so directed to specific problems of Amos' own day, that the modern reader is tempted to mutter, "You had to be there to appreciate Amos!"

For this reason, our first task will be to investigate the editorial history of the book (source and redaction criticisms). It will help us to appreciate anew prophetic literature when we study how it was compiled, edited, and reedited. This redactional study not only informs us about the historical stages in the development of a book like Amos but it also documents the status of prophetic literature within the community of Israel.

[14] At this point you might also want to consider the results of our form-critical examination of the prophetic phrase "Thus says the Lord" in Chapter 2 of this book. Our findings there have implications for the relationship between the prophet and the word (of his message).

[15] I ask this because we normally think of the prophet as a "future-teller" or "fore-teller." As far as you can discern from this illustrative story of Elijah, was the prophet more interested in past, present, or future?

I have chosen the Book of Amos for several reasons. First, the historical Amos was among the earliest prophets (eighth century B.C.E.) whose sayings have been collected. Second, the editorial stages in the Book of Amos are comparable with the history of most of the prophetic books in the Hebrew Scriptures. Third, the problems faced by the historical prophet Amos seem to be ethical issues with which the contemporary reader can easily identify. And, finally, the size of the book is much more manageable for an introductory investigation such as ours than would be the Books of Isaiah, Jeremiah, or Ezekiel.

Redaction-Critical Study of the Book of Amos

The Beginning and End Points in the Redaction of Amos

First, we shall establish the *terminus a quo* and the *terminus ad quem* of the redaction of the book; that is, the *earliest* and *latest* dates clearly witnessed in the editorial history of the Book of Amos.

Read through the Book of Amos in your Bibles. Amos 1:1 can be called the title of the book. It both situates the prophet Amos historically and it makes some observations about its content ("Words" and "Visions"). The prophet Amos lived during the reigns of Uzziah (783–742 B.C.E.) in Judah to the south and of Jeroboam II (786–746 B.C.E.) of Israel to the north.[16] This date situates Amos in the latter half of the eighth century B.C.E.

1. Now study Amos 9:11–15 carefully. What city is referred to in these verses? To what specific historical event does this section refer? (Be sure to justify your answer.) What is the date of this period?

If Amos 1:1 and 9:11–15 set off two different time periods, then what are the two temporal parameters or time limits within which the book was edited? What does this tell us about the relationship between Amos the Prophet and Amos the Book?

---

[16] Remember that after the death of Solomon in 922 B.C.E. his empire split into two parts. For the next 200 years there was to be a large kingdom to the north, whose capital was Samaria, and smaller Judah in the south, whose capital was Jerusalem. Judah worshipped at Solomon's temple on Mount Zion in Jerusalem, whereas Israel went to old Patriarchal shrines at Dan and Bethel, which Jeroboam I (922–901 B.C.E.) had rebuilt.

Further Redactional Activity in the Book of Amos

More subtle evidence exists for different redactional stages within the book. We shall read selections from Amos and then try to differentiate them into groups according to such features as geographical[17] and ethical concerns, the nature of the threatened punishment, etc. The theory is that each of these different groups reflects different editorial activity. By linking the concern of each group with known historical activities in the Old Testament, we can approximately date each redactional effort (ergo, *redaction history*).

Read Amos 3:9–12, 4:1–3, 5:1–3, 8:4–7. (We'll call these **Group A.**) Now answer the following questions:

1. To which northern city are these oracles directed? (Check the map on p. 129.)[18] If one of these passages does not refer to a city, then ask yourself whether the setting and concerns of the oracles are *city* or *countryside.*

2. Look at the references to "Israel" in these sections (3:12, 5:1, 5:2, 5:3). "Israel" is an ambiguous word in the Hebrew Bible. It can refer to three quite different things: (1) It can be another name for the Patriarch Jacob (Genesis 32:28); (2) it can denote the entire group of the 12 tribes united by Moses in their common faith in the God of Sinai; or (3) "Israel" could be the political name for the northern kingdom (922–722 B.C.E.), which broke away from Jerusalem after the death of Solomon. Which one of these three possibilities best fits the above uses of "Israel"? Be sure to support your choice.

3. Of what specific offenses does the text accuse the people? Which segment of society (poor farmers, wealthy aristocrats, royal family, priests, etc.) do these passages especially fault?

---

[17] As you shall see, the three main editorial stages of the book can be oriented around three major cities in the Hebrew Scriptures.

[18] Mention could also be made of 6:1–7; however, the reference to the capital city here in 6:1a is complicated by the parallel reference in 6:1b to Judah's capital on Mt. Zion, although this might be a later addition.

What is the nature of the punishment mentioned in these passages? How extensive will the punishment be? How exactly would you describe the prophet's position: Is he *warning* the accused ("Change or else!") or is he simply *announcing* what is going to happen regardless of what they do?[19]

4.   Can you find any other passages in the Book of Amos that seem similar to these in their geographical references, in the type of accusations they make, in the social makeup of the accused social group, or in the comparable punishments that the prophet threatens?

Now read Amos 3:1–6, 4:4–5, 5:4–6, 5:14–15, 5:21–27, 7:10–15 **(Group B)**.

1.   With which city are these sections in Group B especially concerned?

2.   Contrast the main concerns of these passages (as deduced from their accusations) with those we studied earlier (Group A). In other words, of what offenses does Group B accuse its reader as opposed to the accusations of Group A?

[19] Think of an example. There is a considerable difference between a doctor telling a patient, "You really must stop smoking!" (warning) and his announcing, "You have lung cancer and three months to live!"

3.   How do these new concerns fit in with the particular city with which the

...re of the threat in these verses. Does the prophet warn
...loes he announce imminent and unavoidable destruction?
...ith the nature of the punishment in Group B?

...roup A, there are few references to the office and authority
...nveys the message. However, in Group B there are several
... consider the status of the prophetic messenger (for example,
...nk of any reasons why it is more important to authenticate
...3 than it was in Group A?[20]

...oups can be neatly contrasted by their different use of the *lion*
...the description of the lion in Amos 3:12 with that in 3:8. Can
...rence to either Group A or Group B? Explain your choice. How
... metaphor typify the view of Groups A and B about prophecy
...of punishment in each group?

Important, while the discussion MUST be performed individually—transcribing someone else's discussion will result in a ZERO for the lab grade. the observations may be shared between students,

[20] Let us return to our earlier grim example about smoking and lung cancer. The patient has received the two messages (warning: "Stop smoking!" and announcement: "You have lung cancer!"); which message demands more authentication? Which message calls into question more the qualifications of the physician?

6.   Recall your earlier reading of 9:11–15 (**Group C**). How does the view presented here contrast with the message of both Groups A and B?

What city is mentioned in 9:11–15?

What is the nature of the punishment in 9:11–15?

Summary of the Redaction History of the Book of Amos

Now is the time to piece all of this information together to reconstruct a *redaction-critical* view of the Book of Amos. There seem to have been three major editorial stages that correspond (in chronological order starting with the oldest) to Group A, then Group B, and finally the more "hopeful" restoration picture presented in chapter 9 (Group C). Because it is fairly complicated to ask the beginning student to link each of these stages with events in Israel's history, I shall make some comments in that regard.

Group A probably is made up of the oral prophecies of the historical eighth-century Amos, who preached against the social injustices of the wealthy in Israel's capital city, Samaria. Amos lived during the glorious years of Jeroboam II, after whose death the country quickly declined until its destruction 20 years later. Archaeological excavations in Samaria have confirmed the level of luxury during this period: The houses were spacious and the furniture was often imported and decorated with ivory inlays (Amos 6:4). Amos, however, tells us at what social expense these luxuries were achieved. The wealthy were confiscating the property of the poor, which by biblical law should not pass from a clan (see 1 Kings 21:1–3). This expropriation was achieved by forcing the farmers into debt by forcing them to purchase their needs from the state (iron tools, seed, water). Farmers increasingly lost their agricultural self-sufficiency; they became more dependent on Samaria by being required to grow commercial crops for export (wine and olive oil) to earn hard currency to finance luxury imports (for example, ivory beds). This, ironically, made

This ivory plaque of a sphinx was found in excavations in Samaria. Although it dates from the 9th century B.C.E. it illustrates the luxuries of the capital city described by the 8th-century Amos (6:4). The workmanship is probably Phoenician (the homeland of the contemporary queen Jezebel) and illustrates the dependence of the northern kingdom on international trade.

farmers dependent on the state for food. Their debts increased.[21] The historical prophet announces the imminent destruction of the northern kingdom, which must have seemed preposterous to those enjoying its current prosperity. The oracles of Group A are small disorganized pronouncements that were probably delivered orally to the inhabitants of the capital. The Assyrian destruction of Samaria in 722 B.C.E. meant that the words of Amos had been confirmed (recall the criteria of Deuteronomy 18:21-22).

Group B is primarily interested in cultic matters relating to sacrifice in the northern shrine at Bethel; this stage can probably be dated to around the time of the discovery of the Book of Deuteronomy in the reign of King Josiah (622 B.C.E.). It was this king who destroyed the shrine at Bethel under the instigation of the Deuteronomists (2 Kings 23:15-20). Bethel had been rebuilt by Jeroboam I after the northern kingdom broke from Jerusalem; this rival shrine was the object of the Deuteronomistic Historian's enmity (read 1 Kings 12-13).[22] Even though the northern kingdom had been destroyed a hundred years earlier, Israelites still went to Bethel, which had been spared destruction by the Assyrians. Group B wanted to put a stop to this cultic outrage. This Deuteronomic group adapted and expanded the words of the original Amos, for the authority of this prophet had already been established when his words came true in the Assyrian conquest of 722 B.C.E. Group B formulates its message as a warning: Stop going to Bethel or else! There is still a chance that Yahweh might change his mind (Amos 5:15).

Clearly the last stage of the book (9:11-15)—Group C—stems from the time following the destruction of Jerusalem in 586 B.C.E., and converts the message of judgment (Group A) and warning (Group B) into the possibility of restoration after

[21] There are startling similarities between the economic situation described in Amos A and that of modern developing countries, where, for example, farmers who were formerly self-sufficient are made dependent on large landowners to grow crops only for export (for example, coffee, bananas, cocoa).

[22] Remember that the Deuteronomic movement wanted to centralize all worship in the temple in Jerusalem (Deuteronomy 12).

Sargon II (721–705 B.C.E.). This Assyrian king destroyed Samaria after a three-year seige begun by his predecessor. There is some evidence that Sargon II himself was killed in battle fighting invaders in southern Russia, an event perhaps taunted in Isaiah 14:5–21 (which later was re-addressed to a "king of Babylon"). Sargon II's son Sennacherib would attack Jerusalem in 701 B.C.E.

the destruction of Jerusalem. This group no longer needed any judgment or warning, for recent events had confirmed the danger of being unfaithful. Now there is hope! Although the contributions of this stage are quantitatively quite small, its hopeful ending changes the entire mood of the final book and establishes the promise of hope after punishment.

A Literary-Critical Reading of Amos

The original messages of Amos (Group A), delivered to the gentry of eighth-century Samaria, were probably unorganized and independent *oral* pronouncements. The real literary structuring of the book can probably be attributed to the seventh-century Group B with its affiliations with the Deuteronomic movement. As this was mainly a scribal movement, their contribution was *written* and therefore more susceptible to complex literary arrangement.

Because the literary structure of the Book of Amos is fairly intricate, we shall have to depart somewhat from our inductive approach. The key to its organization lies in Amos 1:1. This title heading for the book is similar to that of almost every prophetic book and was probably the work of the Deuteronomic movement.[23] Archaeological evidence supports the fact that there was a severe earthquake in

---

[23] Notice that the dating formula in Amos 1:1 coordinates the reigns of the kings of Judah and of Israel—this was also common in the Book of Kings, the work of the Deuteronomistic Historian.

Samaria in the eighth century B.C.E.; but would this event have been so vividly remembered that it could have been used as a dating reference by Group B a century later in Jerusalem?

We have to entertain the possibility that this reference (". . . two years before the earthquake") is a literary device that Group B uses to organize the Book of Amos. The earthquake carries considerable theological weight in the Hebrew Bible. God's power in the theophany is often associated with the shaking of the earth: Psalm 29, 1 Kings 19, Psalm 68:7–8.

1.   Where else in Amos is there mention of the earth shaking? (Indeed, this other passage uses the exact same Hebrew word.) What causes the earth to shake in this passage? Where does this earthquake take place?

In terms of the main concern of Group B, why is this second earthquake so significant? Why could it be termed the *climax* of this editorial stage?

2.   The Book of Amos as assembled by Group B can be read as a literary pilgrimage to the cursed shrine at Bethel. We begin in Jerusalem (1:2) and end up at the end of the book in the ruins of the demolished Bethel. Half-way through the book (and our pilgrimage) we are told to avoid Bethel if we want to survive the destruction that will destroy that northern temple (5:4–6). As suggested in Amos 1:1 our pilgrimage begins two years before that final cataclysm at the Bethel shrine. Several passages cleverly chronicle the passage of each of these two years as we approach our decisive showdown at Bethel.

Read Amos 4:6–13 and see if you can mark the passage of the first year by its references to seasonal changes. The Palestinian year began in the early fall with the approach of the rainy season.[24] The reference to warfare in verse 10 suggests springtime when "kings go forth to battle" (2 Samuel 11:1).

[24] The change of the year was marked by the Feast of Succoth, which both celebrated the past harvest and looked ahead to the coming of the new agricultural year, which the returning rains heralded.

Now read Amos 7:1–8:1 and see if you can detect the passage of the second year and the approaching showdown with Yahweh at Bethel.

To be more specific, the appearance of Yahweh at Bethel in Amos 9 seems to be dated to the feast of Succoth. This early fall feast plays an important role in the Book of Amos, and it is a perfect literary device to stress the theme of *decision*, which is central to the message of Group B. Succoth, like the Roman god Janus, looks in two directions: It looks back in celebration to the completed harvest of the old year; but at the same time it looks apprehensively toward the future and petitions God to bring the autumn rains that announce the beginning of the new agricultural year. Many of the hymns in the Book of Amos, which celebrate God's power over the wind and rains, probably stem from a Succoth cult setting: Amos 4:13, 5:8-9, 9:5-6. What perfect irony! Group B could have chosen no better time to announce the destruction of a rival shrine at Bethel, for it was on this festival complex that Jerusalem celebrated the dedication of Solomon's Temple (1 Kings 8:1ff.).

The original announcement of doom by Amos in the eighth century B.C.E. proved true in the events of 722 B.C.E. when the Assyrians leveled the capital of Samaria. These now-authenticated oracles later formed the nucleus of Group B's call to decision. Like the Deuteronomist, B calls his readers (for we now have a written text) to a decision in correct worship: *Either* perish with Bethel *or* return to Solomon's true temple at Jerusalem. By the addition and placement of this material, B has edited A's announcement of unavoidable doom into the future possibility for a new era. Moreover, B has structured the book around the readers' two-year pilgrimage to a decisive Succoth theophany at Bethel. This feast, so decisive in Palestine's agricultural cycle, then becomes a metaphor for the call to decision. After Jerusalem's calamity in 586 B.C.E., Group C held out a message of hope following destruction. And by this small addition, C has changed the tenor of the entire Book of Amos: No matter how much judgment the errant people bring upon themselves, the hope of divine restoration remains.

If this analysis proves true, then the initial impression made earlier in this chapter that a prophetic book is disorganized is not quite true. Most of these books display an intricate organization that was structured at some stage in their redaction. Hence, rhetorical or literary criticism can make us more aware of the structure and focus of these books.

FURTHER READINGS

Prophecy in General

Joseph Blenkinsopp, *A History of Prophecy in Israel from the Settlement in the Land to the Hellenistic Period* (Philadelphia: Westminster, 1983). This book provides an excellent bibliography on prophecy in general and on each of the prophets.

Deuteronomy 18 and 34

Joseph Blenkinsopp, *Prophecy and Canon: A Contribution to the Study of Jewish Origins* (Notre Dame, IN: Notre Dame University Press, 1977), pp. 39-53, 85-95.

Elijah Story

Bernhard W. Anderson, *Understanding the Old Testament,* 4th ed. (Englewood Cliffs, NJ: Prentice-Hall, 1986), pp. 271-278.

Jerome T. Walsh, "The Elijah Cycle: A Synchronic Approach" (doctoral dissertation, University of Michigan, 1982). Much of this present chapter's literary treatment of Elijah is indebted to this sensitive dissertation.

The Book of Amos

Robert B. Coote, *Amos Among the Prophets: Composition and Theology* (Philadelphia: Fortress Press, 1981). Coote's approach in dividing Amos into three main editorial stages (A, B, C) has been incorporated in this text. His book also supplies an excellent discussion of the economic situation reflected in Amos A.

Norman K. Gottwald, *The Hebrew Bible: A Socio-Literary Introduction* (Philadelphia: Fortress Press, 1985), pp. 353-358.

CHAPTER 8
SURVEY OF ISRAELITE PROPHECY

GOALS AND OBJECTIVES: We shall now build on our previous findings to sketch out a more comprehensive understanding of the Israelite prophet. A good way to acquire this overview is to look at all the different approaches and techniques that scholars have used over the last century and a half to study biblical prophecy. The goal in this chapter is not to inundate the student with a flood of names of mostly German academics, but rather to give a sense of the variety of biblical prophecy, which the student can best appreciate by exposure to all these various descriptions of the Israelite prophet, many of which are even contradictory, but all of which capture legitimate features of this complex person.

TERMINOLOGY

The second division of the Hebrew Bible—the Prophets (*Nebi'im*)—was early divided up into the Former and the Latter Prophets. The first category includes the so-called nonwriting prophets; that is, prophets talked about in the Bible but whose writings have not come down to us. These are particularly found in the Deuteronomistic History (Joshua; Judges; 1 and 2 Samuel; 1 and 2 Kings). (Elijah would be an example of a nonwriting prophet.)

The Latter Prophets include all those prophets after whom a biblical book is named; for example, Isaiah and Jeremiah. In a sense, which has yet to be clarified, these books probably contain—at least as a nucleus—the words of the prophets after whom the book was titled.[1] These Writing Prophets are further categorized into *Major and Minor Prophets.* The Major Prophets, so named after the size of their books, include Isaiah, Jeremiah, and Ezekiel. There are 12 Minor Prophets:[2] Hosea, Joel, Amos, Obadiah, Jonah, Micah, Nahum, Habakkuk, Zephaniah, Haggai, Zechariah, Malachi.

[1] In very few cases is there evidence that a "writing" prophet was actually a writer; his pronouncements were usually preserved or recorded by others (see the example of Jeremiah in Jeremiah 36); and these books also include centuries of expansions and further editing.

[2] Judaism considers the 12 Minor Prophets as one biblical book.

The Second Division of the Hebrew Bible

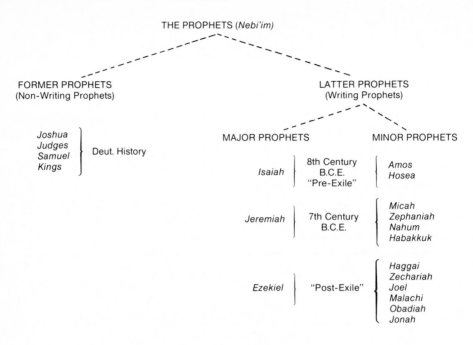

THREE APPROACHES TO THE STUDY OF PROPHECY

Since the methodical investigation of prophecy began two centuries ago, there have been three general focal points in the study of the prophet. The first focused its attention on the prophet as an individual and sought to describe him as a solitary religious rebel in conflict with his age. The second approach centered on the words of the prophet and was more oriented to prophetic language and poetry. The third methodology has paid particular attention to the social interaction of prophecy: With whom in society did the prophet interact? Who in society recognized the prophet's authority? Was the prophet a central or a peripheral figure?

The Prophet as Moral Revolutionary

One of the earliest "modern" treatments of biblical prophecy was by the German Heinrich Ewald (1803–1875), whose study proves the adage that researchers often read themselves into their subject. Although a biblical scholar, Ewald was also regarded as a revolutionary on university campuses because he resisted the attempts of the German Chancellor Bismarck and King Wilhelm of Prussia to form a large German Empire (the "Second Reich") out of the smaller German states. His resistance against the encroachments of Prussia was accomplished at considerable personal cost, and he spent some of his latter years under arrest.

As for Ewald's biblical studies, he saw the Israelite prophet as a mirror image of himself, that is, a "rugged individualist" who fought for universal moral principles against the society of his day.

Ewald, along with his graduate students, stressed that the prophets were *individuals* principally interested in timeless ethical truths that were universally true; according to Ewald, these seers were also responsible for "spiritualizing" a primitive Israelite religion, which supposedly was preoccupied with external rituals, magic, and sacrifices, into that unique example of *ethical monotheism* in the ancient

Near East. In other words, Ewald viewed Israelite religion before the influence of these ancient revolutionaries as almost indistinguishable from the other cults[3] in the ancient world with their focus on priestcraft and sacrifices. At considerable individual cost the prophets supposedly redirected Israelite religion along ethical and moral grounds, so that the society would be judged by its moral conduct before a single deity rather than on such cultic issues as the purity of the sacrificial animals.[4]

Ewald's followers, especially Bernhard Duhm and Julius Wellhausen, further developed their teacher's evaluation of prophecy. In their reconstruction, they emphasized that the prophet reformers were opposed by the priests who supposedly tried to enslave Israelite religion to a sterile and rigid concept of law. Prophets had elevated the Israelite religion, but their reform was endangered by the threat of the priests who sought to damper their revolution by subjecting every conscience to their priestly laws. In this reconstruction, the prophets had been champions of individual responsibility and social justice, but in the end their "spiritualization" of Israelite religion was overcome by the priests whose preoccupation with law created "sterile Judaism." Timeless ethical principles had to yield to an endless series of dated and culturally bound legal details. To support his theory, Wellhausen established the following chronology:

PRIMITIVE RELIGION→   PROPHETIC MOVEMENT→   LAW→   JUDAISM
(cult and sacrifice)   (ethical monotheism)   (priests)

This view of prophecy particularly influenced the conduct of research conducted by Ewald's followers, for whatever data did not fit this perspective were often downplayed or dismissed. Whatever passages in a prophetic book displayed an interest in cultic or liturgical matters were explained as "secondary" because in their view the prophet had broken away from the earlier so-called primitive interest in ritual. As you can see, the argument here becomes circular: A true prophet was not interested in cultic matters, and they construct this nature of the true prophet by eliminating all evidence that does not support this view. Their commentaries preferred those prophetic books with a dominant interest in social ethics; they had difficulty with books which either stressed cultic matters (Haggai) or topics such as revenge (Nahum or Obadiah), which they considered unsuitable for their view of the "religious man," as they termed the prophet.

Their "pick and choose" approach to reading the Hebrew prophets made it clear that they had made their description far too narrow. For many of the writing and nonwriting prophets were not only interested in cultic affairs but were also what we might term "cult prophets"; that is, they were professionals in Israel's worshipping community. Some of the minor prophets in the Bible, such as Habakkuk, Zechariah, Joel, and Nahum, were almost certainly temple officials performing ritual acts of prophecy. As we shall see later in our treatment of the Psalms, many reconstructions of the ceremony of the "Individual Lament" call for a "cult prophet" whose responsibility it was to announce the divine oracle for the complainant. Some of these temple prophets undoubtedly issued warnings to the state on the advisability (or inadvisability) of war, as was common elsewhere in the ancient Near East. In

---

[3] The word "cult" is a word that can cause the student some difficulty. It is not used in its contemporary sense of a fanatical religious group, but rather in its original meaning of "public religious ceremony"; thus, the Roman Catholic Mass could be called "cult."

[4] There is a relationship between *monotheism*—belief in a single deity—and this stress on ethics, for the requirements commanded by a *single* divine voice are clearly less ambiguous than the bewildering dictates of innumerable gods and goddesses in *polytheism*.

fact, the Oracle Against Foreign Nations, which is so common in the prophets,[5] possibly originated as products of temple ceremonies celebrated against state enemies, although they were often reused for a different effect in the books where they are now read. In the story of Elijah we found a prophet who was both interested in sacrifice (1 Kings 18) and in social justice (1 Kings 21).

Even those passages that criticize the cult seem more interested in *reforming* it than in eliminating or superseding it. And so Amos 5:21–24 does not attack the idea of external cult and liturgy, but rather assaults hypocrisy, which clothes itself in ceremonial piety at the expense of social justice (compare Amos 8:4–6). Ewald, Duhm, and Wellhausen were probably also influenced by a type of German Protestantism (Pietism) that downplayed external ceremonies and cult in favor of internal, individual spirituality. They modelled their ideal Israelite prophet after the nineteenth-century German Lutheran Pietist, for whom religion was a matter of the individual private heart and not a public celebration.

Other instances abound in which contemporary concepts affected these nineteenth-century studies of biblical prophecy. In Europe the dominant nineteenth-century intellectual movement, *Romanticism,* stressed the rugged individualist, who was often portrayed as being heroically at odds with society. This ideal was lived by such contemporary figures as Lord Byron, the English poet who fought in the Greek revolution for independence. The cowboy of the American West was a perfect romantic figure; he lived by his own resources, independent from a corrupt society. Undoubtedly Romanticism colored the picture of Ewald's prophet as "a man *outside* society" and led to the de-emphasis of the role of prophet *within* Israelite society.

There is also the likelihood that the anti-Semitism that permeated German academic society of the time affected their reconstruction of the biblical period. And so the chronology of Wellhausen in which the "spiritual" religion of the prophet was "sterilized" by the rigid application of law resulting in Judaism reveals a prejudice (and misunderstanding) of the role of the law in Judaism. Furthermore, as you should already suspect from the treatment of the legal texts in the Book of Exodus (Chapter 5), Wellhausen was mistaken about the antiquity of the Bible's interest in law. Recent research confirms that legal texts are not *later* than the prophetic texts, but were easily as old or older. In fact, major prophets like Jeremiah saw it as their responsibility to return Israel to her foundation in the Torah/Law of Sinai. In light of all this, it became impossible to sustain Wellhausen's argument that law in the Hebrew Scriptures was a late reaction to the prophets.

However, there is still another more serious methodological flaw in the approach of Ewald, Duhm, and Wellhausen. Their portrayal of the prophet depended on their ability to isolate the prophet as a genuine individual personality. They worked on the theory that they could actually reconstruct the personality of the prophet from the biblical book. They had confidence that they could sift out of the Book of Isaiah, for example, the very words of the eighth-century prophet Isaiah, which could then be used to mold their impressions of the personality of Isaiah the individual. The previous treatment of the editorial stages of the Book of Amos should convince the student of the difficulties in isolating the very words of Amos the prophet. So there are really few data from which we could confidently arrive at an impression of the individual prophet from Tekoah. In the final analysis, we have only a *book* to work with and not an *individual*—a book that oftentimes is the product of 400 to 500 years of editing.

---

[5] For example, Amos 1:3–2:8; Isaiah 13, 15–19; Jeremiah 46–50.

Regardless of all the criticism levelled against Ewald, Duhm, and Wellhausen, there is a degree of truth in their view of the prophet. As long as their analysis does not become exclusive, it is true that many of the biblical prophets exhibit an ethical sensitivity unmatched in the ancient world. Israel was not to take advantage of the poor and vulnerable. Even the survival of the state was not worth compromising these social ideals. These figures resisted all religious and political authorities who attempted to take advantage of the vulnerable in Israelite society. (But so did the legal Book of the Covenant!) Whenever contemporary people refer to the courage of the prophet or extol the ethical vision of an Amos, they are recognizing the truth in Ewald's study. Ewald and his followers erred in making their reconstruction the *only* acceptable view of the prophet.

The Words of the Prophet: Prophetic Literature

Many scholars lost confidence in their ability to reconstruct the prophet as individual, because the words of the prophets had been so continuously reedited over centuries. But the awareness of our total inability to arrive at the *person* Isaiah yielded to the positive appreciation of the prophetic *writings: The Book of Isaiah replaced the Prophet Isaiah as the object of study.* In Jeremiah 18:18 Jeremiah attributes law to the priest, counsel to the wise person, and language ("the word") as the characteristic of the prophet. This rediscovery of language (rather than personality) first expressed itself in form criticism, in a new appreciation for poetry and poetic devices, and more recently in the methodology of rhetorical (or literary) criticism.

Herman Gunkel employed form criticism to heighten our awareness of the variety of literary forms employed in the books of the Bible. His work showed how the prophetic books are sources of countless different speech patterns. For example, in the Book of Amos we find the introductory form used by the ancient Near Eastern messenger: "Thus says the Lord . . ."[6]; ironic uses of the call to worship: "Come to Bethel and transgress, to Gilgal and multiply transgression" (4:4); liturgical hymns (5:8-9); funeral songs (5:1-2); and a courtroom trial for a capital offense that required two witnesses (3:9-11); and the ever-present prophetic call scene (7:14-15) in which the prophet receives his divine commission despite his objections.[7]

Many prophetic books were particularly fond of the "controversy speech," called RÎB in Hebrew, in which Israel would be brought to court for violation of the Sinai Covenant (vassal treaty): see Micah 6:1-5, Hosea 4:1-3, Jeremiah 2:9.[8] The presence of this speech pattern demonstrates the importance of the Mosaic Covenant tradition for biblical prophecy; even though there are few specific references to the Sinai Covenant in the prophetic books, it certainly forms the necessary backdrop for the RÎB speech pattern. The people have disregarded their contractual obligations (Sinai), and so Yahweh's representative (the prophet) calls them to judicial account. The conscious efforts in the Elijah story (1 Kings 17-19) to establish a parallelism between Elijah and Moses shows how important it is for the Deuter-

---

[6] See the exercise at the end of Chapter 2 in this book.

[7] For other examples of the prophetic call, see Isaiah 6, Jeremiah 1, and the elaborate theophany and commissioning in Ezekiel 1-3. (Perhaps Ezekiel needed such a "baroque" call as it was unusual to have Yahweh appear in all of his power in a foreign land.)

[8] Interestingly enough, in the Book of Jeremiah it seems that the people have first brought Yahweh to court for having been unfaithful to *his* treaty obligations.

onomic Historian to portray the prophet as representative of the Yahweh in the Sinai Covenant.[9]

The complexity of these forms in any given prophetic book reinforces the impossibility of going beyond these examples of patterned speech to the actual words of any prophet. Furthermore, even if a specific speech pattern does go back to a prophet, we do not have his own personal words, but a form created by his society.[10] Hence, when we study Amos, we are reading the message(s) conveyed by the literary forms in the written *book*. In form criticism we consider speech segments as vehicles for a theological message rather than the person of a prophet.

The use of these literary forms in the prophetic books is quite complicated. Although many of these forms may well date to the original prophet (for example, the funeral dirge in Amos 5:2–3), most of them have been incorporated at different stages of editing. For instance, the call narrative in Amos (7:14–15) probably goes back to Group B, the Deuteronomistic Group, which wrote a century after Amos—and in the southern kingdom of Judah. Many of the call scenes seem to have been written by later groups that were trying to foster the authority of the prophet by dramatizing his summons from Yahweh. (This points out the difficulties involved in using this literary form to reconstruct the psychology of the original prophet.)

Furthermore, when these literary forms have been inserted into their new context, they often acquire fresh, and even ironic, meanings. Amos 1:3–2:8 are examples of the Oracle Against Foreign Nations. Originally these were probably part of war prophecies uttered by a cult prophet in a ceremony against Israel's political foes. We have instances of similar practices in ancient Egypt. However, their inclusion here in Amos is more involved. The oracles begin with a denunciation of Israel's traditional enemies: Damascus, Tyre, Moab, etc.; but the text then unexpectedly names Israel herself. The Book of Amos thereby indicates that Yahweh might very well intervene to destroy his enemies, but understand too that God now considers Israel herself such a foe! A later stage of editing extended this irony to Judah (Amos 2:4–5), at a time when the book was no longer the sole property of the northern kingdom.

Form criticism was also much more willing to use *comparative materials* from elsewhere in the ancient Near East (and even from the results of modern anthropological studies) in its attempt to understand biblical prophecy. Ewald, Duhm, and Wellhausen had not made much use of other prophetic literature both because many of these texts were just then being translated, and because there was a methodological hindrance. These three scholars had portrayed the prophets as *unique* individuals who had raised the religion of the Hebrew Bible to a wholly new ethical plateau. If the prophet were "unique" then it would be impossible to explain these figures by using comparative materials drawn from other religions. But Gunkel examined speech patterns throughout the Near East in order to reconstruct the social situations (Gunkel's *Sitz im Leben*) from which they might have been derived.

Further research into prophetic literature has focused upon the prophet as *poet,* for the majority of all of the Written Prophets were composed in Hebrew poetry. As we learned in Chapter 1 of this text, poetry is not just some sort of "envelope" within which the message is carried, but is inseparable from what is being

---

[9] This parallelism is explicit in Deuteronomy 18:15 ("like me"). However, we must keep in mind that the view of the prophet as guarantor of the Mosaic religion was *not* the only view; some of the prophets were seemingly attached to the royal government and had as their goal the preservation of the interests of the royal Davidic Covenant.

[10] Similarly, the courtroom oath, "I solemnly swear to tell the whole truth . . . ," does not reflect the linguistic creativity of a witness who uses it; rather, it has been placed in the witness's mouth by the legal community.

expressed. And so to understand any prophet adequately—even from the religious perspective of the believer—the reader must appreciate the prophet's poetics. As we learned in the very beginning of this text, poetry differs essentially from referential speech; the prophets cannot be read as if they were merely *talking about* Israel and her historical problems. Poetry functions primarily by talking about language; meaning and references are often quite indirect. The poet chooses a word or phrase because of its ability to evoke all sorts of ideas and moods in the listener or reader. The very sounds of the words can suggest lack of harmony, sadness, enthusiasm, even irony. Isaiah in his parable on the vineyard (Isaiah 5:1–7) plays with the word pairs for "justice (**mishpaṭ**)" and "bloodshed (**mispah**)" and also "righteousness (ṣedaqah)" and "outcry for help (ṣeᶜaqah)" (5:7). You would have expected the one ("Justice" and "Righteousness"), but Israel actually disappointed God by giving "Bloodshed" and an "Outcry." The words' very similarity in sound only highlights their actual contrast.

Part of this sensitivity to "poetics" is an awareness of the use of such devices as parallelism and metaphor. Look at Isaiah 2:6–22. Both the skill of this poem and its meaning are achieved by playing on the vertical dimensions of *high* and *low*. Notice how God is described here (and throughout Isaiah) as "high and lofty" (Isaiah 6:1). Human sin in Isaiah is haughtiness—the human attempt at self-exaltation. In this poem God's exaltation (more philosophically his "transcendence") is continually stressed; whereas everything human that is "lifted up," "exalted," or "lofty" will be brought low: Humans will end up even under the ground! There can really be no appreciation of the "message" of the prophet without sensitivity to poetic devices.

In more recent times, *rhetorical criticism* has brought us beyond form criticism by enabling us to understand the larger literary structure of the prophetic books. Form criticism tended to atomize the books into countless independent literary forms at the expense of any "larger picture." In the last chapter we looked at the possible literary organization of the Book of Amos. It seems that at the second stage of editing (Group B) the book was organized as a two-year pilgrimage from Zion (Amos 1:2) to a theophany at the rival shrine of Bethel. At this Succoth revelation of Yahweh the Bethel temple would be destroyed in the earthquake that accompanied Yahweh's appearance. Readers had a decision to make: They could continue their abominable worship at Bethel and suffer the same consequences as the shrine, or have life by association with Yahweh of Zion (Amos 5:4–5). Rhetorical criticism and its attention to the overall literary structure of a book allows the critique to go beyond one's first impression that the prophet is a veritable smorgasbord of disconnected oracles.

At some stage of their editing most of the prophetic books were organized according to larger structures; and as we have already learned, these structures contribute to meaning by focusing the reader's attention on details intended by the editor/writer. Part of the Book of Isaiah (chapters 40–55) called "Second Isaiah" has been arranged around the inclusion that centers on the Word of God (40:8 and 55:10–11), which can restore life to dried or dead vegetation. This theme would be particularly reassuring to the depressed community of the exiles in the Babylonian captivity, for whom Second Isaiah was written.

Social Aspects of Israelite Prophecy

One of the contributions of form criticism is the awareness that speech patterns (forms) have a corresponding "life situation" (Gunkel's *Sitz im Leben*), that is, a social context in which they would normally be appropriate. This immediately introduces the factor of the social context or contexts of prophecy. The prophet is no longer the timeless religious reformer, no longer the rebellious individual outside society. Perhaps no other research has established the complexity of Israelite prophecy as has modern research into that society's sociological interrelationships. In fact, some of the leading sociologists in the last half-century or more (for example, Max Weber and Peter Berger) have studied biblical prophecy.

Prophet as Peripheral vs. Central Figure

Sociology differentiates between *peripheral* and *central* figures. The former are outside the mainstream of society and often oppose its main institutions; the latter type are part of the "establishment," and their responsibility is to bolster and support society's institutions. They might even be reformers; however, central figures cannot tolerate any radical discontinuity. As you can imagine, an individual can pass in and out of these two roles; thus, the antiwar activist (peripheral) of the 1960s could be today's congresswoman (central). In 1 Kings 22 we encounter biblical prophets of both these types. The 400 prophets summoned by Ahab were central prophets whose job was to support the state; Micaiah, son of Imlah, functioned as a peripheral figure. Many of the biblical prophets were central figures in support of society's main institutions: for example, Haggai, Joel, Nahum, Obadiah, Zechariah chapters 1–8. Others could seek to undermine society radically and to call for a future that was totally discontinuous with the present. Jeremiah said that the Mosaic Covenant was null and void (Jeremiah 11:9–10), and the people could only look forward to being "uncreated" (Jeremiah 4:23–26).[11] A prophet like Isaiah of Jerusalem (Isaiah 1–39) seems to have fluctuated between being peripheral and central, although in general he was interested in "purifying" (see Isaiah 1:25–26), not eliminating, the main royal beliefs in the Zion Tradition and the Davidic Covenant.

Prophet and King

Scholars have noted that the time period for the prophet and the monarch were about the same. One of the first great prophets in the Hebrew Bible was Samuel, who also initiated the monarchy with his anointing of Saul.[12] Shortly after the Judahite kingship died out with the fall of Jerusalem (586 B.C.E.), Israelite prophecy began to decline.

Perhaps this is not a coincidence. Frank Cross has speculated that prophecy functioned as a check on the role of kingship. Power in the 12 tribes prior to the royal period was supposedly held by charismatic judges, that is, by figures who received their authority in the community by being recognized as having God's spirit in them. The period of their authority was limited by the acceptance of the tribe and could not be passed on to offspring.[13] This unstructured, free power base fit the origins of the Israelite tribal assembly, in which no individual could come between the suzerain, Yahweh, and his people. With the establishment of a dynastic

---

[11] Notice that in Jeremiah 4:23–26, Jeremiah seems to be imitating the Creation language of his contemporary, the Priestly Writer.

[12] Although figures earlier than Samuel are called "prophets" in the Hebrew Bible, many of these references are found in later texts that seem to have read the prophetic role into an early context; in any case the "glory period" of Israelite prophecy roughly coincides with the period of the Davidic monarchy.

[13] In fact, the sociologist Max Weber coined the word "charismatic" in order to describe the power of this period in Israelite history.

monarchy, a problem arose. Conservative members of the tribal league feared a radical shift in the power structure of the religious community. The spirit-led charismatic judge was now replaced by a stable, institutionalized king, whose power would regularly be passed on to his son (dynasty). Furthermore, since elsewhere in the ancient Near East the king was the main mediator between the divine and earthly spheres, the king in Israel would easily claim a similar role as mediator between his God and people. According to Frank Cross and others the charismatic role once shared by the tribal judge was continued in the prophet. Thus, in Israel the prophet would preserve the charismatic and spontaneous nature of this intercession as a counterbalance to the institutionalized role of the newly established monarchy.

The tension between king and prophet was quite evident in the saga of Elijah in 1 Kings. The Israelite monarch Ahab and his Phoenician wife, Jezebel, attempted to establish an absolute monarchy; along these lines they fostered Baal worship, for the Canaanite god, Baal, was the patron of earthly kingship. These two assumed all religious matters under their own control. Opposed to their efforts was the Moses-like Elijah whose power came spontaneously from Yahweh. This figure called the people back to their original covenantal obligations. Yahweh alone had absolute power; Baal was utterly impotent! (An ironic situation for a fertility deity.) This charismatic prophetic role could be passed on to others (for example, Elisha) but it was not dynastic.

A stele of the Canaanite god Baal from ancient Ugarit in northern Syria. In one hand he holds a lightning-lance, in the other a war club; he stands on wavy lines symbolizing either the life-giving rain waters which Baal brings to the earth or the god Sea who was conquered by the Canaanite storm god. A diminutive worshipper stands before him.

In many respects the newly emerging prophetic role continued the function of the spontaneous and charismatic judge of the tribal league; he was also a guarantor of the religion of the Mosaic Covenant in an atmosphere in which the power of the royal dynasty appeared supreme. Many of the prophets, but certainly not all, served to check the power of the monarchy and to summon the people back to their legal responsibilities under the Sinai Covenant. Clearly the role of the prophet defined in Deuteronomy 18:15-22 was along these lines, for there the prophet was to continue the role of Moses as intercessor. Just before this chapter, Moses limits the power of the king in one of the earliest examples in human history of a royal constitution (Deuteronomy 17:14-20). The monarchy, especially in Judah under David and Solomon, had fostered a royal ideology, the Davidic Covenant,[14] in which its power flowed directly from God and was unconditional (Psalm 89:27-37). This covenant "obligated" Yahweh to stand by the royal family. Many prophets such as Jeremiah countered this royal ideology with the Mosaic Covenant and accused the people of abandoning their responsibility toward their divine suzerain. In a sense these Moses-like figures functioned as lawyers who used the literary format of the "covenant lawsuit (RÎB)" to announce judgment.

The conflict between these two perspectives is well illustrated in the encounter between the Moses-like prophet Jeremiah and the central (royal) prophet Hananiah in Jeremiah 28. Hananiah spoke like a prophet ("Thus says the Lord . . .") but he was limited to defending the permanence of the monarchy (Jeremiah 28:2-4), for according to Hananiah, Yahweh would restore the royal family, which had been exiled to Babylon in 597 B.C.E. But Jeremiah denounced such musings as an illusion. In Jeremiah 7:1-15, the prophet risked death by entering the Jerusalem temple on Mount Zion and denouncing the people's trust in both the reassurances of the Zion Tradition and in the Davidic Covenants as deception. In order to survive, the people must return to the Mosaic Covenant (see Jeremiah 2), in which they preserve the covenant rather than the covenant (Davidic Covenant) preserving them.

SUMMARY

These last two chapters in the text should at least give the reader an appreciation of the complexities of biblical prophecy. The prophet might have been a supporter of the regime or its opponent, outside of the establishment, or a salaried member of Israel's cult. The prophet might have been recognized as a Moses-like authority figure in society, who delivered a word that literally brought life or death[15]; or the prophet could be a figure held in such low esteem that a parent would rather kill a son than let him be a prophet (Zechariah 13:3). The only common element here is that the prophet in some sense was a spokesperson for the deity. The *word* of Yahweh is what links all of these different phenomena. It was the prophet that announced, "Thus says the Lord."

The freedom with which the original prophet's pronouncements were edited and rearranged over centuries shows how important these people were in Israel's religion. The word that they spoke was considered so dynamic that it was constantly adapted to fit new situations and crises. The problem of the eighth-century Isaiah was with King Ahaz's lack of faith in the Zion Tradition whereby Yahweh would

[14] See Psalm 89, Psalm 132, 2 Samuel 7.
[15] Recall these two motifs in the Elijah saga.

preserve Jerusalem from invasion (Isaiah 7:1-10). Almost three centuries later (about 540 B.C.E.) an anonymous prophet ("Second Isaiah") added 15 chapters (40-55) to reassure the exiles in Babylon that Yahweh was about to perform something that would dwarf the Exodus of Moses: He was about to march them directly across the desert to their beloved Jerusalem. A few years later "Third Isaiah"[16] added other chapters (56-66) to this growing "Isaiah collection" in which was addressed the bickering and infighting within the Jerusalem community of returned exiles.[17] The Book of Isaiah grew over the centuries; and the final book then became a new whole in which judgment (original Isaiah) is now read alongside that of hope and new beginnings ("Second Isaiah").

FURTHER READINGS

Claus Westermann, *Basic Forms of Prophetic Speech,* trans. Hugh K. White (Philadelphia: Westminster, 1967).

Robert R. Wilson, *Prophecy and Society in Ancient Israel* (Philadelphia: Fortress Press, 1980).

[16] It could actually have been the same prophet as "Second Isaiah" only under changed circumstances.

[17] Both of these additions to First Isaiah (approximately chapters 1-39) were probably intended to be read along with First Isaiah and never independently.

THE WRITINGS
Psalmist, Sage, and Short Story

CHAPTER 9
THE PSALMS

GOALS AND OBJECTIVES: The exercises in this chapter help the reader acquire a certain working familiarity with the critical tool of form criticism. The chapter also acquaints the student with the major genres of songs/psalms used in Israelite worship. Thus, the reader should come away not only with an introduction to the Book of Psalms but also with an awareness of the role of the Israelite temple and its ancient services.

The third division of the Hebrew Bible, the Writings, is a catchall that contains—among other works—religious song lyrics (the Psalms), advice about the nature of life and "How to Succeed" (Wisdom Literature), and short stories whose main characters generally exhibit survival skills for the Jewish community during the difficult period of the Second Temple (after 586 B.C.E.). Although many of the Writings were composed before 586 B.C.E., most of them were at least edited during this unsettled time after the destruction of national independence, when the community had to rethink the expression and nature of its central beliefs.

Whenever the people of Israel acknowledged their faith in Yahweh's activities, they broke into songs/poems of praise. When they had been delivered from the armies of Pharaoh at the Red Sea, they responded with the "Song of Miriam" in Exodus 15. Their victory over Sisera at Megiddo led to the "Song of Deborah" (Judges 5). The joy of King David expressed itself in the hymn found in 2 Samuel 22. On a more individual level, when the barren and depressed Hannah was rewarded with the birth of a son, she responded to God's gift with the song of 1 Samuel 2. These examples of poems of joy (or hymns) celebrating the work of their God Yahweh are found throughout the Hebrew Bible and not just in the Book of Psalms (Psalter).

However, Israel also knew defeat and the feeling of being abandoned by God. When struck by military catastrophes, plague, famine, the destruction of her central shrine in 586 B.C.E.; Israel turned to Yahweh with poems of lamentation. Both the affected *community* as well as distraught *individuals* could pour out their sorrow before God, acknowledge their responsibility, or demand an accounting from God ("Why? . . . ?" "How long, O Yahweh . . . ?").

The Hebrew Bible contains both *hymn* and *lament*. These *poems* (more about this shortly), which generally were performed as part of public religious ceremonies (that is, cult), were prayers directed to the national deity Yahweh. As part of religious rites, they were accompanied by music (see Psalm 150) and liturgical actions. Most of these public temple prayers, but certainly not all, were collected into the Book of Psalms. This collection probably happened gradually and after the destruction of the temple. In fact, psalms were still being added as late as Qumran (at the turn of the Era, between B.C.E. and C.E.).

In the present canonical arrangement of 150 Psalms it is difficult to detect any organizational principle. However, at the last stage of assembly, some editor divided the 150 Psalms into five books:[1] Psalms 1–41, 42–72, 73–89, 90–106, and 107–150. Each of these smaller "books" ends with a doxology, or small hymn in praise of God, which closes that particular book and opens the one that follows; Psalm 150, with its ecstatic joy, closes the Psalter as a whole. The Hebrew name of

---

[1] Perhaps in imitation of the five books of the Pentateuch.

the Psalter can be roughly rendered "The Book of Halleluias," which indicates that although these joyous songs of praise or doxologies may be a numerical minority, they have come to characterize the entire nature of the later collection: There may be much sorrow and lament in the Book of Psalms, but the entire Psalter is now conceived of as a praise to Yahweh. The introductory Psalm 1 defines the characteristics of the good person in contrast with the evil person; this probably represents a sort of "editorial preamble" by which an editor indicates that the original book of hymns intended for the *singer* in temple liturgies should now be reinterpreted by the *reader* as a guide to the moral life. This arrangement would lend relevance to the collection even after the temple's role had diminished in Israel's religion.

We can only detect suggestions of earlier collections. What follows represents groupings within the Book of Psalms according to their putative author (David), the song guild that performed them (the sons of Korah or Asaph), the word they use to address God (Elohim or Yahweh), or their literary theme (hymn, lament, etc.):

PSALMS	COLLECTIONS
Psalm 1	
3–41	DAVIDIC PSALMS
42–49	Psalms of Korah
51–72	DAVIDIC PSALMS
73–83	Psalms of Asaph
84–88	APPENDIX: Psalms of Korah
93–99	Yahweh is King
100	Psalm of praise
103–107	Psalms of Praise
111–118	Psalms of Praise (alleluia)
Psalm 119	
120–134	Psalms of Ascent
135–136	Psalms of praise
138–139	Individual psalm of praise
140–143	Individual psalm of lament
145	Psalm of praise
146–150	Psalm of praise

(Psalms 42–83 are Elohistic Psalms; that is, they use the Hebrew word *Elohim* ["God"] to describe the deity.)

At the beginning of most of the Psalms we find an historical superscription (see, for example, Psalm 18:1) or a musical notation (Psalm 22:1). It is questionable whether either type of addition goes back to the time of the original song. The first represents an attempt to link psalms with some incident in the life of King David for which that psalm would have been appropriate. Although not necessarily historical, they can be helpful for telling us how a psalm was understood in very early times. The musical comments are almost completely unintelligible to us today.[2]

Modern scholarship on the Psalms has profited from two observations: First, many of the psalms were not mainly *private* prayer but rather liturgical songs (poetic lyrics) intended for cult celebration in the temple. Second, we have been assisted in our appreciation of the psalms by the methodologies of form criticism developed at the beginning of this century, which helps us better understand the structure and expression of various types of psalms. This aids us in reconstructing the cultic contexts in which various types of psalms were performed.

PSALMS AS TEMPLE SONG LYRICS

It is important for the modern reader of the Book of Psalms to appreciate that the book, with few exceptions, is a hymnal—a collection of poems intended to be sung during the official rites at the temple on Mount Zion in Jerusalem. Because they function as liturgical song lyrics, we should then learn both (1) how Hebrew poetry[3] works and (2) about temple rituals and feast days.

Hebrew Poetry

Concerning the nature of Hebrew poetry, please read the Appendix on Biblical Hebrew Poetry at the back of this text.[4] All poetry functions by calling attention to its language; it usually does this by some form of repetition. If the repetition is of sound, we have *alliteration, consonance, rhyme,* etc. Repetition of word accents in English is called *meter.* Scholars have not been able to detect any meter for Hebrew poetry, which seems to prefer a device called **parallelism**: What the Hebrew language really does is rhyme sentences according to their meaning. Be sure you understand parallelism and its various types (synonymous, antithetic, synthetic) as described in the Appendix in this book.[5] Read the following verses and classify them as either *synonymous, antithetic, or synthetic:*

Psalm 103:2   Bless the Lord, O my soul,
                    and forget not all his benefits . . . .

Psalm 103:1   Bless the Lord, O my soul,
                    and all that is within me, bless his holy name!

Proverbs 21:26   All day long the wicked covets,
                    but the righteous gives and does not hold back.

---

[2] Some of these could have been original, for we possess original clay tablets of ancient Hittite, Ugaritic, and Babylonian hymns that begin with comments on their musical performance.

[3] After all, song lyrics are generally poetic in structure.

[4] Although most of you are probably taking this course to study the religion of Israel found in these books, the course operates on the hermeneutical principle that we can *never* separate literary form from (theological) content. That much of the Hebrew Bible is in poetry (almost all the Prophets) is essential for our understanding of how the Bible conveys its meaning. It is not a (referential) textbook, but rather a collection of poems, songs, oracles, riddles, short stories, chronicles, satires, etc.

[5] There is also an excellent set of articles on Hebrew poetry in the *Interpreter's Dictionary of the Bible* and in its supplemental volume.

Read Psalm 29, which follows below. Analyze it according to the terminology found in Appendix E dealing with poetry. That is, isolate the different lines,[6] indicate *bicola* and *tricola*; comment on the relationship between the cola in a line: synonymous, antithetic, or synthetic parallelism. Is the parallelism complete or incomplete? Do any of these stylistic devices aid us in reading the Psalm?[7]

PSALM 29

Ascribe to-Yahweh, sons-of God,

Ascribe to-Yahweh glory and-strength

Ascribe to-Yahweh the-glory-of his-name.

Worship Yahweh at-the-appearance-of his-holiness.

The-voice-of Yahweh (is) upon the-waters;

  the-God-of glory thunders,

Yahweh (is) upon the-waters vast.

The-voice-f Yahweh (is) with-power,

The-voice-of Yahweh (is) in-majesty.

The-voice-of Yahweh breaks cedars,

Yahweh breaks the-cedars-of Lebanon.

And-he-makes-skip like-a-calf Lebanon,

And-Sirion like an-offspring-of a-wild-ox.

The-voice-of Yahweh cleaves with-flames-of fire,

The-voice-of Yahweh makes-writhe the-wilderness,

Makes-writhe Yahweh the-wilderness-of Kadesh.

The-voice-of Yahweh makes-writhe the-deer (in childbirth),

and-strips the-forest,

and-in-his-temple is seen (?) glory

Yahweh on-the-flood is-seated,

---

[6] You should be aware that the division of the poem into "lines" does not always correspond with the numbering of the verses in your Bibles. Versification is fairly recent.

[7] In what follows I have linked with a hyphen the English words that are represented by a single Hebrew word. Thus there are four Hebrew words in each of the first several cola. I have also translated the lines in their original Hebrew word order.

And-is-seated Yahweh king forever,

Yahweh, strength to-his-people may-he-give,

Yahweh, may-he-bless his-people in-peace.

Temple Cult on Mount Zion

The temple on Mount Zion, which had been built by King Solomon around 940 B.C.E., was the center of worship, especially in the southern kingdom of Judah.[8] Nevertheless, the role of the temple in Jewish life was somewhat different from that of the church or synogogue today. For example, list below some events in the life of a Christian that would be celebrated by liturgical ceremonies conducted in church:

In general, birth, coming of age, marriage, and death seem to have no corresponding ceremony in the Jerusalem temple. Rather, these were private affairs in Judah. The temple was used on the three major pilgrim feast days on which all believers were required to go up to the temple (see Leviticus 23): Feast of Unleavened Bread/Passover,[9] the feast of Pentecost,[10] and the autumnal feast of Booths or Succoth.[11]

[8] Although there were other cult centers in both the breakaway northern kingdom of Israel (922–721 B.C.E.) and in southern Judah, the two southern kings, Hezekiah (700 B.C.E.) and Josiah (622 B.C.E.), both tried to centralize all legitimate worship in Jerusalem.

[9] Originally the feast of Unleavened Bread celebrated the gathering of the year's first harvest, the barley harvest; but it later became linked with Israel's belief that Yahweh had freed her ancestors from slavery in Egypt (the Exodus). The Passover started out as a shepherds' festival that marked the change from winter to spring pasturage. At an early time both feasts became joined (see Exodus 12).

[10] This commemorated Israel's second harvest, the wheat harvest, usually about 50 days (hence *Pente*cost) after the barley harvest.

[11] This feast in early September celebrated the ingathering of the remaining harvest such as fruit. It was a complex of harvest thanksgiving, feast of repentance (Yom Kippur), and New Year, because not only did it round off the previous agricultural year but it also petitioned God to begin a new year by beginning the autumn rains, which prepared the soil for the new crops after months of summer drought.

The temple was also the site for (1) ceremonies celebrating the first fruits of harvest (Deuteronomy 26); (2) lamentations about sickness and disease, which was usually thought to be caused by Yahweh; (3) legal proceedings dealing with guilt or innocence and asylum from revenge due to blood guilt (Exodus 21:12–14); (4) atonement rites to help a person or community recover from guilt; and (5) the fulfillment of vows. The temple was also the scene for royal coronations.

The theology about the status of the temple erected by Solomon on Zion in Jerusalem is found in a complex of traditions called the *Zion Tradition.* This tradition is revealed in the Psalter in such Psalms as 46 and 48. Although the following five constitutive elements may not be found in every instance of a hymn celebrating the temple of Zion, they are thought to be part of the Zion Tradition complex:

1. Mount Zion in Jerusalem is considered to be the mountain on which Israel's God dwells. In the ancient Near East deities were frequently associated with mountains (cf. Zeus and Mount Olympus). Yahweh, originally linked in the Mosaic tradition with Mount Sinai, was reassigned Zion, which was often identified symbolically with Mount Zaphon, a mountain on the present-day border between Syria and Turkey, which was considered the mountain of the old Canaanite deity Baal.[12]

2. Like the mountain of the main Canaanite deity, Zion was regarded as the source of major rivers of paradise which brought fertility to the land. (Even though there are no such rivers near the actual temple.) See Ezekiel 47 and Joel 3:18.

3. At this site (Zion) Yahweh was regarded as having defeated all the threatening powers of (watery) chaos (often seen as dragons and sea beasts). This was, in other words, the center of the world's order.[13]

4. Because of the special presence of Yahweh, Zion was inviolable: no earthly enemy could prevail against this mountain. They would suffer the same fate as the mythological forces of chaos.

5. Zion was the goal of all the nations of the earth which streamed there with gifts in pilgrimage to recognize the power of Yahweh. See Isaiah 2:1-5, Psalm 2:10-11.

These five elements were probably not a *natural* conglomerate, but rather an artificial complex of traditions. The first and third elements, which identified Zion with Baal's Mount Zaphon, were indebted to the Canaanite Baal mythology. The second element is borrowed from the mythology of the Canaanite deity El, whose Mount Ll (pronunciation uncertain) was the source of major rivers. The last two points probably had an historical basis derived from the imperial conquests of David and Solomon (about 950–922 B.C.E.) in which historical enemies were defeated and bore their tribute to Jerusalem. Because the latter two points were really only historically true during the reigns of these two monarchs, it is likely that they were the authors of this cult complex celebrating their new royal shrine in Jerusalem.

---

[12] In Hebrew the word "Zaphon" can also mean "north" because the historical Mount Zaphon was several hundred miles *north* of Israel. This has led many translators to miss the reference in Psalm 48:2, where "in the far north" makes no sense: "North of what?" We have here an identification of Yahweh's Zion with Baal's Zaphon.

[13] Recall that in the Enuma Elish, Marduk celebrated his victory over watery chaos (Tiamat) by establishing his temple and Babylon, his holy city.

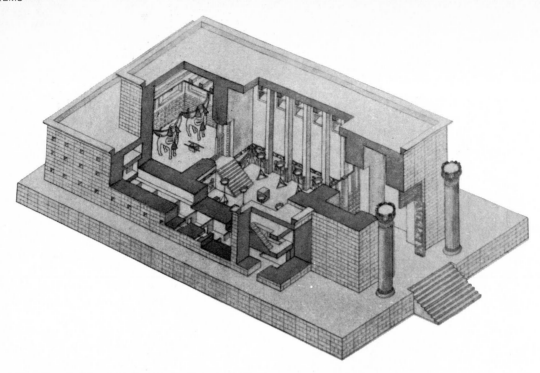

Drawing of Solomon's Temple in Jerusalem. The Temple, constructed by Phoenician artisans, was patterned after Canaanite models in which the temple itself is divided into three chambers: the vestibule, the main sanctuary, and in the back the Holy of Holies, where the Ark of the covenant symbolizing Yahweh's footstool was placed between two guardian Cherubim. (See 1 Kings 5-7.)

SOCIAL ASPECT OF THE PSALMS: FORM CRITICISM

Form criticism studies the social dimensions of biblical literature. Form criticism begins with the observation that the actual *format* of speech (vocabulary and syntax) depends on what is being expressed (content) and the social context.[14] Simply put, the power of the Davidic king in Jerusalem, which was believed to be confirmed directly by God (content), would be described differently (format) when described in a hymn to be recited in the royal temple, in an historical saga, or in a hostile diatribe of a prophet (context).

The form critic wants to compare all biblical passages with similar vocabulary and form of expression in order to theorize about the social context within which such speech was at home: Was it legal language, cultic language, or religious language? In most cases these hypotheses remain highly speculative for we know so little about biblical Israelite society. Furthermore, how the reader uses such information is quite important. A passage might indeed be an example of legal speech, but it might be used ironically and thus not indicate a primary legal context.

In the case of the Book of Psalms, form criticism groups psalms according to similar content and expression (format). The psalms have largely been divided into the following forms (genres or types) based on this research:

Enthronement Hymn

Psalm of Ascent (Pilgrim Songs)

[14] Here scholars often use the German phrase *Sitz im Leben* to describe the social context or particular life situation within which speech takes place.

Entry Liturgy (for example, Psalms 15 and 24)

Zion Hymns

Individual Lament (IL)

Individual Thanksgiving (IT)

Community Lament (CL)

Community Thanksgiving (CT)

Royal Psalms

   Coronations

   Weddings

Form criticism then tries to reconstruct the liturgical ceremony that would have accompanied the recital of that psalm. Because we have little direct knowledge about such ceremonies, reconstruction is based upon (1) references to actions within the psalms themselves, (2) allusions to ceremonies elsewhere in the Bible, and (3) archaeological evidence from religious ceremonies elsewhere in the ancient Near East.

To test how accurate (and dangerous) such claims can be, I have prepared the next exercise. I want you to read the following Christian hymns.[15] They are similar to the psalms in that they are intended to accompany liturgical celebrations and to be sung by the worshipping congregation. I have included only hymns that are for a communion service.[16] I want you to read them through and answer the following questions about their format and content, and I want you—based *only* on these hymns—to try to reconstruct a ceremony of this particular communion service (context). Always support your answers with specific references to the hymns themselves.

COMMUNION HYMNS

[A]

1. At that first Eucharist before you died,
     O Lord, you prayed that all be one in you;
     At this new Eucharist again preside,
     And in our hearts your law of love renew.

Refrain:
     So may we all one bread, one body be;
     Through this blest sacrament of unity.

2. For all your Church, O Lord, we intercede;
     We beg you, make our pride and anger cease;
     Draw us the nearer, each to each we plead,
     By drawing all to you, O Prince of Peace.

[15] These hymns were all taken from the hymnals of a particular Christian denomination, but your lack of familiarity with the ceremonies of this group should cause no alarm. Scholars probably know *less* about the ceremonies of *ancient* Israel than you do about those of this *present-day* denomination. So any lack of familiarity on your part only adds realism to this exercise.

[16] Because I have already grouped these hymns according to a definite, known *context*, that is, a communion service, I have put you at an advantage over the suffering Old Testament scholar who has to labor over such groupings.

3. We pray for those who wander from the fold;
   O bring them back, Good Shepherd of the sheep,
   Back to the faith that filled the saints of old,
   The faith God's holy people still shall keep.

[B]

1. Bread of Heav'n, on thee we feed
   For thy flesh is food indeed;
   Ever may our souls be fed
   With this true and living bread;
   Day by day with strength supplied
   Through the life of him who died.

2. Vine of heav'n, thy blood supplies this blest cup of sacrifice;
   Lord, thy wounds our healing give,
   to thy cross we look and live;
   Jesus, may we ever be
   Grafted, rooted, built in thee.

[C]

1. Father, God of all things living,
   Give us now our daily Bread;
   Thou hast taken our thanksgiving,
   Through they Son, whose blood was shed,
   Jesus, come to us again.
   Thou are life and light to men:
   Let us eat the food you gave us
   On the night you deigned to save us.

2. Lo, a banquet lies before us,
   Flesh and Blood of Christ our King,
   Here is power to restore us,
   Strength when we are wavering.
   Jesus, bids us take and eat;
   Taste and see the Lord is sweet:
   Do thou, Christ, in loving kindness,
   Bind our wounds and heal our blindness.

3. Father, take away all malice,
   As we hold thy holy Son;
   We who feed from Jesus' chalice,
   Joined in him, become as one.
   Welcome Christ, our royal guest!
   Reign supreme in ev'ry breast!
   Share with us your love and power;
   Strengthen us in our last hour.

[D]

1. Members of one Mystic Body,
   Joined in Christ, our Lord and Head,
   Come before your holy altar,
   seeking life through living Bread.
   Make us, Lord, our sins confessing,
   Worthy of your ev'ry blessing.

2. Wheat and wine as gifts we offered,
   Now as gifts to us return;
   God himself as gift is given:
   Food for which our Spirits yearn.
   Lord, our hearts in trust believe you;
   Make us worthy to receive you.

[E]

1. We come to join in your banquet of love.
   Let it open our hearts and break down the fears
   that keep us from loving each other.
   May this meal truly join us as one.

[F]

Refrain:
   Feed on me and never will you hunger:
   Feed on me, and life will never end.

1. Do not work for bread that cannot fill—

2. Moses brought you manna in the desert—

3. I will give my flesh as bread to feed—

[G]

1. I am the bread of life; he who comes to me shall not hunger,
   he who believes in me shall not thirst.
   No one can come to me unless the Father draw him.

Refrain:
   And I will raise him up, and I will raise him up,
   and I will raise him up on the last day.

2. The bread that I give is my flesh for the life of the world,
   and he who eats of this bread, he shall live forever,
   he shall live for ever.

3. Unless you eat of the flesh of the Son of Man, and drink of his blood,
   and drink of his blood, you shall not have life within you.

4. I am the resurrection, I am the life;
   he who believes in me, even if he die, he shall live forever.

5. Yes, Lord, I believe that you are the Christ,
   the Son of God, who has come into the world.

[H]

Refrain:
   Bread that was sown in our hills and valleys now harvested becomes one;
   from all the world gather your people, O God, into the feast of your love.

1. With grateful hearts, we sing our joy
   for knowing Spirit within, among us all;
   life and knowledge, revealed
   through your word: Jesus, the Christ, Emmanuel.

2. Leaven and wheat: so let us be, for others,
   nurturing good with earnest care,
   bringing to birth new life where hope has gone stale,
   faith giving moments to share.

3. Planted, your name becomes our thirst for more,
   being hope to be bread for others' lives,
   vision of what it means to give all that we are:
   this is the seed you have sown.

4. Feast of justice to which all are welcome to share the fullness of our God.
   in Jesus' rising beyond death we've found new springs of hope in our lives.

5. Harvest of peace where love can be the song that heals
   brokenness with listening,
   touching, perceiving in bread of Jesus' life,
   gift to become our flesh as well.

6. Sign of the nearness of one whose life sustains us,
   heart of our heart, creator, friend,
   calling us all to be spirit alive: you, God, our future, lasting life.

[I]

1. O, welcome all ye noble saints of old,
   as now before your very eyes unfold,
   the wonders all so long ago foretold.
   God and man at table are sat down,
   God and man at table are sat down.

2. Elders, martyrs, all are falling down;
   prophets, patriarchs are gath'ring 'round,
   what angels longed to see now man has found.
   God and man at table are sat down,
   God and man at table are sat down.

3. Who is this who spreads the victory feast?
   Who is this who makes our warring cease?
   Jesus, risen Savior, Prince of Peace.
   God and man at table are sat down,
   God and man at table are sat down.

4. Beggars, lame, and harlots also here;
   repentant publicans are drawing near;
   wayward sons come home without fear.
   God and man at table are sat down,
   God and man at table are sat down.

5. Worship in the presence of the Lord,
   with joyful songs and hearts in one accord,
   and let our Host at table be adored.
   God and man at table are sat down,
   God and man at table are sat down.

6. When at last this earth shall pass away,
   when Jesus and his bride are one to stay,
   the feast of love is just begun that day.
   God and man at table are sat down,
   God and man at table are sat down.

Format

I would like you to write down ways of expression common to all these hymns.

1.   Note and *identify* all the speakers or parties mentioned. For example, if direct address is used, or a command, then note who is commanding/speaking. And to whom. This provides some indication of the parties felt to be present in some way at the ceremony.

2.   Is there any common system according to which ideas are organized and arranged? For example, where in these hymns does a wish or request usually occur; where are references to past events usually positioned? Are descriptions of the present (worshipping) community located in any place common to a large number of the hymns? How are the verb tenses arranged: future, present, past?

3.   Is there a preference for a certain grammatical construction, for example, the command? The use of the second person ("you")?

Content

1.   Write down one statement about theology or ideas that are common to all these hymns. What do they say about God, Jesus, the community, etc.?

2.   Which features or events in the life of Jesus do they stress?

3.   What do they say about the past, the present, and the future?

4.   What types of imagery do they prefer?

5.   In a sentence or two, summarize the religious ideas of this communion service based solely on these hymns.

Context

Using only these hymns, try to reconstruct the ceremony at which they might be sung. Try to depict it in as much detail as possible: Who is present; what exactly are they doing?

Conclusions

Based on your ability (or inability) to flesh out the exact details of the religious ceremony reflected in the hymns contained here, describe the benefits and shortcomings of this form-critical methodology.

PSALM TYPES

The Hymn

One of the literary *forms* much used by Israel was the *hymn,* or song of "descriptive praise," as it is termed by Claus Westermann. In fact, the earliest example of Israelite poetry preserved in the Hebrew Bible is the short hymn preserved in Exodus 15:21:

> Sing to Yahweh, for he has triumphed gloriously;
> the horse and his rider he has thrown into the sea.

Already by the twelfth century B.C.E. the hymn resembled its later examples both in the *context* of its recital, its *formal structure,* and in its *content.* The *invocation* to praise Yahweh was addressed by a cult functionary: Miriam, the prophetess, in Exodus 15 and minor Levites in Nehemiah 9:4-5. The performance of the hymn constituted part of a celebration, such as the victory observance in the Book of Exodus. It could also be used in conjunction with a major festival, such as Succoth (Nehemiah 9).

Structure

The *structure* of the hymn was already revealed in miniature in Exodus 15:21. First there was the *invocation,* usually addressed to the participants, to sing praise to Yahweh. The variety of the invocation can be appreciated from a comparison of Psalms 29:1-2, 96:1-2, 148:1-4, 115:1. In the final Psalm 150, the entire psalm is this invocation. Notice here how often the invocation is directed to almost all segments of creation and not just to the believer. Undoubtedly such universalism played an important role in raising the sights of Israelite religion toward a type of universalism. It is probably no coincidence that Second Isaiah (Isaiah 40-55) not only makes the greatest use of the hymn form but is also the most universalist of the Israelite prophets.

The second part of the hymn, the *body,* contains a description of the praiseworthy qualities of the deity. In this main part of the hymn, the divinity is praised in two ways: First, Yahweh is extolled *in himself* for his lordship and majesty. Here we especially find reference to God as creator and as master of all historical events.

Second, Yahweh is celebrated for his solicitude for his people, whom he rescued and preserved. This latter part, which commemorated Yahweh's compassion, was often formulated as a wish.

1.   Read Psalm 113 carefully as an example of the *hymn* format.

Divide it into the structure described above: What is its *invocation*? Its *body*?

In the *body* of Psalm 113, how does it combine the two different types of praise (of the majesty of God *and* of his care for his people)?

What theme or image is used to join together these two approaches to praise?

2.   Read Psalms 33 and 136 and notice their similarity in structure. Fill in the following chart to make their structures more apparent:

	PSALM 33	PSALM 136
INVOCATION		

PSALM 33   PSALM 136

MAIN BODY

    Creator

    Master of History

    Deliverer

    Preserver

      The hymn can be further categorized depending on the circumstances surrounding its performance. A significant number of hymns in the Psalter revolve around the sequence of events celebrating major festivals requiring attendance at the Jerusalem temple on Mount Zion. Certain hymns were performed by pilgrims during their ascent to the temple on Mount Zion during the three major Pilgrim Feasts. These are termed the "Songs of Ascent" (Psalms 120, 122, 125). As reconstructed by form critics, entrance into the temple itself was controlled by priestly attendants at the gate who had to determine that the worshippers fit the cultic requirements of the shrine. (Such entrance rites were common in the ancient Near East, where temple entrance rules were often posted on the outside wall surrounding the sacred enclosure.) Psalms 15, 24, and Isaiah 33:15–16 are possible examples of such "Entrance Songs" performed during this ritual inquiry.

Psalms extolling the Jerusalem sanctuary itself are called "Zion Hymns." During the spring Passover festival the hymns usually celebrated Yahweh's deliverance of his people in the Exodus from Egypt; the Feast of Pentecost commemorated the giving of the Law to Moses on Mount Sinai. During the complex of feasts connected with the fall harvest (the New Year's festival) the psalms honored the kingship of Yahweh, whose rule established the necessary world order to ensure a new agricultural year.

The Lamentation

In the preceding treatment of the hymn you were given the structure common to this genre. Now it is your turn to derive the structure yourself. All the psalms listed below fit into two closely related categories or literary genres. First, separate the two categories and then outline the structure (form) common to most of the instances of each category. You will then be asked questions about the social context of both genres.

Read the following: Psalms 3, 4, 5, 6, 25, 28, 30, 31, 32, 51, 66, 88, 102, 116, 118.[17]

All these psalms can be classified into two literary groups (or genres) based on the three features of format, content, and social context.

Content

Using the criterion of content (their subject matter), divide the psalms cited above into two groups (A and B): (Let the group that has a logical priority be Group A.)

A   B

Format

Outline the literary structure (that is, format) of each type (A and B). Be sure to illustrate these features by reference to verses of actual psalms. This will be only a *general* structure, for not all elements will necessarily appear in each psalm of that group. But it should be as comprehensive as possible. Notice such common literary features as use of the imperative (command), verb tense (past, present, future), the

---

[17] The notes at the beginning of the Psalms, for example, "To the choirmaster. A Psalm of David, when . . ." (Psalm 51), are mostly late additions and cannot be reliably used in these exercises.

order of the various literary parts, use of references to past relations, promises, etc. (You might want to recall what we did with the literary structure of the hymn.)

A   B

1.   Comment on the exact relationship between Psalms 51 and 32; and Psalms 30 and 38.

2.   Contrast these psalms of lament with David's "lament" over his dead friend Jonathan in 2 Samuel 1:19–27. What element of the structure found in the lamentation psalm is missing from David's outcry over the slain Jonathan?

3.   Sometimes a knowledge of the religious literature elsewhere in the ancient Near East can help us better understand a similar literary form in the Bible. Read the following "Prayer to Ishtar," which was written about 1500 B.C.E. Show similarities in *form* and *content* between this Babylonian prayer and a similar genre (A or B above) of biblical psalms.

PRAYER TO ISHTAR

[1.] I pray to you, Lady of Ladies, Goddess of Goddesses,
O Ishtar, Queen of all inhabited places, who preserves all the
living in good order.
O Irnini,[1] you are the exalted one,
O greatest of the Igigi,[2]
You are powerful, you are the Princess, your names are august;

[5.] You are the light of the heavens and of the earth,
the warrior daughter of Suen,[3]
You support arms and decide battle,
You assume all power, you wear the crown of dominion.
O Lady, all your high deeds are illustrious,
they are greater than those of all the Gods!
O Star of the battle cry, who makes even peaceful brothers to
fight,

[10.] Yet you constantly give friendship,
. . . Lady of the battlefield, who strikes down the mountains,
O Gushea,[4] belted with combat, robed with a
frightful appearance,
You send forth judgment with no appeal,
laws for the earth and the heavens;
Chapels, sanctuaries, sacred places, and temples wait on you.

[15.] Where is your name not invoked? Where are your rites not
celebrated?
Where are your ordinances not kept? Where have your temples not
been established?
Where are you not great? Where are you not celebrated?
Anu, Enlil and Ea have exalted you, they have expanded your
dominion among the Gods,
They have elevated you in the Assembly of the Igigi, they have
given you the supreme place;

[20.] At the very mention of your name the heavens and the earth
tremble,
The Gods shake, the Anunnaku[5] are speechless.
The living venerate your majestic name.
For you are great, you are splendid;
The assembly of the Black Heads,[6] the animals,
the living sing of your warrior deeds.

[25.] It is you who pronounce judgment in law and justice on the
people;
You look at the oppressed and on him who has been mistreated, you
restore them each day.
Grant me your favor, Lady of the heavens and earth, shepherdess
of the multitudes;
Grant me your favor, Lady of Holy Eanna,[7] the holy storehouse.
Grant me your favor, Lady with untiring feet and swift knees;

[1] Title of Ishtar.
[2] The assembly of all the great gods.
[3] The moon God.
[4] Title of Ishtar.
[5] Collective name for the great Gods.
[6] A title for humankind.
[7] Name of Ishtar's temple.

[30.]   Grant me your favor, Lady of Battle and of all combats!
O Splendid Lioness of the Igigi, who subdues the Gods in your
wrath,
O more powerful than all princes, you who bridles kings,
You who opens the veils of all young women,[8]
Whether you are in wrath or at peace,
your valiant deeds are great!

[35.]   O brilliant torch of the heavens and earth, brightness over
all inhabited places,
She is furious, irresistible in battle, brave in combat,
Heavenly torch which flames up against the enemies, which
destroys the arrogant,
O whirling Ishtar, who summons the assembly,
Goddess of men, Ishtar of women,
whose plans no one can understand,

[40.]   Wherever you glance, the dead return to life, the sick get
up;
The unfortunate one who wanders astray prospers when he looks
at your face;
I have called upon you, I, your servant, exhausted, miserable,
saddened;
Look upon me, my Lady, and accept my plea,
Look at me faithfully and hear my request;

[45.]   Proclaim my forgiveness, and let your anger towards me be
appeased.
Forgiveness for my wretched body, which is full of disorders and
troubles;
Forgiveness for my sad heart, which is full of tears
and suffering;
Forgiveness for my sad oracles, troubled and in disorder;
Forgiveness for my house without joy, where tears abound;

[50.]   Forgiveness for my spirit, which remains in tears and
suffering!
O Irninitu,[9] savage lion, let your heart become calm!
O angry bull, let your spirit be at peace toward me!
Let your watchful eyes be upon me!
Watch me faithfully with your shining face!

[55.]   Drive away the evil spells from my body, let me see your
brilliant light!
How long, O my Lady, shall my adversaries look upon me with evil?
In their lying and double-dealings, how long shall they plot evil
against me?
Those who persecute me and exult over me rage against me;
How long, O my Lady, shall they the weak and
crippled seek me out?

[60.]   The straggler has gone ahead of me, and I have remained last;
The weak have become strong, but I have become weak;
I toss about like a wave which an evil wind stirs up;
My heart flies and flutters like a bird of the heavens;
I mourn night and day like a dove;

---

[8] Ishtar was the goddess of love.   [9] Diminutive name of Ishtar; see line 3.

[65.]   I am feverish and weep bitterly!
My spirit sorrows with "Oh!" and "Alas!"
What have I done, O my god, O my goddess?
I am treated as one who fears not my god and my goddess;
Sickness, headache, pain, and ruin afflict me;

[70.]   I am afflicted with tribulations, disdain, fulness of fury,
Anger, fury, the hatred of the Gods and of humans.
O my Lady, I have seen dark days, shadowy months,
    years of trouble;
O my Lady, I have seen judgment, chaos, and rebellion;
Death as well as distress hold me in;

[75]   My chapel is in neglect, my sanctuary in neglect;
The silence of death is poured out over my house, my hut, and my
    fields.
As for my (personal) god, his face is turned elsewhere;
My clan is scattered, my hut is broken.
In you, O my Lady, I hope; I have cast my attention towards you;

[80.]   To you I pray; forgive my debt!
Absolve my fault, my guilt, my misdeed, and my deficiencies!
Disregard my misdeed, accept my plea,
Release my bonds, set me free!
Make my step straight, that I might walk radiantly like a lord
    among the living.

[85.]   See to it that at your command the angry god is appeased;
Let the goddess who was angry with me return to me.
Then let my hearth that was dark and smoky shine forth;
Then let my torch that had been extinguished burst into flame;
Then let my clan that had been scattered come together again;

[90.]   Then let my sheep-folds grow larger, my stable expand!
Accept my humiliation; hear my prayers!
Look at me faithfully, and hear my pleading!
How long, O my Lady, will you be irritated and your face be
    turned away?
How long, O my Lady, will you be angry
    and your spirit be in rage?

[95.]   Turn your head which you have set against me; be disposed
    towards a good word;
Like the overflowing waters of a river, let your spirit be calmed
    towards me;
Let me stomp my enemies like the ground;
Overcome those who hate me and place them at my feet.
Let my prayers and my requests come before you;

[100.]   Let your great indulgence be upon me.
Let those who see me on the street exalt your name;
As for me, let me proclaim to the Black Heads[10]
    your divinity and your warrior acts!
Ishtar is great! Ishtar is queen!
The Lady is exalted! The Lady is queen!
Irnini, the warrior daughter of Suen, has no rival!

[10] That is, "humanity."

4.   In one of the two groups (A or B) there is invariably a plea for Yahweh's aid. This petition for help is often accompanied by a *reason why* Yahweh should help the petitioner (called a *motivation clause*). List below some of the reasons given why Yahweh should intervene. Is there any similar "reason for help" given in the "Prayer to Ishtar"? Is there any frequently reoccurring phrase or motif?

Liturgical Context

The next part, the reconstruction of the cultic background (Liturgical Context), of the Psalms is difficult and must always remain quite *hypothetical,* for we know so little about Israel's cultic life. We can only reconstruct the temple liturgy by using the obscure references within the Psalms, much like you are now asked to do. We can also try to find references in other biblical passages that might obliquely clarify a religious ceremony. Sometimes our knowledge of religious ceremonies elsewhere in the ancient Near East can be helpful, for our familiarity with their cult is often much fuller. The questions that follow guide you through the reconstruction of the ceremony that accompanied the individual lament (IL, our original Group A).

      First we shall isolate references to such externals as location (temple, private home, palace, courtroom, etc.) and time. Next we shall look at the dialogue of the different voices/characters often witnessed in these individual laments (IL). Because dialogue is often a clue to the dramatic action of a liturgy, this evidence will be particularly helpful. The movement of dialogue within these IL's can also help us understand the background activity behind the petitioner's sudden change of mood from anguish to confidence that he or she will receive a hearing. Finally, we shall examine evidence outside the Book of Psalms, both in the Bible and elsewhere in the ancient Near East. At each one of these stages or plateaus you will be asked to theorize about the ceremony. (Remember that this "liturgy" is the social context in which the form critic is interested.)

      Reconstruct the *social context* for the individual lament. In other words, describe the religious ceremony (cult) in which each would have been performed! Begin by noticing concrete references describing the location of the lament, time of day, the status of the participants, liturgical activity, etc. Be sure to illustrate your reconstruction with ample reference to the psalms themselves, for in the psalms there seem to be references to activities being liturgically acted out; for example, "I will walk around your alter, O Yahweh." "O Lord, in the morning you hear my voice." "I will enter your house." The following questions should aid you:

1.   Describe the speaker(s), especially the "I." Do you think that this is a real individual or only an editorial "I" that symbolizes the nation or some other group?

2.   How many different speakers are there? (Is there any evidence for a dialogue?) Are there references to someone who has spoken, even though his or her words have not been reported? (This will be further developed later on.)

3.   Describe the concrete situation of the speakers: Are they sick? (if so, of what?); persecuted? (if so, by whom?); attacked by personal or external foes, etc.? How concretely is the situation of the main character ("the sufferer") described?

4.   Read Psalm 6. Notice the sudden change in tone or mood. Where does this change take place? Notice the change in verb tense; where does this take place? In the laments that you have read, there is often a change from doubt to "certainty of a hearing"; try to explain these sudden internal changes using your reconstruction of any accompanying ceremony.

Read related psalms such as Psalm 12 and 60, which deal with the complaints of the community rather than with those of an individual. How do the speakers and dialogue witnessed in these two psalms clarify the ceremony and activities behind our group of psalms?

5.   Picture the location of the speakers. Do you have evidence where the psalm is being delivered? Describe the stance of the speaker (sitting, kneeling, etc.).

6.   Describe the time of day. (If a longer period of time is mentioned, describe this.)

7.   Describe any references to an accompanying ceremony: things mentioned as happening, things happening "offstage" or presumed to have just occurred. You are being asked here to collect *all* the clues that will help you reconstruct the ceremony accompanying the words. (This is the most difficult question; you really have to play detective here! It is similar to a non-Catholic trying to reconstruct the Roman Catholic Mass using just the hymnal in the pews!)

Evidence for the IL Ceremony from Outside the Psalter

Now let us try to clarify further our idea of the liturgy. The form critic—remember, it is the form critic who is interested in reconstructing the social situation or ceremony behind the words—can often clarify a psalm by studying references outside the Book of Psalms. Many of these passages may not only use similar wording but also refer to the actual ceremony. And so there is evidence elsewhere in the Bible that seems to refer to cultic happenings akin to what you may have reconstructed in the preceding exercises.

1.   Read 1 Samuel 1:1—2:10. How do these two chapters help you understand the two groups of psalms isolated above?

2.   Study Hosea 14:1–7. Carefully reconstruct the different voices in this passage. Who speaks in 14:4? Who is speaking in 14:1–2, and who is invited to petition Yahweh in verses 2, 3? Now consider these voices as part of a *drama* (remember that a cultic ceremony is really a drama: words and actions); compare this drama in Hosea with the drama narrated in the Samuel passage above. Explain your answer.

3.   Read Lamentations 3:49–60. How does this "lamentation passage" fit in with the drama that you have reconstructed thus far?

4.   Many scholars think that large sections from the exilic prophet Second Isaiah (Book of Isaiah 40–55) were influenced by the individual lament ceremony that you have been trying to reconstruct. Read Isaiah 41:8–13, 14–16; 43:1–4, 5–7; and 44:1–5. What place would these passages have played in any such reconstructed ceremony?

5.   The form critic can also use comparative materials drawn from elsewhere in the ancient Near East. Read the following prophetic text of an oracle concerning the Assyrian king Esarhaddon (669 B.C.E.). Show how it is similar both to the Isaiah texts above and to the various speakers in your drama.

> I, the goddess Belit of Arbela, (say) to the king's mother, "Because you have complained to me (saying), 'What is to the right, what is to the left you place in your bosom; but where is the offspring of my heart? You let him be chased through the open country.' Now, O King, fear not! The royalty is in you, the might is in you indeed!"
> (James Pritchard, *ANET*, p. 450)

The Royal Psalms

Royal psalms include many of the varieties we have already studied. For example, there were royal laments (Psalms 22, 89), which were no different from the other laments except the "I" appears clearly to have been a king. There were the corresponding royal thanksgiving psalms (Psalms 18, 118). There was even a thoroughly secular psalm that celebrated a dynastic wedding with a Phoenician princess (Psalm 45). As you would expect, some psalms were related to the king's preparations for war (Psalm 20); many of these psalms also invoke the Zion Tradition, for the principle of the temple's inviolability could only reassure the monarch residing in the palace next to the Zion Temple.

Read Psalms 2, 72, 101, and 110, which have been linked with the Judean king's coronation. Study these psalms and then answer the following questions to help you reconstruct the biblical theology about the role of the monarch.

1.   What evidence is there that Psalm 101 is a *royal* psalm; that is, it refers to the king?

Some scholars would understand Psalm 101 as an actual example of the text of the "decree of Yahweh" referred to in Psalm 2 and as the "testimony" used in the coronation of King Jehoiada in 2 Kings 11:12. If so, then how would Psalm 101 have functioned in the coronation ritual?

2.   Read about the coronation of Solomon in 1 Kings 1:32–40. Where does the first part of the ceremony take place?

Could this explain the reference in Psalm 110:7?

According to the author of Genesis 2:4–3:24, where was the Garden of Eden located? (*Clue*: read Genesis 2:13.)

Relate the role of this stream with one of the elements of the Zion Tradition referred to earlier.

3.   Use Psalms 2, 72, and 110 to establish the theology of the king's role in Judean society. Be specific and illustrate from the texts.

Mark the different speakers in Psalm 110. How does this help us reconstruct the coronation ceremony? What does it say about the source of royal power in Judah?

When exactly does the king become Yahweh's son?

4.   How do these psalms help us understand the hymn in Isaiah 9:2–7a?

FURTHER READINGS

John Hayes, *Introduction to the Psalms* (Atlanta: Abingdon Press, 1967).

Herman Gunkel, *The Psalms* (Facet Books, Biblical Series 19; Philadelphia: Fortress Press, 1967).

J. J. M. Roberts, "The Davidic Origin of the Zion Tradition." *Journal of Biblical Literature* 92 (1973) 329-344.

____. "Zion Tradition," in *Interpreter's Dictionary of the Bible Supplementary Volume*, 985-987.

CHAPTER 10
THE WISDOM MOVEMENT

GOALS AND OBJECTIVES: This chapter serves to acquaint the student with the wide array of biblical literature attributed to the "Wisdom School," which the student will investigate by a close reading of two representative sapiential books, Proverbs and Qoheleth (also called Ecclesiastes). You will read passages that both stress an ordered, predictable universe (Proverbs) and those that question such stability (Qoheleth). These two extreme world views reveal the complexity of the intellectual and religious movement called Wisdom.

DIFFICULTIES IN STUDYING WISDOM

It is enigmatic but true that one of the most important intellectual and literary movements within the Bible, the *Wisdom Movement,* is also the least understood and appreciated. This becomes especially ironic because Wisdom offers theological and religious reflections that are remarkably in tune with those of the contemporary study of religion, which focuses on the broad ecumenical scope of religion, on the cosmopolitan interrelationship among world religions, on questions of doubt, on the relationship between the natural environment and humankind, and on human autonomy and material advancement. All of these interests were at the heart of Wisdom in the Hebrew Bible.

Wisdom and Salvation History

Until recently the Wisdom Tradition was denigrated for several reasons: First, it did not fit in with the standard direction of biblical theology that stressed the central role of the Mosaic Sinai Covenant. This was supposed to be the center of the Hebrew Bible around which every other movement revolved. All of biblical theology was summed up by the German word *Heilsgeschichte,* or "Salvation History," for the Bible supposedly recounted the sequence of events (history) whereby Israel's God made promises to the early fathers of Israel, then created a people as his own possession on Mount Sinai, and finally settled them upon the land of Palestine promised centuries before to the Patriarchs Abraham, Isaac, and Jacob. This linear/historical characterization of biblical theology was strengthened by its supposed contrast with the cyclical, nonhistorical, repetitive *nature myths* operative elsewhere in the ancient Near East. Because, until after 200 B.C.E. in the apocryphal works of Ben Sirach and the Wisdom of Solomon, the Wisdom Movement made no clear mention either of Sinai, the Promise to the Patriarchs, a covenantal relationship with Yahweh, or the temple cult, it was dismissed as mostly a *secular* movement. It was the sum of "human wisdom" in contrast to the "divine revelation" witnessed in Salvation History.

Many biblical scholars have also faulted the Wisdom Movement for its fundamental reliance on *order* in the cosmos; supposedly, in this regard, it lacks the dynamic, even disruptive, force of more traditional Yahwistic religion, as witnessed in the Law and Prophets, which had within it the power to challenge order and the accepted status quo. In a world dominated by myth, with insistence on the timeless and recurrent, the Exodus supposedly was a symbol that God was capable of interrupting events and of dramatically changing the status of a people: God could do something totally new! And so to many biblical scholars Wisdom, with its insistence that order and stability pervade all, seemed diametrically opposed to the radical challenge of the rest of the Hebrew Bible.

Wisdom and the Foreign Connection

Another reason why the Wisdom Tradition was denigrated was the striking similarity both in *content* and in *literary form* between Israelite wisdom and traditions in her pagan surroundings—especially in Egypt—that made sapiential "orthodoxy" supremely suspect. For example, large sections of the Book of Proverbs (Proverbs 22:17–24:22) have probably been translated from the work of the Egyptian sage Amen-em-opet. Israel herself recognized the preeminence of Wisdom among her neighbors (1 Kings 4:29–34), and one of the Israelite Wisdom books, namely Job, has non-Israelite heroes. Proverbs 30:1 and 31:1 attribute their list of sayings to Agur and Lemuel, non-Israelites from Massa. Thus, the absence of citations from Israel's own peculiar religious tradition (often reduced by scholars to the theological center of Covenant), coupled with affinities for foreign materials, has tended to relegate the Wisdom Movement to the sidelines as a foreign contamination. How could there be "divine relevation" in such borrowed, secular material?

Wisdom and the Canon of the Bible

A third factor that worked against the acceptance of this tradition was the matter of *canonicity*. If we limit, as we shall, the extent of this movement to the Books of Job, Qoheleth (Ecclesiastes), Proverbs, Ben Sirach (Ecclesiasticus), and the Wisdom of Solomon, a problem emerges. The last two books, Sirach and the Wisdom of Solomon, are not in the canon of the Hebrew Bible. That means, these two books are not part of that list of books agreed to around the beginning of the second century of the Common Era, which is authoritative for the Jewish religion. The latter two are, of course, also dropped from the canon of Old Testament biblical books used by Protestants, for they too have accepted the Jewish list. Only the Roman Catholics and Greek Orthodox accept Sirach and the Wisdom of Solomon as canonical or authoritative. Their contested status has relegated them to a category called either **Deuterocanonical** ("second canon") or **Apocrypha** ("hidden books"). Because almost one-half of the Wisdom corpus was suspect to Jewish and Protestant scholars, study of the entire movement suffered. The emergence of the ecumenical spirit following the Second Vatican Council has helped erase Protestant and Jewish suspicions concerning the Apocrypha in the Catholic Bible.

How Does One Define "Wisdom"?

Still another problem that has hindered the investigation of the Israelite Wisdom Tradition is the difficulty that scholars encounter in trying both to define the term "wisdom" and to delimit its extent in the Bible. Definitions of ḤOKMAH ("wisdom") extend from the very terse ("ability to cope") to a more comprehensive definition:

> The quest for self-understanding in terms of relationships with things and the Creator . . . on three levels: (1) nature wisdom which is an attempt to master things for human survival and well-being, and which includes the drawing up of onomastica and study of natural phenomena as they relate to man and the universe; (2) juridical and *Erfahrungsweisheit* (practical wisdom) with the focus upon human relationships in an ordered society or state; and (3) theological wisdom, which moves in the realm of theodicy, and in so doing affirms God as ultimate meaning.[1]

Scholarly efforts to detect the influence of this biblical movement, which has been so difficult to pin down with a definition, have been equally controversial. To some, evidence of sapiential editing or composition extends from the primeval history in Genesis 1–11 and the Joseph story (Genesis 37, 39–50) to the writing of the history of the kings of Israel and Judah. Even the book of Deuteronomy is held to be the product of the sages. Other researchers, this author included, find it more profitable to restrict the Wisdom literary corpus to the Books of Proverbs, Job, Qoheleth (Ecclesiastes), Ben Sirach (Ecclesiasticus), and the Wisdom of Solomon. In the following exercises we are forced by the space constraints of an *Introduction* to confine our treatment to the Books of Proverbs and Qoheleth (also called Ecclesiastes). These two works, however, will suffice to acquaint the student with the broad and often contradictory nature of Israelite Wisdom.

DEFINING WISDOM

Let us try to derive from the Book of Proverbs an understanding both of the troublesome term "Wisdom" and of its main concerns. The Hebrew word for wisdom (ḤAKAM) broadly defined means "to be skilled, proficient" (compare the artisans imported for Solomon from Tyre in 1 Kings 7:13ff., who are described as ḤAKAM). What, however, remains to be learned from the Wisdom corpus is the precise sense in which the "wise/skilled" person may be said to be ḤAKAM.

1.   Read Proverbs 1–9. This section probably represents the preface of the postexilic editors who assembled the various collections that follow. Here we find the understanding of the editors about the meaning of ḤOKMAH ("wisdom").

Read through these chapters and mark the occurrences of the word "wisdom"; write out a definition that would account for all the uses you have encoun-

---

[1] J. Crenshaw, "Method in Determining Wisdom Influence upon 'Historical' Literature," *Journal of Biblical Literature,* 88 (1969): 130.

tered. (Be sure to make use of your knowledge of Hebrew poetical parallelism, for these proverbs are poetry; oftentimes the author's concept of a term will be further developed in the parallel colon.) Make your definition as specific and concrete as possible. Be sure to justify it with regard to the biblical text.

Compile a list of terms used by the poet in parallelism with "wisdom." How does this list further our understanding of the term?

Read the important introduction to the Book of Proverbs (1:2–7), probably composed by its postexilic editor. The following translation from W. McKane, *Proverbs* (Philadelphia: Westminster, 1970) captures the tenor of the major vocabulary employed by the Wisdom Movement (important words in italics).

> (2) To take note of *wisdom* and *instruction*, to grasp *perceptive sayings*. (3) To receive *effective instruction*, righteousness, justice, and equity; (4) to give *shrewdness* to the *untutored*, *knowledge* and *resourcefulness* to the youth—(5) the *wise man* listens and appropriates more *wisdom* and the *perceptive* man learns the ropes. (6) To grasp a *proverb* and an *allusion*, the words of the wise and their *riddles*. (7) The *fear of Yahweh* is the beginning of *knowledge*; fools despise *wisdom* and *instruction*.

If these verses reflect the editor's purpose in compiling the Book of Proverbs, state in your own words what is the objective of the Wisdom Movement as stated by this unknown editor.

What human faculties are most involved in this process of "becoming wise"? In other words, according to the text, where in the human person does this specific type of proficiency called **ḤOKMAH** reside? Is it in the *hands* of the artisan? In the *clever speech* of the courtier? In the *mind* of the intellectual? (Remember that the Israelites considered the "heart" to be the center of intelligence and understanding.)

2.   Suppose you overhear a doctor giving the following advice to a patient: "Abstain from sugar and refrain from a diet high in carbohydrates, limit your calories, and try to get as much exercise as possible." Hearing this, a person could readily infer that the problem being addressed is obesity, which poses a health problem. Diet is being suggested as the answer to the question, "What should an overweight person do to improve his or her life?" Back to Proverbs! Throughout Proverbs 1–9 the editor offers a solution, or course, recommended to alleviate a problem or to answer a question. What is this *unstated* question that lies behind the solution being recommended in these first nine chapters of Proverbs? The editor of chapters 1–9 offers a whole series of recommendations. What exact question is the editor trying to answer? Or what problem is the editor trying to resolve by writing this book?

Notice all the references to the term "life" in the early section of Proverbs (2:19, 3:13–18, 5:6, 8:35, 10:11, 10:16–17, 11:19, 11:30). What *exactly* do the passages understand by "life"? What characteristics make up this "life"? Does the answer to this question help you better formulate your previous answer regarding the unspoken issue behind the answers/recommendations of Proverbs 1–9?

Read Qoheleth (or Ecclesiastes) 2:3; how does Qoheleth's search compare with the "question to be answered" in the Book of Proverbs?

3.   Many scholars maintain that wisdom is *anthropocentric,* that is, unlike the Book of Psalms, the interests of the Book of Proverbs are supposedly oriented toward the human rather than toward God. Let us test whether this is true of our introductory section in Proverbs 1–9. Here we find God mentioned several times. How exactly does God function with regard to humans in these passages? To begin with a specific example, look at Proverbs 3:7–10. In this passage where is the author's real interest: In God or with humans? Explain your response and look for other examples that support your position.

4.   In Proverbs 1–9 the editor offers his students countless recommendations. On what authority? Why should the reader listen to this advice? The source of authority is quite clear for the prophet, who continually reminds his listener, "Thus says Yahweh!" But on whose authority should the reader listen to these proverbs?

How do the "motivation clauses" contained in Proverbs 24:16 and 21–22 help you understand the authority behind these proverbs?

THE MAIN MOTIFS OF THE WISDOM MOVEMENT

What areas of life fell within the scope of Israelite Wisdom? Again, let us turn to the Book of Proverbs. In Proverbs 2 the final editor, who wrote the introductory Proverbs 1–9, offers a small sample of some of the main motifs in the book as a whole. In the left-hand column below you will see the main sections in Proverbs, chapter 2; to its right, in the second column, describe the main concerns of each of those sections in chapter 2. In the third column list passages in Proverbs 3–9 that elaborate on each of those motifs. In the fourth and right-hand column cite at least one passage in the older parts of the Book of Proverbs, that is, in chapters 10–22:16

and 25–29, that take up these motifs.[2] (In this exercise try to withdraw yourself a little from specifics, and just indicate broad categories. Thus, you might classify several maxims under the motif of "stability/order within authority.")

In this exercise you gradually move from the main motifs listed in the "table of contents" (Proverbs 2) of the final editor to that editor's complete introduction (Proverbs 3–9) and finally to the main subjects considered in the oldest levels of the book (Proverbs 10–22:16 and 25–29), for which that editor wrote his nine-chapter preface.

MAIN MOTIFS IN THE BOOK OF PROVERBS

I MAIN SECTIONS IN PROVERBS 2	II MAIN MOTIFS OF EACH SECTION IN PROVERBS 2	III SIMILAR MOTIFS IN PROVERBS 3-9	IV SIMILAR MOTIFS IN PROVERBS 10–22:16; 25-29
2:1-8			(At least one citation!)
2:9-11			
2:12-15			
2:16-19			

[2] You will notice that we are proceeding according to the natural divisions within the book itself: Proverbs 2 provides a thumbnail sketch of the total introduction in Proverbs 1–9, which then introduces the larger collections.

MAIN MOTIFS IN THE BOOK OF PROVERBS (cont.)

I MAIN SECTIONS IN PROVERBS 2	II MAIN MOTIFS OF EACH SECTION IN PROVERBS 2	III SIMILAR MOTIFS IN PROVERBS 3-9	IV SIMILAR MOTIFS IN PROVERBS 10-22:16; 25-29
2:20-22			

THE WISDOM VIEW OF THE WORLD

A proper understanding of Wisdom begins with the assumption that lies behind the Chaos Myth witnessed so often in the Book of Psalms: This world is an ordered reality. The Israelite assumes harmony (Hebrew **ṢEDAQAH**) in the spheres of (1) nature, (2) human society, and (3) in the religious relationship between believers and their deity; indeed, all three of these areas were held to form an interrelated harmony, whose accord stemmed from the activity of Yahweh as Creator.

The Works of Yahweh have existed
  from the beginning by his creation,
And when he made them,
  he determined their divisions.
He arranged his works in an eternal order,
  and their dominion for all generations;
They neither hunger nor grow weary,
  and they do not cease from their labors.
They do not crowd one another aside,
  and they will never disobey his word. (Sirach 16:24-28)

For another example of Yahweh's ordering of Creation, read Psalm 104. Indeed, the frequency of the Creation motif in Wisdom literature attests to the centrality of this concept as the keystone to Hebrew **ṢEDAQAH**, which can significantly refer to cosmic order, political legitimacy and social justice, and divine grace.[3]

1. Read Proverbs 8:1-36.

Who is speaking in this section? That is, who is the "I/me" in verses 4, 15, 16, 17, 20, 22, 23, etc.?

---

[3] This order was called *MA'AT* in Egypt and *ME* in Mesopotamia.

Describe Wisdom's role at Creation in Proverbs 8:22–31.

Compare the view(s) of the world reflected in Psalm 104 with that behind Proverbs 8:22–31.

The sages maintained that the wise person (**ḤAKAM**) successfully integrated him or herself into this created order, whether on the level of the natural universe which one sought to understand, or in the sphere of human relationships, where one believed in an orderly society.[4] Psalm 37 describes this order on the level of human

---

[4] The final editor of the Book of Proverbs may have concretely demonstrated his belief in the order within the world by his arrangement of its parts (redaction criticism):

PART I	Proverbs 1–9	235 lines
	2–7 form 7 columns of 22 verses each (= number of the letters of the Hebrew alphabet). These form the "7 columns" in Wisdom's house of Proverbs 9:1	
PART II	Proverbs 10:1—22:16	375 lines
	Solomon's Collection. The word "Solomon" in Hebrew adds up to 375! (The letters of the Hebrew alphabet have numerical value.)	
PART III	Proverbs 22:17—24:34	97 lines
	Sayings of the Wise People	
PART IV	Proverbs 25–29	139 lines
	Sayings of men of Hezekiah. "Hezekiah" = 130 in Hebrew!	
	Appended Material	86 lines
Total lines		932 lines

In Proverbs 1:1 we are introduced by the editor to the book of *Solomon,* son of *David,* king of *Israel.* These three proper nouns in Hebrew add up to 930, if we assign the Hebrew letters their numerical values. If these occurrences are not mere chance, as seems to be the case, then the editor by his careful arrangement of the sections sought to establish a paradigm of literary order mimicking his concept of the universe. Such a concept of a numerical symbolism of cosmic order was also found in his Greek contemporary Pythagoras.

affairs, where such **ṢEDAQAH** assumes the shape of the ethical doctrine of *retribution*. This concept has been well expressed in G. von Rad's book on Wisdom:

> The most characteristic feature of her (Israel's) understanding of reality lay in the first instance in the fact that she believed man to stand in a quite specific, highly dynamic, existential relationship with his environment.[5]

1.   Find at least three proverbs in the Book of Proverbs that show concern for *order* or *harmony* in the areas of (1) nature, (2) human social interaction, and (3) the relationship between the believer and Yahweh.

Nature:

Human social interaction:

Believer and Yahweh:

Order and Mastery

The wise sought to discover the continuity between the natural world around them and human activities. This effort results in the frequent number of *similitudes* in the Book of Proverbs, which liken some human characteristic with nature (6:6–8, 26:1–3, 30:18–33). But the sage hopes "to control" or "master" his or her situation by detecting this interwoven tapestry, much as today's scientists study genetics in the hope of eventually exercising control over gene expression. Knowledge of the *likenesses* throughout Creation can yield *control* and *harmony* to the sage.

[5] G. von Rad, *Wisdom in Israel,* trans. by James D. Martin (Nashville: Abingdon Press, 1972), p. 301.

Order and Disorder

However, we must never lose sight of the fact that wise people of the ancient Near East were not Pollyannaish. They, like us, were perfectly aware of the evils and *disorders* that pervaded their experience of the world. The very literary nature of the *proverb* appears to recognize this. The proverbial aphorism portrays both a *concrete/ specific* and a *generalized* situation. In fact, the charm and effect of the proverb depends on this mixture. "A well-fed person will disdain honey" (Proverbs 27:7). Here we have a concrete observation that also aspires to the generalized observation that the content can afford to be choosy; the concrete proverb, however, is obviously more noticeable in its specific formulation. This specificity, however, also prohibits the proverb from posing as a universal truth. The typical proverb easily allows exceptions; and so, we all might well have experienced successful and wealthy people who are not so picky. In one dramatic case two contradictory proverbs are placed alongside each other:

> Do not answer a fool when he speaks nonsense, lest you too, are reduced to his level. Answer a fool when he speaks nonsense, lest he suppose himself to be a wise person. (Proverbs 26:4–5)

Although proverbs suggest cases of widespread validity, they do not purport to offer absolute laws of nature.

> Since any given proverb may or may not be appropriate in a particular situation, their truth is conditional and relative, not absolute. They can not be taken as unambiguous statements of "that which really is."[6]

Supposedly the official Yahwist religion of Israel tended to "defamiliarize" its believer, that is, to disorient believers from comfortable familiarity and expected order. This is often contrasted with proverbial wisdom, which typically represents the ordinary and everyday. Nevertheless, many proverbs, which argue from *analogy,* likewise seek to "defamiliarize" and disorient precisely by unexpected and startling relationships drawn between normally unassociated ideas. This is particularly true of the numerical proverbs, which associate a specific number of seemingly unrelated items.

> Three things there are which are too wonderful for me, four which I do not understand: the way of a vulture in the sky, the way of a serpent on the rock, the way of a ship out at sea, and the way of a man with a woman. (Proverbs 30:18–19)

The sage delights in astonishing comparisons:

> The way of an adulteress is this: she eats, then wipes her mouth and says, "I have done no harm." (Proverbs 30:20)

Such allegories prod the reader to stop and think on the unusual association of a casual meal with casual sex.

[6] John J. Collins, "Proverbial Wisdom and the Yahwist Vision," *Semeia*, 17 (1980) 6.

The wise folk of the Near East were also aware of such limitations inherent in human wisdom as to preclude the formulation of immutable natural laws:

> There is no wisdom, no understanding, no counsel against Yahweh. The horse is made ready for the day of battle but victory belongs to Yahweh (Proverbs 21:30-31). The plans of the mind belong to man, but the answer of the tongue comes from Yahweh. (Proverbs 16:1)[7]

The limitation of human wisdom did *not* represent an intrusion of Yahwism into the Wisdom Movement, for sages elsewhere were equally aware that even wise people could not uncover unexceptionable, predictable laws. And so the Egyptian sage Amen-em-opet remarked, "One thing are the words which men say, another is that which the god does." And a Babylonian sage observed, "The will of a god is difficult to find out." The uncertainty of experience prompted Amen-em-opet to state that "man knows not what the morrow is like."

The very use of the literary format of the *proverb* is probably significant. The wise person sees reality mirrored in thousands of disconnected, discreet little observations—many of which are even contradictory. There are no general or always-applicable rules—just countless observations, none of which applies to every circumstance at all times. In other words, the very choice of the literary style of the "proverb" is itself an observation about reality. Even today the proverbial style is a favorite of philosophers and thinkers (Wittgenstein, Kafka, Nietzsche, for example) and theologians (Pascal) who believe that the times do not justify the smugness of capturing life in general rules and principles.

> I will write here my thoughts without order, although not in confusion without design: This is the true order, and it will always mark my goal by disorder itself—I would honor my subject too much if I treated it in order, because I want to show that it is incapable of it. (Blaise Pascal, *Pensées* 71)

REDACTION CRITICISM OF THE BOOK OF PROVERBS

As we have already suggested, the Book of Proverbs is composed of different collections stemming from different time periods (see Proverbs 25:1) and even different countries (Proverbs 30:1, 31:1). Chapters 10:1–22:16 and 24:23–29:27 seem to have been separate sources. These documents were probably combined by an editor (redactor) who appended an introduction (Proverbs 1-9) and arranged the hymn to the woman of valor (31:10-31) at the conclusion. These two sections form a sort of *inclusion* in that the images of the "wise woman" (chapter 31) or "wisdom as woman" (chapters 1-9) come to prominence by this placement. Chapters 1-9 contrast wisdom as a woman calling and enriching her disciples (1:20 ff., 3:13-18, 8:22-36) with the "strange/foreign woman" (2:16-19, 5:3-8, 7:10-23) who brings death and deception. Chapter 31 sings the praises of the woman who prudently manages her household;[8] her praise even extends to the center of male power, the city gates (31:31).

Before this post-586 B.C.E. editing of the book, "wisdom" had been closely identified with the monarchy. Read the legends in 1 Kings 3:1-14 and 4:29-34.

---

[7] See Proverbs 16:2, 9; 19:14, 21; 20:24.

[8] Surprisingly, in Proverbs 31:21 the term used is "*her* house," which almost seems a play on the normal Hebrew expression "patriarchal house" (**bêt 'ab**).

Whatever the truth behind these stories, it remains clear that wisdom was *par excellence* an attribute of the successful king.[9] Although Psalm 72 does not use the Hebrew word **HAKAM** ("wise"), it is clear that the king was the guarantor of the social stability (**SEDAQAH**) identified with **HOKMAH** ("wisdom").

The postexilic redaction of the Book of Proverbs, however, has transferred the attention of the Wisdom Tradition away from the now defunct royal court into the home administered by the Israelite woman (Proverbs 31). As we shall see in the emergence of the so-called short stories of Ruth and Esther in the next chapter of this text, in the period after the Exile and when the Book of Proverbs was finally edited, women seem to replace men as the focal point of the new community.

> In a situation where the male mediator of justice [the king] is ineffective—indeed, in this case, lost forever—[female Wisdom] does what Israel had literally come to expect its women to do: she matter-of-factly steps in and makes her own work do for both God's and men's. The tradition does not, moreover, end with her but continues in the later stories of Esther and Judith. . . . Given the lack of real political power in Judah at this time, the feminization of wisdom enhanced its ability to reflect accurately Israel's situation with respect to its foreign masters while at the same time holding out a viable hope for a new kind of "power" defined in terms of faith rather than politics, and located in the home rather than in a national government.[10]

SAPIENTIAL LITERARY FORMS

The Wisdom Movement expressed itself in a myriad of literary forms depending on the social circumstances in which life skills (**HOKMAH**) were being taught (form criticism). The table below offers a sample of such forms and the probable original setting for each.

SOCIAL SITUATION AND LITERARY FORM

SOCIAL SETTING	LITERARY FORMAT	PURPOSE
Family and Clan	Hortatory and Proverbs	Mastery of Life
Royal Court	Didactic	Educate Select
Scribal School	Dialogue and Admonition	Reflection and Speculation

DESCRIPTION OF LITERARY FORMS

PROVERB A *proverb* is a short saying that exists in a variety of forms: (1) sentence (Proverbs 10:6); (2) instruction, exhortation, or admonition (Proverbs 3:25-)[11]; (3) numerical (Proverbs 6:16-19); (4) comparison or exclusion (Proverbs 12:9, 15:16-17); (5) and antithetical proverb (Proverbs 10-15).

[9] The superscriptions in Proverbs 1:1, 10:1, and 25:1 recall the close association between Solomon and wisdom.

[10] Claudia Camp, "Wisdom and the Feminine in the Book of Proverbs" (Doctoral Dissertation, Duke University, 1982), pp. 312, 313.

[11] Notice how often these are accompanied by *motive clauses,* which demonstrate their didactic orientation.

SOCIAL SITUATION AND LITERARY FORM

DESCRIPTION OF LITERARY FORMS (CONT'D)

RIDDLES	A *riddle* functions as a verbal paradox that is presented as a model of reality itself. Its clearest form in the Hebrew Bible is in Judges 14:10-18; but we also can find examples in Proverbs 23:29-35; 23:27; 16:15; 20:27; 25:2-3; 27:20; 5:1-6—all of which have merely to be reformulated in an interrogative format: What is . . . ?
FABLES AND ALLEGORIES	The *fable* is characterized by a cast of characters that are animals or plants and thus approach the ludicrous; for example, see Judges 9:8-15. The *allegory* is a story, all the elements of which have a double meaning. See Proverbs 5:15-23 and Qoheleth 12:1-6.
HYMN AND PRAYER	*Hymns* are especially prevalent in Sirach (for example, 42:15—43:33). Especially important in this literary form are hymns that celebrate Yahweh's creation in Wisdom: Proverbs 1:20-33; 8; Sirach 24:1-22; Wisdom of Solomon 6:12-20; 7:22—8:21. Many of the Psalms seem to have been formulated or edited by the sages: See Psalms 1, 112, 127.
DIALOGUE	The Book of Job uses the *dialogue* format, which was so common in sapiential literature in the ancient Near East.

THE BOOK OF QOHELETH

The Book of Qoheleth (its Hebrew name) or Ecclesiastes (its Greek and English title) is one of the most puzzling, but beguiling, books in the Hebrew Scriptures. It provides almost no usable evidence for the historical-cultural critic. The narrator's name, "Qoheleth," is not a proper name at all but apparently a title or office, although it is not used anyplace else in Hebrew; it is derived from a root (**QHL**), meaning "to gather" or "to assemble." "Qoheleth" has sometimes been translated as the "Preacher," for this root is often used of the worshipping "assembly"; and so Qoheleth was the one who presided over the congregation, that is, the "Preacher." Because Qoheleth does not seem particularly interested in worship or cult, perhaps he was a "collector" of students, that is, a philosopher of the day who "gathered" around himself disciples. However, this cryptic "assembler" also portrays himself as the great King Solomon (1:1)[12]—although he never actually uses that name. In reality, this guise, upon which Qoheleth never really insists, seems fictional; for the Hebrew language of the book stems from a period at least 500 years after Solomon. The book also lacks unambiguous references to historical events that could provide the historical critic with a handle by which to date the book.

The religious stance of the book is equally perplexing. Qoheleth avoids the mention of elements specific to Israel's religion: the Zion Tradition, Sinai Covenant, the Prophets, Moses, Yahweh; to our narrator, God is the impersonal "deity." His tone, with its emphasis on life's boundaries imposed by the certainty of death, is so grim that some scholars have said that the book serves to warn believers how far astray they can go before they must heed the more obviously religious books of the

---

[12] After all, who else was "the son of David, king in Jerusalem"?

Bible: that is, the book serves as a "bad example"! The reader can see how unusual the religion of Qoheleth is by examining an editor's postscript in 12:9–14.[13] This postscript seems to be an attempt to bring the book more in line with customary religion, which by this time was the Law of Moses and its commandments (Qoheleth 12:13: "Fear God and keep his commandments!"). The addendum was probably composed by someone who was assembling the Wisdom Literature into a collection ("the sayings of the wise"), which then had to be related to the authoritative Law of Moses (the Pentateuch). It functions then in a similar way to such editorial comments as Malachi 4:4 and Hosea 14:9.

The literary critic also has problems with the Book of Qoheleth. Not only are there apparent contradictions (compare 7:4 with 8:15 and the morbid 3:19–21 with 12:7), but also the work seems to lack clear structure and literary organization. Thus, literary critics can proceed in two ways. One way would be to form an intuition of the meaning of a work and *then* follow up with an attempt to show how the structure of the work communicates that intuited meaning. This approach works when the piece is straightforward; for example, it might have worked in our reading of the Creation account in Genesis 1:1—2:4a. However, this "direct" method is far too subjective when the reader faces more complex passages such as the Book of Qoheleth. A second way would be to avoid *predetermining* the author's thesis; let us put our search for structure or literary organization first; we can speculate later on the meaning(s) conveyed once we have determined these structural patterns. This is obviously going to be difficult in a work that seems to lack any organization; but in fact, Qoheleth might be one of the most carefully structured books in the Hebrew Bible.

The questions that follow are divided into four groups. The first group will assist the student to establish the extent of Qoheleth's text (text criticism). If there have been additions or alterations to this original text, you must determine these, for they would obviously affect your efforts to outline the author's own structure. The second set of study questions will guide you through your efforts to sketch the literary patterns of the book.[14] Third, I shall call your attention to the author's uses of certain key words in the book. Finally, you will then begin to build on these data to speculate on the thesis or meaning of the work.

The Text of the Book of Qoheleth

1.   Read through the Book of Qoheleth carefully, including any introduction or footnotes found in your particular edition of the Bible.

2.   Let us consider the possibility of later additions to the text. Many scholars think that 12:9–13 was written by another author (possibly by several authors).

First, do verses 9–13 stand *within* or *without* the overall structure of the book? Ancient writers particularly liked to employ inclusion[15] as a device to delimit the literary boundaries of the work. Look at 12:8; where else in the book does the

---

[13] For our purposes here it is really irrelevant how many editors might have contributed to these ending verses; the addition(s) provide a commentary on how the previous material in 1:1—12:8 was considered.

[14] Remember, at this stage do not worry about the *meaning* of the book.

[15] *Inclusion* is the device whereby an author begins and ends his or her work using the same phrase, word, sentence; often this phrase mentions significant motifs in the book.

phrase "Vanity of vanities, says Qoheleth, all is vanity" occur? Does this evidence help us determine the status of 12:9–14?

Let us check whether these verses (12:9–14) agree with the sentiment found in the rest of the Book of Qoheleth. Remember to be quite specific in your responses; always justify your answers by referring to the biblical text itself.

Would Qoheleth agree with the sentiment expressed in 12:13 that "This is the sum of the matter, when all has been heard: Fear God and keep His commandments; for this applies to everything!"? Explain your answer.

What does Qoheleth say about divine judgment? Would he agree with the statement, "For God will bring every deed into judgment, with every secret thing, whether good or evil" (12:14)?

Read the latter part of Qoheleth 11:9: "But know that for all these things God will bring you into judgment." Does this statement fit into its present context? How exactly does it resemble 12:14? Is the phrasing of this passage in 11:9 (especially "bring into judgment") found anyplace else in the book besides 12:14? What does this say about the status of this passage in 11:9?

3.   Look at 12:1. The Hebrew text says "Remember also your Creator in the days of your youth."

One small change in the Hebrew word for "your Creator" would yield "your grave." Which do you think was the original reading? Base your answer on both the context of the poem in which it now appears (11:9–12:7) and on the general tone of the book.

4.   Now, by way of summary, why do you think these changes might have been made in the book?

The Literary Structure of the Book of Qoheleth

The Book of Qoheleth employs inclusion on several levels.[16] First, the leitmotif, or central theme, of the book is signaled by the refrain in verses 1:2 and 12:8. Next, there is an inclusion set up by use of poetic bookends, for the book is bracketed by two poems, one at the very beginning in 1:3–11, and the final poem in 11:7–12:7. (These poems also encapsulate the entire thesis of the writer, but more about that later.) The author then has a double introduction (1:12–15 and 1:16–18) in which both parts exhibit identical patterns: an introductory statement, the phrase "all is vanity and a chasing after wind," and finally the quoting of a proverb. (The two proverbs together testify to the unavoidable frustration that confronts humans.)

And so the body of the Book of Qoheleth extends from 2:1 through 11:6. The structures that I have already indicated above suggest that this book is much more carefully organized than at first glance. The following questions will focus your attention on the structural features in the main body of the piece. We shall still suspend ideas on the *meaning* of Qoheleth until after these preliminary investigations.

1.   It appears that the best indication of the structure of Qoheleth is to be found in its use of refrains, those constantly recurring phrases. Go through your text of Qoheleth and, using colored markers, mark off in 2:1–11:6 the following phrases[17]:

(All is/was vanity) and a striving after wind

Not find out/who can find out (the good)

Not know/who knows (what comes after him).

---

[16] Qoheleth 1:1 is really just the title of the book and should be left out of consideration.

[17] Notice that the phrase "this (also) is vanity/all is vanity/all that comes is vanity" (see 2:15, 19, 21, 23; 3:19; 4:8; 5:9; 6:2; 7:6; 8:10, 14; 11:8) serves a structural function: It sets aside subtopics within the major divisions that you are about to establish.

2.   The first part of the book seems organized around the first refrain "(All is/ was vanity) and a striving after wind." (The refrain comes at the end and closes off the preceding section.) If so, where exactly does this first half of the book end?

List below the different sections that comprise the first half of Qoheleth as determined by the use of this refrain.

Literary critics always want to be sure that structures that they detect are not purely subjective. Thus, let us test our evidence. The existence of these divisions can be further confirmed by reading each and seeing if it is also unified around a general issue. In other words, does each section more or less treat a coherent topic? If so, try to give each section a one-sentence title that captures its theme. What common theme do *all* of these sections in the first half of the book treat? How well is this common theme reflected in verse 2:3?

3.   Look carefully at verses 6:10–12. They state that the human has no knowledge of what the deity has done for two reasons: (1) The human cannot find out what is good; and (2) the human cannot know what is to come afterwards. These latter two reasons form the rallying points for the last half of the book.

Notice how 7:1–8:17 is arranged around the refrain "not find out/who can find out" (the good for humans). What structural device indicates that 8:17 completes this section dealing with the search for the "good?"[18]

Most of this section seems to be an examination of *traditional wisdom*; for example, using proverbs in an attempt to "find out" the good, after which we all search for fulfillment. These traditional teachings, however, do not seem to give us any clear direction. How does Qoheleth indicate the shortcomings and failures of this wisdom? Is the wise person mentioned in 7:7–12 in a *better* position to know what is good than anyone else?

Now let us look at 9:1–11:6 and the use of the refrain "do not know/who knows." Notice that once again our refrain appears three times at the end of this section. Did the motif about our inability to know the future appear in the first half of the book?

4.   Why would our inability to discover what fulfills us ("the good") and to know the future paralyze or frustrate our efforts to control our lives? How does this observation fit in with the theme common to the investigations of the first half of the book?

[18] Notice how often the word "good" occurs in the section 7:1–8:17. In fact, the English word "better" used so often in the proverbs in 7:1–10 translates the Hebrew expression "good than."

5.   So far we have ignored another very important refrain. Look at all the times that Qoheleth recommends *pleasure* or *enjoyment* (2:24–26; 3:12, 22; 5:18–19; 8:15; 9:7; 11:8-9). First of all, what do you think the author means by "enjoyment"? Is it a wild hedonistic orgy? Relate his recommendations of enjoyment to the structure which you have already established. Secondly, how do these "pleasure" refrains interact with that overall pattern?

Key Words in the Book of Qoheleth

1.   Look at the following list of important words in Qoheleth. From what sphere of human endeavor have they been taken; in other words, are these words as a whole religious terms, economic, political, educational?

Profit	Toil	Business
Money/Silver	Portion	Success
Wealth	Owner	Deficit

Go through the Book of Qoheleth and see if you can mark these and other instances that support your answer. In summary, then, what *metaphor* does the author use to describe human life?[19]

The author of the Book of Qoheleth may use a certain metaphor to describe human life, but does he indicate whether he thinks that metaphor is really suitable or not? Is that particular way of looking at life *helpful* or is it in fact the *problem* itself according to Qoheleth? Be sure both to explain your answer clearly and to refer to the text itself. (As you can see we are moving closer to the meaning of the book.)

[19] If the writer uses—indeed, stresses—vocabulary derived from one particular field, then this indicates that the writer sees life *metaphorically* along the lines of that field. For example, the politician who constantly uses language such as "the ball's in my opponent's court," "he fields a good team," and "he's a team player" obviously sees politics according to a sports metaphor.

2. Of the 35 times that the word "toil" is used in the book, 24 are found in the first half. Based on just these statistics, it would seem safe to claim that the first half of Qoheleth is concerned with evaluating human "toil." First, what does Qoheleth mean by "toil"? How is it different from work? Next, what is the author's judgment on the value of human effort/toil? What precisely is there about "toil" that makes it suspect to the author?

3. Qoheleth frequently uses the word "lot" (Hebrew **heleq**): 2:1[20]; 3:22; 5:18, 19; 9:9. Explain what you think he means by this "lot." Where does a person's lot come from? Who is responsible for "allotting" it?

4. We have established that the word *toil* represents a major concept in the book. It is equally important to appreciate the relationship between the word "toil" and the important words "lot" and "profit/gain/advantage." In the following passages, *toil* occurs with either the word "lot" or with "profit":

TOIL

Profit/Advantage: 1:3; 2:11; 3:9; 5:16

Lot: 3:22; 5:18, 19; 9:9

In the Book of Qoheleth, one's toil can be viewed as either "lot" (5:18–19) or as "profit" (2:11). What is the difference between the two types of toil? And why is one type of human effort preferred over the other?

5. The author of Qoheleth clearly uses the word "vanity" so frequently that it has become the hallmark of this book. What exactly does this word mean *in terms of the book itself*? Elsewhere in the Bible this word (Hebrew **hebel**) means "fog," but this does not exactly tell us how it functions within this particular book. Read

---

[20] The RSV translates **heleq** here as "reward."

through Qoheleth and mark all the occurrences of the word "vanity." Then try to come up with a better English word that captures exactly how Qoheleth seems to use it. You might try by substituting the value X for it and then try to find a good idiomatic English expression to substitute for this X.[21]

The Meaning of the Book of Qoheleth

1.   Let us examine the two poems that serve to support the heart of the book like bookends. In a sense the entire thesis of Qoheleth is personified in the poems in 1:3–11 and 11:7–12:7.

2.   Read the first poem and note the description of nature in verses 4 through 7. If you were to convert this verbal picture to a diagram, how would you draw the dynamics of these natural forces? For example, as a straight line? What adjectives best describe the natural processes?

It seems that the poet offers these natural images of the wind blowing, the sun rising and setting, streams running to the sea, etc., as an answer to the initial question, What do humans gain by all their toil (verse 3)?[22] How do these examples put a limit on all human toil?

[21] In Hebrew the expression "X of X's" (for example, "Song of Songs" or "Vanity of Vanities") indicates the "best possible example of X"; in other words, the best example of a "song," the best example of a "vanity."

[22] The question in 1:3 provides the context in which the remainder of the poem is to be read.

Earlier you divided the book into two halves, which were oriented around different refrains. Show how the different themes in this first poem agree with the various sections of the body of the book. Explain your answer.

3.   Where else in the Book of Qoheleth does the author use examples from nature in order to counsel humans about their attitudes toward life?

4.   In this first poem, Qoheleth seems to warn the reader that there can be no profit in human toil because there is neither progress, novelty, remembrance of the past, nor foreknowledge of the future. Now read the second poem (11:7—12:8).

Notice that this beautiful poem separates into the two distinct themes of pleasure and death: the advice to enjoy youth (11:7-10), and the admonition to recall that there will be an end to even this delight as the body grows old (12:1-8). How do these two themes fit in with both sections of the body of the Book of Qoheleth?

5.   Now look at the two poems together and mark the movement of their argument. The first starts out by stressing the pointlessness of human labor and toil; the second then recommends that we enjoy our youth, but then reminds us that even this joy is not an *absolute* because it will eventually be checked by age and death.

I think that this dynamic (Negative evaluation, Enjoy!, Qualification) is carried into the body of the work. Look at sections 2:18-26; 3:16—4:3; 5:9—6:6;

6:7–9. Show how the dynamic movement of the two poems is carried over into these sections.

Is the ultimate meaning of life for Qoheleth pleasure? Has the author raised pleasure and enjoyment to that ultimate good for which he was searching in 7:1—8:17?

6. Do you think that the Book of Qoheleth is primarily pessimistic,[23] that is, that it presents a negative view of human life; or can it be seen as offering a positive view? Explain your answer.

As you recall, the Book of Proverbs was a guide for acquiring life in its fullest sense; this seems to have been an objective for the Wisdom Movement; does the Book of Qoheleth share this goal? Or is it a counter-book, a work directly opposed to the goal of a book like Proverbs?

[23] As most scholars do.

7.   Both Proverbs and Qoheleth base the authority of what they say on human experience.[24] How does Qoheleth's use of *experience* differ from that of Proverbs? Whose experience is often cited in Proverbs; whose in Qoheleth?

Why would Qoheleth disallow that long chain of experience passed from one generation to another?

8.   Now for the true test! State in a few sentences what you think is the *thesis* of the author of the Book of Qoheleth.

FURTHER READINGS

Wisdom Literature

Bernhard W. Anderson, *Understanding the Old Testament*, 4th ed. (Englewood Cliffs, NJ: Prentice-Hall, 1986), pp. 570–603.

James L. Crenshaw, *Old Testament Wisdom: An Introduction* (Atlanta: John Knox, 1981).

Norman K. Gottwald, *The Hebrew Bible: A Socio-Literary Introduction* (Philadelphia: Fortress Press, 1985), pp. 563–582.

Gerhard von Rad, *Wisdom in Israel* (New York: Abingdon Press, 1973).

---

[24] In the Prophets, the authority is based more directly in the revealed word of the deity ("The Word of Yahweh!"); although there are passages in Proverbs that suggest divine revelation, in general the wise person's counsels should be obeyed because they conform to obvious human experience.

J. Coert Rylaarsdam, *Revelation in Jewish Wisdom Literature* (Chicago: Chicago University, 1946). This is an excellent book that shows how the Wisdom Movement sought to reconcile itself with the Torah.

James G. Williams, *Those Who Ponder Proverbs: Aphoristic Thinking and Biblical Literature* (Sheffield, England: Almond, 1981). This is a study of the literary nature of the proverb used in the Bible.

The Book of Qoheleth

Edwin Good, *Irony in the Old Testament* (Sheffield, England: Almond, 1981), pp. 168-195.

Addison Wright, "The Riddle of the Sphinx: The Structure of the Book of Qoheleth," *Catholic Biblical Quarterly,* 30 (1968): 313-334.

____ , "The Riddle of the Sphinx Revisited: Numerical Patterns in the Book of Qoheleth," *Catholic Biblical Quarterly*, 42 (1980): 38-51.

CHAPTER 11
THE JEWISH SHORT STORY
Ruth, Esther, and Judith

GOALS AND OBJECTIVES: This chapter studies some of the last writings to achieve canonical status in the Hebrew Bible; in fact, the Book of Judith never did acquire such authority. Chapter 11 furthers the student's use of literary criticism; it also acquaints the reader with the historical and religious situation in the Jewish community during those dark days after the return from Babylonian Exile that are otherwise so poorly documented. In these three stories the culturally perceived "weakness" of women becomes a symbol for new concepts of power.

The centuries after the return from the Babylonian Exile (538 B.C.E.) were difficult politically and religiously. The glorious New Exodus promised by Second Isaiah (chapters 40–55) and the (re-)fulfillment of the threefold divine promise heralded by the exilic Priestly Writer seemed empty. Those returning from the Babylonian Exile found themselves in immediate conflict with the majority of the people who had stayed in Palestine after its devastation by Nabuchadnezzar in 586 B.C.E. The main issue was, Who would assume leadership of the community now that the Davidic Dynasty was no longer in power? The destroyed Temple of Solomon was indeed to be rebuilt—in fact, the Persian King Cyrus had given funds for its reconstruction. However, which line of the priesthood would assume control of the new shrine? Where they the Levites, who were a Mosaic priesthood or the Zadokites who traced their lineage at least as far as David's appointee Zadok? Furthermore, there were still supporters of the Davidic family who hoped to restore a survivor of that dynasty to the throne.[1] Obviously, any such efforts would be interpreted by the Persian overlords as a rebellion to be suppressed.

All of these destabilizing factors were compounded by the religious problem of reconciling the current diminished situation with the more grandiose theology of the monarchy. How could the people adapt the "eternal" divine promises of a permanent dynasty in Jerusalem (Davidic Covenant) with the foreign occupation of

---

[1] See the Prophets Haggai and Zechariah (chapters 1–8), who both wished to restore the situation *prior* to 586 B.C.E. They urged the immediate completion of the new temple, the restoration of an independent Davidic Dynasty, and power for the old royal Zadokite priesthood.

the promised land? How could they reconcile the exalted status of Mount Zion (Zion Tradition) with the perilous situation after 586 B.C.E.?

Furthermore, the Israelites had to face the problem of their relationship to other peoples and gods. Who was Yahweh compared to Marduk or, later under the Greeks, compared to Zeus Olympios? There was also the dilemma of Jews living outside of Palestine (the *Diaspora*). After 586 B.C.E., Jews had settled over the entire eastern Mediterranean in Asia Minor, Egypt, and Mesopotamia. How could they worship Yahweh apart from the promised land and temple, which had been the center of the Priestly, Deuteronomistic, and Chronicler religious visions?

Under Persian control (about 540–330 B.C.E.), much of this turmoil had been addressed by the reforms of Ezra, which resulted in adoption of the Law (Pentateuch). After Alexander the Great conquered the Persian Empire, this area was to be ruled by a succession of Hellenistic states, which combined Greek culture with Near Eastern features to result in the uniquely cosmopolitan civilization called *Hellenism*. This culture proved particularly seductive to many Jews. Many thoroughly accommodated their religion to this new movement; others fiercely resisted its encroachments; nevertheless, almost all used its thoughts and language as a vehicle for reexpressing Yahwistic religion.

During the late postexilic period (about 400–100 B.C.E.) we encounter two significant developments, one literary and the other theological: the evolution of the *short story literary genre* in the Bible, and a focus on the *woman as savior of Israel.*[2] All three of the stories covered in this chapter—Ruth, Esther, and Judith[3]—are examples of this new literary type, the short story, in which we follow a small group of characters through a single brief plot to its resolution. Scholars can point to early examples of similar stories in Genesis 24, 38, the Joseph saga in Genesis 37, 39–50, and the Davidic succession story in 2 Samuel 9–20 and 1 Kings 1, 2. However, these stories had been embedded in larger books and had been interwoven into a larger literary fabric. The three examples in this chapter were totally independent books. Although their dating remains an object of considerable controversy,[4] the emergence of this story type, which imitates historical tales, seems late.[5]

The Hebrew Scriptures had already noted important women (Deborah, Miriam, Huldah, Bathsheba, etc.), but never before had women played such a central role throughout an entire plot. Furthermore, in these three books women are forced to assume the part of liberator *precisely because* men have failed. These late stories even emphasize the contrast between *male* and *female* virtues: The male values of military prowess (Book of Judith), regal control (Book of Esther), and economic/social clout (Book of Ruth) are incapable of providing for the Jews and are superseded by a beautiful widow (Judith), a comely and assertive queen (Esther), and a sexually aggressive foreigner (Ruth). In all three of these stories the main weapon of the heroine is her female sexuality. All three women—a foreigner, an orphan, and a widow—are described as stereotypes of weakness in a world perceived as dominated by males; nevertheless, by beauty, cunning, and assertiveness they save both themselves and the Jewish people whether at home in Israel (Books of Judith and Ruth) or in the Diaspora (Book of Esther). These three books are perfect models for the weak postexilic community that existed in a hostile environment. The old reliance on military prowess and the Davidic dynasty had failed the nation, which must now look for strength within its own apparent debility.

As you study these books, keep in mind that each had a different concept of liberation. Although all three women were *liberators,* ask yourself: From *what* type of oppression did each free her people? Describe the nature of the enslavement in each book, for "freedom" is defined in terms of "freedom *from what*?"

Also consider the attitudes in the three books toward non-Jews, who play obvious and decisive roles in each book. Because Judah and Israel were no longer independent states in control of their own destinies, the believers found themselves either scattered throughout the eastern Mediterranean (the Diaspora) or clustered

---

[2] In the previous chapter we have already seen that the final edition of the Book of Proverbs, with its stress on "the wise woman/wisdom as woman," had moved wisdom away from its original context in the royal court into the Israelite home.

[3] The Book of Judith belongs in the collection called the *apocrypha* (or *Second Canon* by Roman Catholics), a group of books that belong in the canonical (authoritative) lists of some religious groups (for instance, Roman Catholicism), but is not included in the canon or Bibles of either Judaism or Protestantism.

[4] The Book of Ruth is dated all the way from premonarchical to postexilic times.

[5] The literary genre "short story" is loosely used here. Basically, it is a short, fictional narrative in which a single hero faces a problem that is usually resolved by story's end after considerable suspense. Often such a story imitates an historical account (Books of Esther and Judith) or focuses on small, everyday scenes (Book of Ruth). Short stories usually evidence considerable literary intricacies. Although there is still considerable debate on the exact literary genre of these works (see Further Readings), "short story" is perhaps the most usable and most neutral term.

in small villages in Palestine vulnerable to the whims of distant overlords. In either case the believer had to face the issue of the relationship to the Gentile. This information can help you form an idea about the different ways in which postexilic Judaism related itself to the gentile world in which it was immersed.

In all three books the motifs of "food and banquets" appear at decisive moments in the stories. The resolution of famine occurs on a threshing floor amidst piles of harvested grain (Book of Ruth); the decreed fate of Jews in the Persian Empire changes dramatically at Esther's banquets for Haman and the King (Book of Esther); the city of Bethuliah and the temple are saved at Holophernes's banquet for Judith (Book of Judith). In all three of these cases, a vulnerable woman entered a menacing scene as a supplicant, but emerged in complete control. Why do you think these authors chose these similar moments—the banquet—in order to "disempower" the apparently powerful and to "empower" the so-called weak?

STUDY QUESTIONS FOR THE BOOK OF RUTH

Please answer *in writing* the following questions. Your task is to move from literary considerations, with which the Book of Ruth abounds, to the theology that these features express. First, chart out the literary features to which the questions below call attention. Second, try to formulate a thesis for the meaning of the book that takes as many of these elements into consideration as possible.

1.   The Book of Ruth can be divided roughly into five major scenes: "Journey From and Return to Bethlemen," "In the Field of Boaz," "At the Threshing Floor," "At the City Gate," and "Birth of the Child."

Study the following transition verses and indicate exactly how they mark the transition from the scene they complete to the scene that follows: Ruth 1:22, 2:23, 3:18, 4:13.

2.   How are the following features in the first scene (chapter 1) resolved or taken up in the final scene (Ruth 4:13–22): (a) the chronological dating in the beginning to the time of the Judges (notice where the RSV Bible places the Book of Ruth in its sequence of books); (b) the ten-year stay in Moab with its recurring themes of death and sterility; and (c) the loss of the two "boys" in Ruth 1:5? (This verse refers to the adult children of Ruth by the Hebrew word for "boys," not by the expected word "sons" as has been translated in the RSV.)

THE JEWISH SHORT STORY: RUTH, ESTHER, AND JUDITH **259**

List and then comment on all the examples of symmetry between scene 1 (Ruth 1) and scene 5 (Ruth 4:13–22).

3. List and comment on all the examples of similarity and difference between scene 2 (Ruth 2) and scene 3 (Ruth 3).

4. From a literary point of view, why does the narrator never have Naomi and Boaz meet? It seems their paths must have crossed, and yet the author never has them meet in the story. Why? How does this affect Ruth's role in the short story?

5. There are similarities drawn between Ruth and the Patriarch Abraham in the Book of Genesis. Read Genesis 12 and list resemblances between Ruth and the first Patriarch. What could such a comparison express?

Read the blessing in Ruth 4:11, 12. Ruth is compared here with Rachel, Leah, and Tamar. Read about these three women in the Book of Genesis (chapters 29, 30, 38). Can you see any similarities between their lives and Ruth's? In view of the preceding scene at the threshing floor,[6] do you detect any irony in the com-

---

[6] Although it is probably significant that the references here are so veiled, I prefer the interpretation in which the encounter between Ruth and Boaz at the threshing floor is understood as sexual: "feet" here probably refers to the male genitals.

parison implied by this blessing? How does this blessing relate to the question about comparing Ruth to the Patriarchs?

6.   Note the development in the ways in which Ruth is addressed throughout the book. She calls herself by different names in 2:10, 2:13,[7] 3:9; and she is addressed differently by others in 2:5, 2:8, 3:11, and finally in 4:11. How does this progression mark other developments in the book?

7.   Explain the legal status of both the Redeemer and of the Levirate Marriage in Israelite society. For this, consult the *Interpreter's Dictionary of the Bible.* (Remember that the Book of Ruth is a short story, *not* a technical legal treatise. Therefore you cannot demand *referential* legal accuracy in the book's discussion of Israelite regulations.)

Let me offer my interpretation of the pivotal scene at the city gate in chapter 4. I read the Hebrew of the crucial verse 4:5 a little differently: "The day that you acquire the field from the hand of Naomi, *I* also acquire Ruth the Moabitess . . . in order to restore the name of the dead to his inheritance." Here Boaz exploits both legal strategies: The next of kin would acquire Naomi's (really Elimelech's) field as Redeemer: A fair profit since Naomi apparently has no prospects of offspring to claim the field later. Boaz then announces his Levirate Marriage to Ruth in order to restore Naomi's dead offspring. If Boaz and Ruth have any children, they would have a right to reclaim the field from the Redeemer. The Redeemer promptly loses interest. This also explains why the child born of Ruth is in a real sense Naomi's boy (4:14).

---

[7] Here Ruth calls herself a **shiphah** ("maidservant"); in 3:9 she will call herself an **'amah.** There is evidence that a **shiphah** represents a lower social status. In a grave inscription near Jerusalem dating from around 700 B.C.E., a royal steward mentions that he has been buried with his **'amah;** it is unlikely that he would have chosen to announce his eternal rest with a mere **shiphah!**

Does this knowledge help explain the happenings on the threshing floor?

Recall that the Book of Ruth describes *two* women desperately in need of help. How do these two customs (Redeemer and Levirate Marriage) provide for both women? Who in the book is the Redeemer? Who is the Levir? (Remember that the arrangement in the Book of Ruth is unparalleled in the Hebrew Bible—but this is a short story, not a law journal!) Which character thought of a way to help *both* women? Where is this plan first put forward?

8.   The Book of Ruth abounds in a series of words that only appear twice, or at least infrequently; these can be said to round out the themes of the story. Below is a list of such instances. (Some of these Hebrew words are repeated with different meanings; for instance, **KANAPH** in 2:12 means "wings," but in 3:9 it means "corner of a blanket.") Discuss the role of each in expressing the theme of the book:

"boys"	1:5, 4:16
ḤESED, "kindness"/"loyalty"	1:8, 2:20; 3:10
security/"home"	1:9, 3:1
cling/attach/stay close	1:14, 2:8; 2:21, 23
lodge/"spend the night"	1:16, 3:13
brought back/restorer	1:21, 4:15
empty	1:21, 3:17
substance/worth	2:1, 3:11; 4:11
take special note/regard	2:10, 2:19
wings/"blanket corner"	2:12, 3:9

These paired words are also very important for making a statement about how God functions in the Book of Ruth (theology). In the above list, note those passages in which God is either portrayed as accomplishing something or else is being asked (through prayer) to accomplish something. Who later on in the story *actually* performs that same task? What does this pattern say about how God operates in the world of the Book of Ruth?

9.   According to the Book of Ruth, how are Orpah and the unnamed Redeemer in chapter 4 similar? Did they do anything wrong? How does the following proportion help us understand their roles: Ruth:Orpah::Boaz:Unnamed Redeemer?

10.   What exactly are Ruth's *two* acts of **ḤESED** ("kindness," "loyalty") to which Boaz refers in 3:10?

11.   What is the book's attitude toward non-Jews?

12.   Your last task is more difficult. I want you now to write down what you think is the *thesis* of the Book of Ruth, what it is trying to express. The best expression of its thesis will take into consideration most of the literary features commented on above.

In what sense could Ruth be seen as a model of deliverance for the Jewish community living during the times after the Exile? From what would she save them?

Reread the poem to the "Woman of Valor" that ends the final edition of the Book of Proverbs (31:10–31). Compare Ruth with this ideal woman.

Why would such female models have spoken to the situation of post-exilic Judaism?

What does the Book of Ruth say about the community's responsibilities if they are to survive these difficult days? According to Ruth, what is the nature of these responsibilities?

STUDY QUESTIONS FOR THE BOOK OF ESTHER

1.   The Book of Esther has the appearance of an *historical* event. What indications lend the book this historical semblance?

What evidence is there that despite its historical veneer the Book of Esther is probably fictional? In other words, are there indications within the text that suggest that this book is *not* real history?

2. Look at the organization of the book. How do banquets/drinking bouts provide the main literary structure for the book?

Notice that there are *two* Purim feasts celebrated in chapter 9: one in the provinces and another the next day in Susa (9:17–18). How do the two feasts fit in with the overall structuring of feasts/banquets in the Book of Esther?

What always happens at these banquets?

3. Observe the *Law* motif in the book (everything has to be done according to the "law"). Liberation in the Book of Esther frees Jews from the burden of oppressive and unyielding human laws.

Notice that even drinking must be in accordance with "law" (1:8). How does the king show that even he is bound by law? (Look especially at chapters 1, 8!)

Who ultimately has power to manipulate the law—a power that even the king lacks?

How is this person able to violate the law without punishment or any disrespect for the state?

4.   *Kingship* and *royal power* form the other important motifs in the Book of Esther, which contains the Hebrew verbal root for "king" in almost each verse of the book.

Show some of the ways that the royal power theme is handled in the book. How does this motif touch each of the main characters? How is each character (Mordecai, Esther, Ahasuerus, and Haman) related to the theme of royal power?

Mordecai is related by his genealogy to King Saul (compare Esther 2:5 and 1 Samuel 9). Haman too is affiliated with King Saul by his genealogy (compare Esther 3:1 and 1 Samuel 15). Why would Mordecai not be linked with David, the more popular monarchical figure? (Think about the role of the Davidic monarchy in the time *after* the Exile.)

How does this link with the rejection of Saul in 1 Samuel 15 explain Esther 9:10, 16?

Does Esther remain loyal to her husband, King Ahasuerus? Does she betray his trust? Relate your answer to this question to the book's view on royal authority suggested to its postexilic readers.

How does the "royal power" achieved by Esther and Mordecai (see 8:15) in the book compare with the former power exercised by the Davidic monarchy in Jerusalem during its preexilic independence? What fresh views of authority does this new royal model offer the postexilic Jewish community?

5. Recall our earlier definition of *irony*. Give some examples of irony in the book.

How does this irony help convey the thesis of the book? Describe how this literary device would be a perfect tool with which to describe the situation of postexilic Judaism.

Discover examples of the motif "high/low" and "raise/fall" in the book. For example, why does Haman wish to kill Mordecai? What exact deed causes Haman's downfall? Was Haman's gallow high enough? How does this motif convey much of the book's irony?

6.   When in the book (chapter and verse) does Esther change from being the passive queen, who is little more than a sex object, to the leader of her people's destiny?

What causes Esther to assume control?

When precisely (chapter and verse) does Esther decide to reveal her Jewish identity? Relate this answer to the previous question about her assumption of control.

7.   Describe the book's understanding of Judaism.

8.   In what ways is the Feast of Purim *like* and *unlike* the Feast of Passover, which celebrates the Exodus from Egypt?

Notice that the Exodus from the Land of Egypt described in the Book of Exodus comes after the Joseph story at the end of Genesis. How is the story of Esther similar to that of Joseph?

Compare the dates for Passover (Leviticus 23), which commemorated the Exodus from Egypt, and the date for commemorating the liberation of the Jews in the Book of Esther (3:13, 9:1–2). Do the two seem related by their dating?

9.   Most commentators have been disturbed by the fact that God is not mentioned once in the entire book. Does the book have a theology (that is, a view about God's activity in the world) even though it does not mention God, nor even such typically Jewish religious topics as the Law of Moses, prayer, Jewish dietary laws, etc.? Explain your answer carefully.

How could this silence about God fit in with the thesis of the author?

Notice how many decisive things happen by "chance." List them. What does this say about the author's view about how the Jewish Diaspora is protected?

How is the portrayal of God's activity in Esther *similar* to that in the Book of Ruth?

10.   Read the Additions to the Book of Esther in the Apocrypha. (Perhaps you will find this at the back of your RSV.) How do the theologies of the Additions differ from the regular book?

Do you detect a different attitude toward non-Jews in the Additions than in the regular Book of Esther? Be sure to support your answer.

How does this attitude of the Greek Additions toward non-Jews reflect a situation for its community that is different from that for the Hebrew Book of Esther?

Reread the description of *apocalyptic* in Chapter 4 of this text. What elements are there of this literary genre in the Greek Additions to Esther? Can you explain how the social situation within the Jewish community might have contributed to the emergence of apocalyptic elements?

12. Let us put all of this literary information together. What is the thesis of the Book of Esther?

STUDY QUESTIONS FOR THE BOOK OF JUDITH

As can be detected by the mood of the Book of Judith, relations with the Hellenistic kingdom of Syria under the Seleucid dynasty[8] were particularly strained during the time when the Book of Judith was written. Somewhere between 175–163 B.C.E. the Syrian monarch Antiochus IV Epiphanes persecuted the Jews of Palestine and sought to establish his dynastic deity, Zeus Olympios, on Mount Zion. These events form the background to the latter half of the Book of Daniel. Undoubtedly the author of Judith has thinly veiled this arrogant king under the name of that archfiend Nabuchadnezzar, who had first desecrated the temple.

1. Judith, the heroine of the book, does not even appear until chapter 8. To many scholars the first part of the book (chapters 1–7) is a boring, irrelevant addition. However, it seems to introduce many important themes that are developed in the latter half of the book.

First, let's form some *preliminary* ideas about both the literary structure of Judith and about its meaning. Notice the chapter in which we are first introduced to Judith. Does this suggest how the book should roughly be divided? If any book is divided into two parts, what type of message could be conveyed by such a bipartite division? (The following questions should help you determine how this two-part literary division functions in the case of the Book of Judith.)

---

[8] The Seleucid kings were successors of Seleucus, one of Alexander the Great's generals.

Do you find any links or symmetries between the two parts of the book? (Notice, for example, that a 34-day period is given for the military plans of both the Assyrians and the Israelites in 7:20 and 15:11. Also, both sections talk about "by the hand of. . . .")

2.   Trace the motif of "fear/dread/terror" in part one (chapters 1–7) and part two (chapters 8–16) of the book. Who inspires or causes "fear" in the respective parts?

List all the military terms and statistics that appear in part one of the book. How do these support the strong motif of *fear* in these first seven chapters? What effect does this Assyrian power have on its victims?

Who is "fearful" in the second part of the Book of Judith (chapters 8–16)?

3.   Trace the motif "Lord"[9] through the two parts of the book. Who is predominantly Lord or God in chapters 1–7? Who in chapters 8–16?

[9]Among Hellenistic Jews who spoke Greek, the word "Lord" (*kyrios*) was the normal translation for the Hebrew name for the deity Yahweh.

Do you find passages in which there is definite (and probably intended) ambiguity about the person to whom the word "Lord" actually refers? How does this ambiguity suggest *irony*? How does this irony in the use of the word "Lord" play an important role in the thesis of the book?

4.   List all the banquet scenes in the Book of Judith. How do these scenes develop the theme of the book about power and lordship?

5.   Write down all the passages that talk about what "the hand" accomplishes (for example, "by my hand," "by the hand of a woman," etc.). The "hand of Yahweh" plays an important role in the account of the Exodus from Egypt (Exodus 3:19,20; 13:9); Yahweh uses the hand of Moses to execute his plan in the Book of Exodus (14:26, 27). What role does this phrase play in the Book of Judith? How does it recall the Exodus theme?

How is Judith 2:12 ironic given the second half of the story?

6.   Can you point out other examples of irony in the Book of Judith? (This really should be easy. There are few books so full of dark irony as the Book of Judith.)

Why do you think that the literary device of irony is so suitable for the religious situations addressed by the postexilic books of Esther and Judith?

7.   Contrast the theology of Uzziah with that of Judith.

The encounter of the "wise man" and the woman is a typical scene in the Bible (for example, Job 2:9, 10). How is the encounter in Judith different? (All three of these books—Ruth, Esther, and Judith—reverse gender stereotypes!)

8.   How does the book contrast male "strength" with female "strength"?

Show how "beauty" is an important motif in part two of the Book of Judith (chapters 8–16). (Judith's cosmetic preparations in chapter 10 are a satire on the dressing of the warrior for battle as described so often in a work like Homer's *Iliad.*) How does it contrast with the military motif in part one (chapters 1–7)?

9.   What is the thesis of the Book of Judith?

        For which Jewish readership would the book speak: Palestinian or Diaspora
Jews?

What is the book's attitude toward non-Jews?

10.   You have now read three short stories, two of which come from the third
division of the Hebrew Bible—the Writings. These narratives spoke to the needs of
that vulnerable postexilic Jewish community.[10] Using these three works, describe as
concretely as possible the problems of both the Palestinian and Diaspora Jews. What
were some of the solutions recommended by these short stories? In other words,
describe how a Jew could express his or her religion in postexilic Palestine. Describe
the same thing in the postexilic Diaspora.

	PROBLEMS	SOLUTION
PALESTINIAN JUDAISM		

[10] Even if a book such as Ruth had been written earlier during the Davidic monarchy, its
particular relevance during postexilic times contributed to its incorporation into the Writings of
the Jewish Canon.

                        PROBLEMS   SOLUTIONS

DIASPORA
JUDAISM

FURTHER READINGS

General Readings

John F. Craghan, "Esther, Judith and Ruth: Paradigms for Human Liberation," in *Biblical Theology Bulletin,* 12 (1982): 11-19. This excellent article compares all three books and has been influential on the approach taken in this chapter.

Susan Niditch, "Legends of Wise Heroes and Heroines," in *The Hebrew Bible and Its Modern Interpreters* (Chico, CA: Scholars Press, 1985), pp. 445-463. This review article discusses dates, theology, and the literary genres of these short stories.

The Book of Ruth

Stephen Bertman, "Symmetrical Design in the Book of Ruth," *Journal of Biblical Literature,* 84 (1965): 165-168.

Jan Wojcik, "Improvising Rules in the Book of Ruth," *Proceedings of the Modern Language Association,* 100 (March 1985): 145-153.

Phyllis Trible, *God and the Rhetoric of Sexuality* (Philadelphia: Fortress Press, 1978), pp. 166-199. This chapter is an expansion of Trible's article "Two Women in a Man's World" in *Soundings,* 59 (1976): 251-279.

The Book of Esther

Sandra Beth Berg, *The Book of Esther: Motifs, Themes, and Structures* (Missoula, MT: Scholars Press, 1979).

The Book of Judith

John Craghan, "Judith Revisited," *Biblical Theology Bulletin,* 12 (1982): 50-53. This is an excellent survey article with a bibliography on recent studies on Judith.

Toni Craven, "Artistry and Faith in the Book of Judith," *Semeia,* 8 (1977): 75-101. This is one of the best literary studies available on the Book of Judith.

APPENDIX A
JEWISH AND CHRISTIAN CANONICAL BOOKS

A.

JEWISH CANON OF THE BIBLE (= HEBREW BIBLE)

1. Genesis
2. Exodus
3. Leviticus   **TORAH/PENTATEUCH**
4. Numbers
5. Deuteronomy

6. Joshua
7. Judges
8. 1 and 2 Samuel   FORMER PROPHETS
9. 1 and 2 Kings

10. Isaiah
11. Jeremiah
12. Ezekiel
13. The Twelve
    Hosea
    Joel
    Amos
    Obadiah
    Jonah   LATTER PROPHETS   **PROPHETS**
    Micah
    Nahum
    Habakkuk
    Zephaniah
    Haggai
    Zechariah
    Malachi

14. Psalms
15. Job
16. Proverbs
17. Ruth
18. Song of Songs
19. Qoheleth (Ecclesiastes)
20. Lamentations   } WRITINGS
21. Esther
22. Daniel
23. Ezra-Nehemiah
24. 1 and 2 Chronicles

B.
THE CHRISTIAN BOOKS OF THE OLD TESTAMENT

Protestant Canon of the Old Testament	Roman Catholic Canon of the Old Testament

Apocrypha or Deuterocanonical Books in Italics

Protestant Canon	Roman Catholic Canon
1. Genesis	1. Genesis
2. Exodus	2. Exodus
3. Leviticus	3. Leviticus
4. Numbers	4. Numbers
5. Deuteronomy	5. Deuteronomy
6. Joshua	6. Joshua
7. Judges	7. Judges
8. Ruth	8. Ruth
9. 1 Samuel	9. 1 Samuel
10. 2 Samuel	10. 2 Samuel
11. 1 Kings	11. 1 Kings
12. 2 Kings	12. 2 Kings
13. 1 Chronicle	13. 1 Chronicles
14. 2 Chronicle	14. 2 Chronicles
15. Ezra	15. Ezra
16. Nehemiah	16. Nehemiah
	17. *Tobit*
	18. *Judith*
17. Esther	19. Esther + *Additions*
18. Job	20. Job
19. Psalms	21. Psalms
20. Proverbs	22. Proverbs
21. (Qoheleth) Ecclesiastes	23. (Qoheleth) Ecclesiastes
22. Song of Solomon (= Song of Songs)	24. Song of Solomon
	25. *Wisdom of Solomon*
	26. *Ecclesiasticus* (= *Wisdom of Ben Sirach*)
23. Isaiah	27. Isaiah
24. Jeremiah	28. Jeremiah
25. Lamentations	29. Lamentations
	30. *Baruch & Letter of Jeremiah*
26. Ezekiel	31. Ezekiel

THE CHRISTIAN BOOKS OF THE OLD TESTAMENT (CONT.)

Protestant Canon of the Old Testament	Roman Catholic Canon of the Old Testament
	Apocrypha or Deuterocanonical Books in Italics
27. Daniel	32. Daniel + *Additions:* *Story of Susanna* *Song of the Young Men* *Bel and the Dragon*
28. Hosea	33. Hosea
29. Joel	34. Joel
30. Amos	35. Amos
31. Obadiah	36. Obadiah
32. Jonah	37. Jonah
33. Micah	38. Micah
34. Nahum	39. Nahum
35. Habakkuk	40. Habakkuk
36. Zephaniah	41. Zephaniah
37. Haggai	42. Haggai
38. Zechariah	43. Zechariah
39. Malachi	44. Malachi
	45. *1 Maccabees*
	46. *2 Maccabees*

APPENDIX B
ENUMA ELISH

The Enuma Elish (EE) is not really a typical Near Eastern creation myth; rather, it is a piece of religious (and political) propaganda extolling the supremacy of the Babylonian god Marduk. Marduk was not one of the original main gods in the Mesopotamian pantheon—a distinction belonging rather to such deities as Enlil, Anu, and Ea. These latter gods had been linked with very ancient Sumerian cities that had held power at the dawn of Mesopotamian history (before 3000 B.C.E.). Because Babylon's arrival at power in the north had been late (1800 B.C.E.), beginning with Hammurabi, her city god, Marduk, had not been listed among the main older gods. When Babylon assumed supremacy, her god's fate was also elevated. And so there arose a need to explain Marduk's recent increased status. (Notice in the EE that this increase is achieved at the expense of Ea, Anu, and Enlil, whose power Marduk assumes and whose names are all but absent in the EE.)

Both Genesis and the Enuma Elish arose in similar circumstances. The Babylonian Creation story was written around 1100 B.C.E., ironically during the reign of King Nabuchadnezzar I, whose namesake was to destroy Jerusalem 500 years later. In 1200 B.C.E. the Assyrians had conquered Babylon and removed the statue of Babylon's chief deity, Marduk, to Assyria. This political and religious catastrophe was not avenged until the reign of Nabuchadnezzar 100 years later when Assyria was defeated and the statue returned. This event was celebrated by the writing of the Enuma Elish, which attempted to explain how Marduk, who was considered throughout Mesopotamia to be an insignificant deity, could rise to such power. And so, like the Priestly Creation story, the Enuma Elish was a work of political propaganda composed after a religious calamity. Both foster views about their respective creator gods, which were at variance with the norm.

Unlike the P account in Genesis, the EE begins with a *theogony,* a story about the origin or birth of the gods. Because the EE is solely interested in Marduk, this theogony is restricted to the direct ancestors of Babylon's god. Like Genesis, the account begins with water covering everything; since the origin of the gods is seen in terms of "birth," water is portrayed as the god Apsu, the god of fresh water, and the goddess Tiamat, goddess of the salt-water seas. When they mingle their waters together (sexual intercourse), Lahmu and Lahamu emerge. These gods derive from the Akkadian word for "silt," and their birth probably reflects the common Mesopotamian experience of land (silt) emerging at the juncture of the freshwater Tigris and Euphrates rivers at the salt-water Persian Gulf. (In fact, so much silt has been deposited at this marshy point that the ancient seacoast is now hundreds of miles inland.)

As soon as land (silt) is born, then we have reference points for the horizon, which is seen from the point of the sky, Anshar, and of the earth, Kishar, thus keeping a pair of deities who beget Anu, the sky god and the first god of the regular Mesopotamian pantheon. Anu in turn fathers Ea (also called Nudimmud—"maker of the gods"). Ea was considered the god of craft and art.

At this point in the EE theogony quickly passes into *theomachy*, or war between the gods. Apsu's rest was disturbed by the newer divine generation; and so despite the attempt of Tiamat to calm him, Apsu and his minister Mummu waged war against the younger gods. Apsu's quest for peace (I:40) ironically leads to his permanent rest at the hand of Ea (I:60–69). Ea then uses the body of Apsu as a site for his temple. There Ea and Damkina give birth to the god Marduk. (There is a pun on his name in I:101, 102.)

Eventually Tiamat is aroused to avenge her slain mate (I:124–131). She and her allies create an army of demons to do battle against the younger gods (I:132–143). When Ea proves helpless against the onslaught of Tiamat, the panicky younger god turns to the newborn Marduk for help.[1]

EARLY GENERATIONS OF GODS (I:1-20)

When on high the heaven had not yet been named, (I:1)
below the first-set earth had not been given a name,
Only primordial Apsu, their begetter,
And the matrix, Tiamat, she who bore all of them,
were intermingling their waters; (5)
Before the bog had formed, and no island could be found,
When no gods whatever had yet been created,
When no god had yet been given a name,
Then it was that the gods were formed within them.
Lahmu and Lahamu were brought forth, they were called by
   name; (10)
While they grew up and became mighty,
Anshar and Kishar were formed, exceeding them.
They lengthened the days, increased the years.
Anu was their heir, the rival of his fathers;
Anshar made his son Anu in his own likeness. (15)
Anu begot in his image Nudimmud.
This Nudimmud was of his fathers the master;
His ears were wide open, wise, mighty in strength,
stronger than his own grandfather, Anshar.
He had no rival among the gods, his brothers. (20)

WAR BETWEEN APSU AND EA (I:21-78)

The brother gods banded together,
They confused Tiamat as they danced back and forth,
Yes, they worried Tiamat to the core of her heart

---

[1] The translation that follows is the author's.

They perturbed the gods in the Abode of Heaven by their
  boisterous behavior.
Apsu could not lessen their clamor (25)
And Tiamat was speechless before them.
Their activities were noisome to her.
Their behavior was not pleasant; they were overbearing.
Then Apsu, the begetter of the great gods,
Cried out, addressing Mummu, his minister: (30)
"O Mummu, my minister, who gladdens my spirit,
Come here and let us go to Tiamat!"
They went and sat down before Tiamat,
Exchanging advice about the gods, their first-born.
Apsu, opening his mouth, (35)
Said to resplendent Tiamat:
"Their ways are truly noisome to me.
By day I find no relief, nor sleep by night.
I will destroy, I will smash their ways,
That quiet may be restored. Let us have sleep!" (40)
As soon as Tiamat heard this,
She was furious and called out against her husband.
She cried out furious, as she raged all alone,
She took the evil of this right to her heart.
"What? Should we destroy what we ourselves created? (45)

Although their ways indeed are most troublesome, let us be kindhearted!"
Then Mummu answered, giving counsel to Apsu;
Ill-wishing and ungracious was Mummu's advice:
"Do destroy, my father, their troublesome doings.
Then you shall find rest by day and sleep by night!" (50)
When Apsu heard this, his face grew radiant
Because of the evil he plotted against the gods, his sons.
He embraced Mummu by the neck
And sat him down on his knees to kiss him.
Now whatever they had plotted between them, (55)
Was repeated to the gods, their first-born.
When the gods heard this, they wandered around in distress,
They became dazed and lapsed into silence.
Surpassing in intelligence, accomplished, resourceful,
Ea, the all-wise, saw through their scheme. (60)
A comprehensive plan against it he devised and set it up,
He artfully made his surpassing and holy spell against it.
He recited it and made it subsist in Apsu's waters,
he poured sleep upon him, so that he lay sound asleep.
When Apsu he had made prone, drenched with sleep, (65)
Mummu, the adviser, was dizzy with sleeplessness.
Ea loosened Apsu's band, tore off his crown,
Removed his glory and put it on himself.
Having bound up Apsu, Ea slew him.
Mummu he bound and locked up. (70)
He then established his dwelling upon Apsu,
Ea seized Mummu, holding him by the nose-rope.
After Ea had conquered and struck down his foes,
Had established the triumphal annihilation of his enemies,
He rested in his sacred chamber in deep sleep, (75)
He named it "Apsu," for shrines he assigned it.
There he established his cult hut.
Ea and Damkina, his wife, settled there in grand style.

BIRTH OF MARDUK (I:79-104)

In the sanctuary of the fates, the abode of the divine
   plans,
The god was engendered, most able and wisest of all the
   gods, (80)
In the heart of Apsu was Marduk created,
In the heart of Holy Apsu was Marduk created.
Ea, his father, begot him;
She who bore him was Damkina, his mother.
He sucked the breasts of the goddesses. (85)
The nurse that nursed him filled him with awesomeness.
Robust was his figure, sparkling the glance of his eyes.
Already from his birth he was manly, he was mighty from
   the very beginning.
When Anu has grandfather saw him,
He became jubilant, he beamed, his heart filled with
   gladness. (90)
Anu made him perfect, giving him double divinity.
He was exceedingly tall above them, surpassing them in
   everything.
His shape was perfect beyond comprehension,
Incomprehensible, difficult to behold.
Four were his eyes; four were his ears; (95)
When he moved his lips, fire blazed forth.
Large were all four hearing organs,
And the eyes, in like number, scanned all things.
He was the loftiest of the gods, surpassing was his
   stature;
His members were enormous, he was exceedingly tall. (100)
"My little son, my little son!
My son, the Sun! Sun of the heavens!"
Clothed with the splendor of ten gods, he was exceedingly
   strong,
As the 50 Fears were heaped upon him.

Like any grandfather, Anu then presents his grandson Marduk with toys, in this case the four winds. The winds stir up Tiamat (who is, remember, the Sea). Tiamat is also reminded of the outrage committed against her consort Apsu and so is finally goaded to battle. She appoints Kingu as her commander and new spouse.

TIAMAT'S PREPARATIONS FOR WAR (I:105-61)
Anu brought forth and begot the fourfold wind (105)
And turned them over to his grandson to let him play.
He created dust and allowed the storm to blow it around;
Anu caused a wave to disturb Tiamat.
Tiamat was roiled, day and night the gods were astir.
They suffered restlessness with each storm.
Their hearts plotted evil, (110)
They said to Tiamat, their mother:
"When they killed Apsu, your lover,
You did not help him but stayed still.
Now (Anu) created the four dread winds, (115)

Your innards are so roiled that we cannot sleep.
Apsu, your lover, was not on your mind
and Mummu, who has been bound! You kept aloof!
You are not our mother, you wander around in a daze,
We cannot go to sleep. You do not love us! (120)
. . . pinched are our eyes,
Lift the yoke that leaves us no peace. Let us have rest!
. . . to battle. Avenge them!
. . . and annihilate them!"
When Tiamat heard these words, she was pleased (125)
"Our sleep (?) you have given. Let us make monsters,
. . . and the gods in the midst . . .
. . . let us do battle and against the gods . . . !"
They thronged and marched at the side of Tiamat.
Enraged, they plotted incessantly night and day, (130)
They are prepared for battle, furious, raging,
They form a council to prepare for the fight.
Mother Hubur, she who fashions all things,
Added weapons without rival, bore dragons,
With sharp teeth, merciless fangs. (135)
She has filled their bodies with venom for blood.
Roaring dragons she has clothed with terror,
Has crowned them with splendor, making them like gods,
So that whoever looks at them shall perish in terror,
That, with their bodies reared up, none might turn them
  back. (140)
She set up the Viper, the Dragon, and the Sphinx,
the Great-Lion, the Mad-Dog, and the Scorpion-Man,
Mighty lion-demons, the Dragon-Fly, the Centaur—
Bearing weapons that were merciless, fearless in battle.
Firm were her decrees, they were irresistible. (145)
Altogether 11 of this kind she brought forth.
From among the gods, her first-born, who formed her
  assembly,
She elevated Kingu, magnified him among them.
Leadership of the army and command of the assembly,
The raising of weapons for the encounter, advancing to
  combat (150)
She entrusted the generalship to Kingu.
She entrusted all these into his hands as she seated him
  on the throne:
"I have cast for you a spell,
  raising you up in the assembly of the gods.
I have placed in your hand the dominion over all the
  gods.
May you be truly exalted, be you my only spouse! (155)
Your command shall prevail over all the Anunnaki!"
She gave him the Tablet of Destinies, fastened on his
  chest:
"As for you, your command shall be unchangeable, your
  word shall endure!"
As soon as Kingu was elevated, possessed of the rank of
  supreme god,
For the gods, his sons, the fates were decreed: (160)
"Let your word calm the fire,
Let your venom as it collects humble the powerful!"

SUMMARY OF II:1–III:138

As soon as the new gods learn of Tiamat's plan, they try to frustrate it. Unlike the previous time when Ea easily defeated Apsu, now the foe, Tiamat, is much more formidable and better prepared. The younger gods make two desperate attempts at stopping Tiamat before arriving at a successful plan.

Anshar sends Ea to make the first attempt to subdue Tiamat. Ea's attempt, however, fails and he returns in defeat. Then Anshar dispatches Anu to accomplish this task but cowers at the mere sight of the fierce Tiamat. At last Anshar summons Marduk.

Marduk is ready to take advantage of the situation. Thus, when he steps forward and is asked to kill Tiamat, he brags that the rest of the gods are afraid of a mere woman. He alone will kill her, he says, if he is given supreme command over all the gods.

Anshar agrees and immediately sends for Lahmu and Lahamu to ratify the decision. On hearing the full story of Tiamat's behavior, Lahmu and Lahamu are quite troubled. They go quickly to Anshar's house where they attend a banquet. After they become drunk, they cede to Marduk the absolute power he requested. They then give him a constellation to demonstrate that Marduk truly has the powers they have delegated to him.

MARDUK'S VICTORY (IV:1–122)

They erected a princely throne for Marduk. (IV:1)
He sat down facing his fathers to receive rulership:
"You are the most honored of the great gods,
Your decree is unrivaled, your command is Anu [that is,
   divine].
You, Marduk, are the most revered of the great gods, (5)
Your decree is unrivaled, your word is divine.
From this day your orders shall be unchangeable.
To raise or bring low—these shall be within your power.
Your word shall be true, your command shall be
   unimpeachable.
No one among the gods shall go against your
   determinations! (10)
Support is a necessity for the sanctuary of the gods,
Let your sacred place be established in their
   sanctuaries!
O Marduk, you are indeed our avenger.
We have granted you kingship over the entire universe.
Sit in assembly, may your word prevail. (15)
May your weapon not fail; let it smash your foes!
O Lord, spare the life of him who trusts in you,
But shed the life of the god who embraces evil!"
Having placed a Constellation in their midst,
They addressed themselves to Marduk, their first-born: (20)
"Lord, truly let your decree be first among the gods.
Just speak to destroy or create; it shall be.
Open your mouth: the Constellation will vanish!
Speak again, and the Constellation shall be whole!"
At the word of Marduk's mouth the Constellation vanished. (25)
He spoke again, and the Constellation was restored.

When the gods, his fathers, saw the power of his word,
Joyfully they did homage: "Marduk is King!"
They conferred on him scepter, throne, and royal robes;
They gave him irresistible weapons that overwhelm the
    foes: (30)
"Go and cut Tiamat's throat!
May the winds bear her blood hither as tidings of joy!"
The Lord's destiny thus fixed, the gods, his fathers,
Sent him on the road to obtaining full obedience.
He constructed a bow, designed it as his weapon, (35)
Attached the arrow firmly on its bowstring.
He raised the mace, grasped it with his right hand;
Bow and quiver he hung at his side.
In front of him he set the lightning,
With blazing flame he filled his body. (40)
He then made a net to put Tiamat in.
He stationed the four winds so that none of her might
    escape,
The South Wind, the North Wind, the East Wind, the West
    Wind.
The gifts of his (grand-)father Anu, he brought to the
    side of the net,
He brought forth Imbulla "the Evil Wind," the Whirlwind,
    the Hurricane, (45)
The Fourfold Wind, the Sevenfold Wind,
the Cyclone, the Matchless Wind;
Then Marduk set forth the winds he had brought forth,
the seven of them.
They followed him to disturb the inside of Tiamat.
Then the Lord Marduk raised up the Flood-Storm, his
    mighty weapon.
He mounted the terrifying chariot (drawn by) the
    irresistible storm demons. (50)
He harnessed and yoked it to a team-of-four:
The Killer, the Relentless, the Trampler, the Swift.
Their lips were parted, their fangs carry venom.
They were tireless and skilled in destruction.
On his right he posted the Smiter, fearsome in battle, (55)
On the left the Combat, which repels all the zealous.
He was wrapped in a coat of mail inspiring terror;
With his fearsome sheen his head was turbaned.
The Lord Marduk proceeded, went on his way,
He set his face towards the foaming Tiamat. (60)
In his lips Marduk held a spell;
A plant to counteract poison was grasped in his hand.
Then they milled about him, the gods milled about him,
The gods, his fathers, milled about Marduk,
the gods milled about him.
The Lord approached to scan the inside of Tiamat, (65)
And of Kingu, her consort, in order to perceive their
    plans.
Marduk kept looking at Tiamat until his judgment became
    confused,
His resolution scattered, his actions distraught,
And when the gods, his allies and auxiliaries,
Thus beheld their hero and leader,

their vision too became blurred. (70)

Tiamat emitted a cry, without turning her neck,

Framing blandishments in her lips—they were lies:

"You are honored, O Lord,

since the gods have taken their stand with you.

They have gathered to their place, and now they are here
    with you."

Thereupon, the Lord, raised the Flood-Storm, his mighty
    weapon, (75)

To enrage Tiamat he sent word as follows:

"Why do you assume a friendly attitude outwardly,

Although you have charged your heart to stir up a fight?

The sons have withdrawn, their fathers acted with
    disrespect,

While you, who have born them, hate your offspring! (80)

You have appointed Kingu as your spouse,

Conferring on him the rank of Anu, not rightfully his.

Against Anshar, the king of the gods, you seek evil;

Against the gods, my fathers, you have confirmed your
    wickedness.

Your forces are drawn up, your weapons strapped on, (85)

Stand up, that you and I might meet in single combat!"

When Tiamat heard this,

She was like somebody possessed; she took leave of her
    senses.

In fury Tiamat cried out aloud.

To the roots her legs shook both together. (90)

She recites a magic charm, keeps casting her spell,

While the gods of battle sharpen their weapons.

Then joined issue Tiamat and Marduk, wisest of gods.

They strove in single combat, locked in battle.

The Lord Marduk spread out his net and had her
    surrounded, (95)

The Evil Wind, which followed behind, he let loose in her
    face.

When Tiamat opened her mouth to swallow the wind,

He drove in the Evil Wind so she couldn't close her lips.

As the raging winds filled her belly,

Her insides were blown up, and her mouth was wide open. (100)

Marduk shot his arrow, it tore into her belly,

It cut through her insides, splitting her in half.

He bound her, Marduk extinguished her life.

He cast down her corpse to stand upon it.

After he had slain Tiamat, the leader, (105)

Her army was smashed, her troops were broken up;

And the gods, her helpers who marched at her side,

Trembling with fear, turned around,

And fled to save their own lives.

Marduk hemmed them in,

tightly surrounded without possibility of escape. (110)

He shattered their weapons.

Thrown into the net, they crouched in the trap;

They crept into the corners, they are full of moaning.

Bearing his wrath, they were held imprisoned.

And the eleven creatures which Tiamat had charged with
   awe, (115)
The whole band of demons that marched at her right,
Marduk put nose-ropes on them, he tied their arms.
He stood in triumph upon them and their allies.
And Kingu, who had been made their chief,
He bound and counted him among the dead gods. (120)
He took from him the Tablet of Destinies, not rightfully
   Kingu's,
Marduk sealed them with a seal and fastened them to his
   breast.

CREATION OF SKY AND EARTH (IV:123-146)

When Marduk had vanquished and subdued his adversaries,
When he had enslaved the conceited foe,
After he had wholly established Anshar's triumph over the
   foe, (125)
After he had achieved Nudimmud's desire, then valiant
   Marduk
Strengthened his hold on the captured gods,
And turned back to Tiamat whom he had bound.
Lord Marduk walked on the legs of Tiamat,
With his merciless mace he crushed her skull. (130)
When he had severed the arteries of her blood,
The North Wind bore it to unknown places.
On seeing this, his fathers were joyful and jubilant,
They brought gifts and presents to him.
Then Marduk calmed down inspecting her corpse, (135)
That he might cut the monster in two and create ingenious
   things.
He split her in half like a dried fish:
He set up half of her and roofed the sky with it,
He then drew a limit and posted guards.
He commanded them not to allow her waters to escape. (140)
Marduk crossed the heavens and surveyed the regions.
He squared Apsu's quarter, the abode of Nudimmud,
As the lord measured the dimensions of Apsu.
And as a replica of it set up the Great Abode called
   Esharra
The Great Abode, Esharra, which he made in the sky. (145)
Anu, Enlil, and Ea he made occupy their places (temples).

CREATION OF STARS AND GODS' STATIONS (V:1-22)

Marduk created stations for the great gods, (V:1)
Fixing their astral likenesses as the Constellations.
He determined the year by designating the zodiac:
He set up three constellations for each of the 12
   months.
After defining the days of the year by means of heavenly
   figures,

He established the station of Nebiru to determine their
  heavenly bands, (5)
That none might transgress or fall short.
Alongside it Marduk set up the stations of Enlil and Ea.
Having opened up the gates on both sides,
Marduk strengthened the locks on both the left and the
  right. (10)
In Tiamat's belly he established the zenith.
He bade the Moon to come forth, entrusting the night to
  him.
He designated him as adornment of the night to delimit
  the days:
And every month unfailingly he marked off by a crown.
"When the new moon is rising over the land, (15)
You shall shine with horns to signify six days,
on the seventh day appear as a half-crown.
And then let periods of fifteen days be counterparts,
two halves each month.
When the sun overtakes you at the base of heaven,
Wane step by step, reverse your growth. (20)
At the time of disappearance you should approach
the course of the sun,
And on thirtieth you shall again stand in opposition to
  the sun."

SUMMARY (VERSES 23ff.)

At this point the text is fragmentary. But enough remains to reveal that Marduk
continues to create "marvelous things." He pokes out Tiamat's eyes, and the Tigris
and Euphrates rivers flow from them. He forms mountains out of her breasts. Then
he drills holes in them, allowing springs to gush forth. Finally, as a memorial to his
conquest of Tiamat, he turns her 11 monsters into statues and places them at the
gate of the Apsu. After these events are described, there is a gap in the text. The
story then resumes on Tablet VI:

CREATION OF THE HUMAN RACE (VI:1-44)

When Marduk hears the words of the gods, (VI:1)
He decided to create something clever.
Opening his mouth, he addresses Ea
What he had carefully planned, he now gave as advice:
"I will knot arteries and create bones. (5)
I will make of it the primal-human, 'Human' shall be its
  name.
Truly 'primal-man' I will create.
He shall be burdened with the toil of the gods that they
  might rest!
I will improve the organization of the gods.
Together they should be honored
although they are divided into two groups." (10)
Ea answered him, speaking a word to him,

Giving him another plan for the relief of the gods:
"Let one of their brothers be handed over;
He alone shall perish that humankind be fashioned.
Let the great gods be here in Assembly, (15)
Let the guilty be handed over that they may endure."
Presiding graciously, Marduk issues instructions.
To his utterance the gods obey.
King Marduk addresses a word to the Anunnaki: (20)
"If your former statement was true,
The word you speak to me should be true!
Who was it that conceived the uprising,
And made Tiamat rebel, and join battle?
Let him be handed over who contrived the uprising. (25)
His guilt I will make him bear. But you all shall dwell
   in peace!"
The Igigi, the great gods, replied to him,
To the King of the Gods of Heaven and Earth,
counselor of the gods, their lord:
"It was Kingu who contrived the uprising,
And made Tiamat rebel and join battle." (30)
They bound him and took him before Ea.
They inflicted the punishment on him, opening his blood
   vessels;
With his blood they created humankind.
Ea imposed the service and then let free the gods.
After Ea, the wise, had created humankind, (35)
Had imposed upon it the service of the gods—
That work was beyond comprehension;
As artfully planned by Marduk, did Nudimmud create it—
Thereupon Marduk, the king of the gods, divided
All the 600 Anunnaki into upper and lower
   groups. (40)
He assigned the Upper Gods to Anu to guard his orders,
Three hundred in the heavens he appointed as a guard.
Likewise he set up the organization of the netherworld:
Thus he settled in heaven and in the netherworld 600 gods.

SUMMARY OF VI:45—VII:144

When Marduk finished putting order into the universe, the gods propose that a sanctuary (the city of Babylon) be built for them all. After they complete the job, they praise the weapons Marduk used to slay Tiamat. Then they proclaim the duties of the human race, which includes paying homage to Marduk and supplying sustenance to all the gods. Finally, they recite Marduk's 50 Sumerian names, each of which indicates something of Marduk's achievements. For example, he is called "Ziukkinna" because "he established the heavens," and "Lugallanna" ("The King whose Strength is Outstanding among the Gods"). Finally, the gods give Marduk the title, "Fifty," to encompass all the characteristics of his 50 names: "With the title 'Fifty' the great gods proclaimed Marduk whose names are 50 and made his way supreme." The gods also proclaimed Marduk as the embodiment of the older deities, Ea, Enlil: ". . . Marduk, the Enlil of the gods."

STUDY QUESTIONS ON THE ENUMA ELISH

1.   Notice the emphasis on "naming" in the first part of the Enuma Elish. Compare this with Genesis 2:4a–3:24. Who does the naming in Genesis?

2.   Do you notice any development in the origin of the gods? What types of gods are created first? Is Ea any different from the very first gods?

3.   Why does Tiamat go to war against the younger gods? Who is Kingu?

4.   Describe in detail what Marduk does with Tiamat's corpse. How is this similar to the Creation in the P account of Creation in Genesis?

5.   Why does Marduk create humans? Of what raw materials are the humans made? What does this say about the Babylonian view of humans?

Compare the nineteenth-century Frankenstein myth with the creation of humans in the EE. How are Frankenstein and the primitive-human similarly flawed? In other words, why does the Frankenstein monster do evil? Does this explain human evil in the EE?

6. In Genesis 1:1–2:4a the *word* of God is important. Is there any stress on the creative power of Marduk's word in the EE?

7. Compare the role of the astral bodies (sun, moon, stars) in the two Creation accounts (EE and P).

8. In general, how do the EE and P accounts differ in their view of the cosmos?

APPENDIX C
MESOPOTAMIAN FLOOD STORY

Utnapishtim said to him, to Gilgamesh:
"I will reveal to thee, Gilgamesh, a hidden matter
And a secret of the gods will I tell thee: (10)
Shurippak—a city which thou knowest,
[(And) which on Euphrates' [banks] is situated—
That city was ancient, (as were) the gods within it,
When their heart led the great gods to produce the flood.
[There] were Anu, their father,
Valiant Enlil, their counselor,
Ninurta, their assistant,
Ennuge, their irrigator.[183]
Ninigiku-Ea was also present with them;
Their words he repeats to the reed-hut:[184]   (20)
'Reed-hut, reed-hut! Wall, wall!
Reed-hut, hearken! Wall, reflect!
Man of Shuruppak,[185] son of Ubar-Tutu,
Tear down (this) house, build a ship!
Give up possessions, seek thou life.
Forswear (worldly) goods and keep the soul alive!

Aboard the ship take thou the seed of all living things.
The ship that thou shalt build,
Her[186] dimensions shall be to measure.
Equal shall be her width and her length.   (30)
Like the Apsu thou shalt ceil her.'[187]
I understood, and I said to Ea, my lord:
'[Behold], my lord, what thou hast thus ordered,
I will be honored to carry out.
[But what] shall I answer the city, the people and elders?'[188]
Ea opened his mouth to speak,
Saying to me, his servant:
'Thou shalt then thus speak unto them:
"I have learned that Enlil is hostile to me,
So that I cannot reside in your city,   (40)
Nor set my f[oo]t in Enlil's territory.
To the Deep I will therefore go down,
To dwell with my lord Ea.
[But upon] you he will shower down abundance,
[The choicest] birds, the rarest[189] fishes.
[The land shall have its fill] of harvest riches.

---

[183] More specifically, "inspector of canals," cf. *Creation Epic*, VII, 62.

[184] Presumably, the dwelling place of Utnapishtim. Ea addresses him through the barrier of the wall.

[185] Line 11 has the uncommon form Shurippak instead.

[186] The Akkadian for "ship" is feminine, although without the grammatical feminine ending.

[187] For the description of the subterranean waters of the Apsū cf. *Creation Epic,* IV, 62.

[188] cf. my remarks in *Studies in the History of Culture* (1942), 60.

[189] I take these genitive forms to denote the superlative, in accordance with Semitic usage. The literal sense would be "[A choice of] birds, a hiding of fishes."

[1] Text and notes taken from *ANET*, pp. 93–95, translated by E. A. Speiser.

[He who at dusk orders] the husk-greens,
Will shower down upon you
a rain of wheat.'' '[190]

With the first glow of dawn,
The land was gathered [about me].
(too fragmentary for translation)   (50-53)
The little ones [carr]ied bitumen,
While the grown ones brought [all else]
that was needful.
On the fifth day I laid her framework.
One (whole) acre[191] was her floor space,[192]
Ten dozen cubits the height of each
of her walls,
Ten dozen cubits each edge of the square
deck.[193]
I laid out the contours (and) joined
her together.[194]
I provided her with six decks,   (60)
Dividing her (thus) into seven parts.
Her floor plan I divided into nine parts.
I hammered water-plugs into her.[195]
I saw to the punting-poles and laid in
supplies.[196]
Six 'sar' (measures)[197] of bitumen I poured
into the furnace,
Three sar of asphalt [I also] poured inside.
Three sar of oil the basket-bearers carried,
Aside from the one sar of oil which the
calking[198] consumed,
And the two sar of oil [which] the boatman
stowed away.
Bullocks I slaughtered for the [people],   (70)
And I killed sheep every day.
Must, red wine, oil, and white wine[199]
[I gave the] workmen [to drink], as though
river water,

That they might feast on New Year's Day.
I op[ened . . .] ointment, applying (it)
to my hand.
[On the sev]enth [day] the ship was completed.
[*The launching*] was very difficult,
So that they had to shift the floor planks[200]
above and below,
[*Until*] two-thirds of [*the structure*][201]
[*had g*]one [*into the water*].

[Whatever I had] I laded upon her: (80)
Whatever I had of silver I laded upon her;
Whatever I [had] of gold I laded upon her;
Whatever I had of all the living beings
I [laded] upon her.
All my family and kin I made go aboard
the ship.
The beasts of the field, the wild creatures
of the field,
All the craftsmen I made go aboard.
Shamash had set for me a stated time:
'When he who orders unease at night,[202]
Will shower down a rain of blight,
Board thou the ship and batten up
the entrance!'
That stated time had arrived:
'He who orders unease at night, showers down
a rain of blight.'   (90)
I watched the appearance of the weather.
The weather was awesome to behold.
I boarded the ship and battened up
the entrance.
To batten down[203] the (whole) ship,
to Puzur-Amurri, the boatman,
I handed over the structure together with
its contents.

---

[190] Restored from lines 87, 90. As has long been recognized, these lines feature word plays in that both *kukku* and *kibāti* may designate either food or misfortune; cf. C. Frank, *ZA*, XXXVI (1935), 218. Wily Ea plays on this ambiguity: To the populace, the statement would be a promise of prosperity; to Utnapishtim it would signalize the impending deluge.

[191] cf. Heidel, *EG*, 82, n.170.

[192] Schott and Landsberger, *ZA*, XLII (1934), 137.

[193] The ship was thus an exact cube, cf. Heidel, *EG*, 82, n.173.

[194] Or ''fashioned.'' ''Contours,'' lit. ''outside shape.''

[195] For O. Neugebauer's explanation of the plugs cf. *ZA*, XLII, 138.

[196] Lit. ''the needful.''

[197] Var. ''three *šar*.'' The *šar* was the number 3,600. If the measure understood with it was the *sūtu* (seah), each *šar* designated about 8,000 gallons; cf. Heidel, *EG*, 83, n.178.

[198] For *niqqu* cf. A. Salonen, *Die Wasserfahrzeuge in Babylonien* (1939), 149, n.2.

[199] See A. Poebel, *ZA*, XXXIX (1929), 149.

[200] Read *ge-er-má-dù*, with Salonen, *op. cit.*, 93. I take the sense to be, however, that the weight had to be shifted around (*uštabbalu*) on the upper and lower decks (*eliš u šapliš*) to make the launching possible.

[201] Because of the masculine suffix (*šinīpat-su*), the antecedent cannot be the feminine *eleppu* ''ship.'' Perhaps *ekallu*, as in line 95.

[202] The true bearing of the word plays mentioned in lines 46-47. In order to reflect the rhyme of the Akkadian, which the two halves of this line contain—perhaps to bring out the proverbial content—I have translated here *līlāti* as ''night,'' instead of ''evening, dusk.''

[203] Lit. ''to calk,'' cf. Salonen, *op. cit.*, 152. This expression seems to mean here ''to put the finishing touches to.''

With the first glow of dawn,
A black cloud rose up from the horizon.
Inside it Adad thunders,
While Shullat and Hanish[204] go in front,
Moving as heralds over hill and plain.   (100)
Erragal[205] tears out the posts;[206]
Forth comes Ninurta and causes the dikes
          to follow.
The Anunnaki lift up the torches,
Setting the land ablaze with their glare.
Consternation[207] over Adad reaches
          to the heavens,
Who turned to blackness all that had been light.
[The wide] land was shattered like [a pot]!
For one day the south-storm [blew],
Gathering speed as it blew,
          [submerging the mountains],
Overtaking the [people] like a battle.   (110)
No one can see his fellow,
Nor can the people be recognized from heaven.
The gods were frightened by the deluge,
And, shrinking back, they ascended
          to the heaven of Anu.[208]
The gods cowered like dogs
          Crouched against the outer wall.
Ishtar cried out like a woman in travail,
The sweet-voiced mistress of the [gods]
          moans aloud:
'The olden days are alas turned to clay,
Because I bespoke evil in the Assembly
          of the gods.
How could I bespeak evil in the Assembly
          of the gods,   (120)
Ordering battle for the destruction
          of my people,
When it is I myself who gave birth
          to my people!
Like the spawn of the fishes they fill the sea!'
The Anunnaki gods weep with her,
The gods, all humbled, sit and weep,
Their lips *drawn tight*,[209] [. . .] one and all.
Six days and [six] nights
Blows the flood wind, as the south-storm
          sweeps the land.
When the seventh day arrived,
          The flood(-carrying) south-storm

subsided in the battle,
Which it had fought like an army.   (130)
The sea grew quiet, the tempest was still,
          the flood ceased.
I looked at the weather: stillness had set in,
And all of mankind had returned to clay.
The landscape was as level as a flat roof.

I opened a hatch, and light fell upon my face.
Bowing low, I sat and wept.
Tears running down on my face.
I looked about for coast lines in the expanse
          of the sea:
In each of fourteen[210] (regions)
          There emerged a region(-mountain).[211]
On Mount Nisir[212] the ship came
          to a halt.   (140)
Mount Nisir held the ship fast,
          Allowing no motion.
One day, a second day, Mount Nisir held
          the ship fast,
          Allowing no motion.
A third day, a fourth day, Mount Nisir held
          the ship fast,
          Allowing no motion.
A fifth, and a sixth (day), Mount Nisir held
          the ship fast,
          Allowing no motion.

When the seventh day arrived,
I sent forth and set free a dove.
The dove went forth, but came back;
Since no resting-place for it was visible,
          she turned round.
Then I sent forth and set free a swallow.
The swallow went forth, but came back;   (150)
Since no resting-place for it was visible,[212a]
          she turned round.
Then I sent forth and set free a raven.
The raven went forth and, seeing that
          the waters had diminished,
He eats, circles, caws, and turns not round.
Then I let out (all) to the four winds
          And offered a sacrifice.
I poured out a libation on the top
          of the mountain.

[204] For this reading of the names of the two heralds cf. *CT*, XXXV, 7, lines 19–20.

[205] i.e. Nergal, god of the netherworld.

[206] Of the world dam.

[207] The term *šuḫarratu*, with the elative element *š*-, does not mean "rage," but "stark stillness, bewilderment, consternation." cf. line 131, below.

[208] The highest of several heavens in the Mesopotamian conception of the cosmos.

[209] Var. "covered."

[210] Var. "twelve."

[211] cf. Oppenheim, *Orientalia*, XVII (1948), 54; for *nagū* see H. and J. Lewy, *HUCA*, XVII (1943), 11–15.

[212] For the identification of Mount Niṣir with modern Pir Omar Gudrun, cf. my report in *AASOR*, VIII (1926/27), 17–18.

[212a] More exactly "appeared," from *(w)apū*, in view of the repeated writing with *p*.

Seven and seven cult-vessels I set up,
Upon their pot-stands I heaped cane,
    cedarwood, and myrtle.
The gods smelled the savor,
The gods smelled the sweet savor,   (160)
The gods crowded like flies about the sacrificer.
When at length as the great goddess[213] arrived,
She lifted up the great jewels which Anu had
    fashioned to her liking:
'Ye gods here, as surely as this lapis
    Upon my neck I shall not forget,
I shall be mindful of these days, forgetting
    (them) never.
Let the gods come to the offering;
(But) let not Enlil come to the offering,
For he, unreasoning, brought on the deluge
And my people consigned to destruction.'
When at length as Enlil arrived,   (170)
And saw the ship, Enlil was wroth,
He was filled with wrath over the Igigi gods;[214]
'Has some living soul escaped?
    No man was to survive the destruction!'
Ninurta opened his mouth to speak,
    Saying to valiant Enlil:
'Who, other than Ea, can devise plans?[215]
It is Ea alone who knows every matter.'
Ea opened his mouth to speak,
    Saying to valiant Enlil:
'Thou wisest of gods, thou hero,
How couldst thou, unreasoning, bring on
    the deluge?
On the sinner impose his sin,   (180)
    On the transgressor impose
    his transgression!

(Yet) be lenient, lest he be cut off,
Be patient,[216] lest he be dis[lodged]!
Instead of thy bringing on the deluge,
    Would that a lion had risen up
    to diminish mankind!
Instead of thy bringing on the deluge,
    Would that a wolf had risen up
    to diminish mankind!
Instead of thy bringing on the deluge,
    Would that a famine had risen up
    to l[ay low] mankind!
Instead of thy bringing on the deluge,
    Would that pestilence[217] had risen up
    to smi[te down] mankind!
It was not I who disclosed the secret
    of the great gods.
I let Atrahasis[218] see a dream,
    And he perceived the secret of the gods.
Now then take counsel in regard to him!'
Thereupon Enlil went aboard the ship.
Holding me by the hand, he took me
    aboard.   (190)
He took my wife aboard and made (her)
    kneel by my side.
Standing between us, he touched
    our foreheads to bless us:
'Hitherto Utnapishtim has been but human.
Henceforth Utnapishtim and his wife shall be
    like unto us gods.
Utnapishtim shall reside far away, at the mouth
    of the rivers!'
Thus they took me and made me reside
    far away,
    At the mouth of the rivers.

[213] Ishtar.

[214] The heavenly gods.

[215] An allusion to one of the common epithets of Ea.

[216] For *šadādu* in the sense of "heed," and the like, see XII, 32.

[217] Lit. "Erra," the god of pestilence.

[218] "Exceeding Wise," an epithet of Utnapishtim.

THE REASON FOR THE BABYLONIAN FLOOD

The cuneiform tablets, or better yet the *fragments* of these clay tablets, are confusing about the causes of the Flood in Babylonian literature. Most of the pieces drawn from different ages and localities seem to suggest a struggle between the two Mesopotamian gods Enlil and Ea/Enki. Ea has created humankind and is sympathetic and protective, whereas Enlil plots humankind's destruction through drought, starvation, and eventually a flood. Much of Enlil's hostility toward humans arose from their multiplication on the earth with the accompanying noise that disturbed Enlil's sleep. That divine hostility can be sensed in the following fragment from Tablet II of the Atra-Hasis story, which contains the original Flood Account used by Gilgamesh.

Enlil heard their noise and addressed the Great Gods: "The noise of humankind has become too much for me; with their noise I am deprived of sleep. Stop supplies for the people! Let there be a lack of vegetation to satisfy their hunger!"

When Ea frustrated Enlil's attempts to starve humans, Enlil eventually sent the flood.

APPENDIX D

TREATY BETWEEN MURSILIS AND DUPPI-TESSUB OF AMURRU

PREAMBLE

1. These are the words of the Sun[1] Mursilis, the great king, the king of the Hatti land, the valiant, the favorite of the Storm-god, the son of Suppiluliumas, the great king, the king of the Hatti land, the valiant.

HISTORICAL INTRODUCTION

2. Aziras[2] was the grandfather of you, Duppi-Tessub. He rebelled against my father, but submitted again to my father. When the kings of Nuhasse land[3] and the kings of Kinza[4] rebelled against my father, Aziras did not rebel. As he was bound by treaty, he remained bound by treaty. As my father fought against his enemies, in the same manner fought Aziras. Aziras remained loyal toward my father [as his overlord] and did not incite my father's anger. My father was loyal toward Aziras and his country; he did not undertake any unjust action against him or incite his or his country's anger in any way. 300 (shekels of) refined and first-class gold, the tribute which my father had imposed upon

your father, he brought year for year; he never refused it.

3. When my father became god[5] and I seated myself on the throne of my father, Aziras behaved toward me just as he had behaved toward my father. It happened that the Nuhasse kings and the king of Kinza rebelled a second time against me. But Aziras, your grandfather, and DU-Tessub,[6] your father, [did not take their side]; they remained loyal to me as their lord. [When he grew too old] and could no longer go to war and fight, DU-Tessub fought against the enemy with the foot soldiers and the charioteers of the Amurru land just as he had fought with foot soldiers and charioteers against the enemy. And the Sun destroyed them.

(gap in which the reign of DU-Tessub was dealt with)

6*. (DU-Tessub recommends his son as his successor:) "[. . . When I die, accept my son] Duppi-Tessub as your vassal."

7*. When your father died, in accordance with your father's word I did not drop you. Since your father had mentioned to me your

---

[1] Sun is the title with which the Hittite king is addressed.

[2] The king of Amurru who is well known from the Amarna letters.

[3] The region between Halba (Aleppo) and the Orontes River.

[4] Qadesh on the Orontes, today Tell Nebi Mendo.

[5] i.e. died.

[6] The first part of the name is an ideogram, the Hurrian pronunciation of which is not known; in this case even the meaning of the ideogram is obscure.

[1] Text and notes taken from *ANET*, pp. 203–205, translated by A. Goetze.

name *with great praise*, I sought after you. To be sure, you were sick and ailing, but although you were ailing, I, the Sun, put you in the place of your father and took your brothers (and) sisters and the Amurru land in oath for you.

FUTURE RELATIONS
OF THE TWO COUNTRIES

8*. When I, the Sun, sought after you in accordance with your father's word and put you in your father's place, I took you in oath for the king of the Hatti land, the Hatti land, and for my sons and grandsons. So honor the oath (of loyalty) to the king and the king's *kin*! And I, the king, will be loyal toward you, Duppi-Tessub. When you take a wife, and when you beget an heir, he shall be king in the Amurru land likewise. And just as I shall be loyal toward you, even so shall I be loyal toward your son. But you, Duppi-Tessub, remain loyal toward the king of the Hatti land, the Hatti land, my sons (and) my grandsons forever! The tribute which was imposed upon your grandfather and your father—they presented 300 shekels of good, refined first-class gold weighed with standard weights—you shall present them likewise. Do not turn your eyes to anyone else! Your fathers presented tribute to Egypt; you [shall not do that!]

(gap)

MILITARY CLAUSES

9**.[7] [With my friend you shall be friend, and with my enemy you shall be enemy. If the king of the Hatti land is either in the Hurri land,[8] or in the land of Egypt, or in the country of Astata,[9] or in the country of Alse[10] —any country contiguous to the territory of your country that is friendly with the king of the Hatti land— (or in) any country contiguous to the territory of your country that is friendly with the king of the Hatti land—(as) the country of Mukis,[11] the country of Halba[12] (and) the country of Kinza[13]—but turns around and becomes inimical

toward the king of the Hatti land while the king of the Hatti land is on a marauding campaign—if then you, Duppi-Tessub, do not remain loyal together with your foot soldiers and your charioteers and if you do not fight wholeheartedly; or if I should send out a prince (or) a high officer with foot soldiers and charioteers to reenforce you, Duppi-Tessub, (for the purpose of) going out to maraud in an] other c[ountry— if then you, Duppi-Tessub, do not fight wholehea]rtedly (that) enemy with [your army and your charioteers] and speak as follows: "I am under an oath of loyalty, but [how am I to know] whether they will beat the enemy, or the enemy will beat them?"; or if you even send a man to that enemy and inform him as follows: "An army and charioteers of the Hatti land are on their way; be on your guard!"—(if you do such things) you act in disregard of your oath.

10**. As I, the Sun, am loyal toward you, do you extend military help to the Sun and the Hatti land. If an evil rumor originates in the Hatti land that someone is to rise in revolt against the Sun and you hear it, leave with your foot soldiers and your charioteers and go immediately to the aid of the king of the Hatti land! But if you are not able to leave yourself, dispatch either your son or your brother together with your foot soldiers (and) your charioteers to the aid of the king of the Hatti land! If you do not dispatch your son (or) your brother with your foot soldiers (and) your charioteers to the aid of the king of the Hatti land, you act in disregard of the gods of the oath.

11**. If anyone should press you hard, Duppi-Tessub, or (if) anyone should revolt against you, (if) you then write to the king of the Hatti land, and the king of the Hatti land dispatches foot soldiers and charioteers to your aid—(if you treat them in an unfair manner[14]), you act in disregard of the gods of the oath.

12**. If they take Hittites—foot soldiers and charioteers—through Duppi-Tessub's territory and Duppi-Tessub provides them while passing through (his) towns with food and

---

[7] The bracketed first part of the section is here restored from the treaty between Mursilis and Tette of Nuhasse (*KBo*, 1, 4 etc. in Akkadian, translated by Weidner, *loc. cit.*, 58 ff.). It is possible that not all the geographical names were the same here.

[8] Upper Mesopotamia between the Euphrates and Assyria.

[9] The region at the bend of the Euphrates south of Jerablus.

[10] The region on the upper Tigris.

[11] Its capital is Alalha, the ancient name of Atchana (Tell Açana) east of Antakya.

[12] Aleppo.

[13] Qadesh on the Orontes, today Tell Nebi Mendo.

[14] Inadvertently omitted by the scribe.

drink—(if that army) engages in any misconduct—pilfering in his country or his towns or in an attempt at deposing Duppi-Tessub from his kingship—it acts in disregard of the oath.

DEALINGS WITH FOREIGNERS, ETC.

13**. If anyone of the deportees from the Nuhasse land or of the deportees from the country of Kinza whom my father removed and myself removed escapes and comes to you, (if) you do not seize him and turn him back to the king of the Hatti land, and even tell him as follows: "Go! Where you are going to, I do not want to know," you act in disregard of your oath.

14**. If anyone utters words unfriendly toward the king or the Hatti land before you, Duppi-Tessub, you shall not withhold his name from the king. Or if the Sun (iii) gives you an order in secrecy (saying): "Do this or that!" (if) that order cannot be executed, petition about it on the spot (stating): "This order I cannot execute and will not execute" and the king will *reconsider* it then and there. But if you do not execute an order which can (well) be executed and deceive the king, or (if) you do not keep to yourself the word which the king told you in secrecy, you act in disregard of the oath.

15**. If a country or a fugitive takes to the road and while betaking themselves to the Hatti land pass through your territory, put them on the right way, show them the way to the Hatti land and speak friendly words to them! Do not send them to anyone else! If you do not put them on the right way, (if) you do not guide them on the right way to the Hatti land, but direct them into the mountains or speak unfriendly words before them, you act in disregard of the oath.

16**. Or if the king of the Hatti land is getting the better of a country and puts them to flight, and they come to your country, if then you desire to take anything from them, ask the king of the Hatti land for it! You shall not take it on your own! If you lay hand on it by yourself or conceal it, (you act in disregard of the oath).

17**. Furthermore, if a fugitive comes to your country, seize him! . . .

(gap)

INVOCATION OF THE GODS[15]

18**. [The Sun-god of Heaven, the Sun-goddess of Arinna, the Storm-god of Heaven, the Hattian Storm-god, Seris (and) Hurris,[16] Mount Nanni (and) Mount Hazzi,[17] the Storm-god of [. . .], the Storm-god of Halab, the Storm-god of Zippalanda, the Storm-god of Nerik, the Storm-god of Lihzina, the Storm-god of Hissashapa, the Storm-god of Sabina, the Storm-god of Tahaya, the Storm-god of Bettiyarik, the Storm-god of Samuha, the Storm-god of Hurma, the Storm-god of Saressa, the Storm-god of . . . , the Storm-god of Uda, the Storm-god of Kizzuwatna, the Storm-god of Ishupitta, the Storm-god of Nuhasse;

the Patron-god, the Hattian Patron-god, Zithariyas, Hapantalliyas, the Patron-god of Karahna, the Patron-god of the shield, Ea, Allatum, Telepinus of Durmitta, Telepinus of Tawiniya, Telepinus of Hanhana, Ishtar the Mighty, Askasepas;

Sin, lord of the oath, Ishara, queen of the oath, Hebat, queen of heaven, Ishtar, Ishtar of the battlefield, Ishtar of Nineveh, Ishtar of Hattarina, Ninatta (and)] Kulitta, the Hattian Warrior-god, the Warrior-god of Ellaya, the Warrior-god of Arziya, Yarris, Zampanas;

Hantidassus of Hurma, Abaras of Samuhas, Katahhas of Ankuwa, the Queen of Katapa, Ammammas of Tahurpa, Hallaras of Dunna, Huwassanas of Hupisna, Tapisuwa of Ishupitta, the "Lady" of Landa, Kunniyawannis of Landa, NIN.PISAN.PISAN of Kinza, Mount Lablana,[18] Mount Sariyana,[19] Mount Pisaisa, the Lulahhi gods (and) the Hapiri[20] gods, Ereskigal, the gods and goddesses of the Hatti land, the gods and goddesses of Amurru land, all the olden gods, Naras, Napsaras, Minki, Tuhusi, Ammunki, Ammizadu, Allalu, Anu, Antu, Apantu, Ellil, Ninlil, the mountains, the rivers, the springs, the great Sea, heaven and earth, the winds (and) the clouds—let these be witnesses to this treaty and to the oath.

---

[15] The bracketed part is again taken from the treaty with Tette of Nuhassi, see n.7.

[16] The two bulls of the Storm-god.

[17] Mons Casius near Ugarit.

[18] The Lebanon.

[19] The Hermon.

[20] Much discussed in connection with the question as to whether the Hapirū (widely quoted as Habirū), who are ubiquitous in cuneiform texts of the times, are to be equated with the Hebrews.

CURSES AND BLESSINGS

20**. The words of the treaty and the oath that are inscribed on this tablet—should Duppi-Tessub not honor these words of the treaty and the oath, may these gods of the oath destroy Duppi-Tessub together with his person, his wife, his son, his grandson, his house, his land and together with everything that he owns.

21**. But if Duppi-Tessub honors these words of the treaty and the oath that are inscribed on this tablet, may these gods of the oath protect him together with his person, his wife, his son, his grandson, his house (and) his country.

APPENDIX E
BIBLICAL HEBREW POETRY

Because so much of the Hebrew Bible is written in poetry,[1] it is important that even the beginning student have some awareness of the nature of **biblical poetry**. Keep in mind that such an awareness is not secondary, not something added to the so-called real meaning like frosting on a cake. The meaning of a passage actually depends in many cases on an appreciation of its poetry.

As you recall from the discussion on the functions of language in Chapter 1, the biblical author has freely determined that his or her particular text function as *poetry*. To disregard this is to risk missing the purpose of that passage. Poetry works differently from referential literature.[2]

When the purpose of communication is to call attention to itself, we term that function *poetry*. Unlike referential communication, poetry does not *primarily* direct attention beyond itself to some external referent; rather, it focuses the listener/reader on the actual means of communication (words or sounds). Poetry in all languages tries to make the means of communication conspicuous; one of the main devices for accomplishing this is *repetition*. Poetry can repeat similar end sounds at predictable intervals, which we call *rhyme*.

In many languages this repetition is called *meter* (from the Greek word for "measurement"). In French and Japanese, for example, the poet repeats the same number of syllables in each line (isosyllablism). Besides its frequent use of rhyme repetitions, English poetry also employs the stress accent of the words in set patterns of accented and unaccented syllables (for example, iamb or dactyl); a certain number of such sets is repeated in each line. Greek or Latin poetry preferred to mark the quantity of syllables, that is, the relative length it took to pronounce syllables (long or short). These long or short syllables were repeated in a set pattern.

---

[1] For example, besides the books of Psalms, Proverbs, and the Song of Songs, the Prophets (Minor and Major), Lamentations, and sections in the Pentateuch and in the historical books of the Former Prophets are written in poetry.

[2] An excellent example of this difference in the Hebrew Bible can be seen in a comparison of a poetic text (Judges 5:1–31) and its prosaic, referential counterpart (Judges 4:12–22). Although both passages talk about the same battle, each is quite different.

Scholars have not been able to agree on similar types of meter in biblical Hebrew poetry. However, there is a type of repetition that is typical of biblical poetry that can be detected even in translation.[3] Hebrew poetry is made up of lines that divide into at least two, often three, clauses, which are called a *cola*. A line that is composed of two cola is called a **bicolon**; a three-cola line is termed a *tricolon*.[4] Read Psalm 19. Notice that many "verses" (or "lines") are made up of two clauses ("cola"); for example, verses 1, 2[5]:

(verse 1): 1. The-Heavens are-telling the-glory-of God 2. And-the-work-of his-hands is-proclaiming the-firmament.

(verse 2): 1. Day to-day pours-forth speech, 2. And-night to-night declares knowledge.

Study the relationship between the two cola in each line. The second colon seems to repeat or advance the thought of the preceding one. In the eighteenth century, Bishop Lowth called this feature of Hebrew poetry "Parallelism of the Members."[6] And so typically in each line of Hebrew poetry the first colon will be followed by one, sometimes two (in the case of the tricola), clauses or cola that develop or repeat the thought and words of the first colon. This repetition (Bishop Lowth's "Parallelism of the Members") is one of the most noticeable features in biblical poetry. As you reread Psalm 19 you should become immediately aware of this almost antiphonal repetition.

Scholars are keenly interested in studying the correspondence between these cola. If the two (or three) cola say the same or similar things, then we have **synonymous parallelism**, as is the case in the two lines above taken from Psalm 19. (Other examples: Isaiah 1:3a; Amos 5:24). Notice the close similarity between cola 1 and 2 in both lines.

If the two cola say the exact opposite, then we have **antithetic parallelism**, which is best found in such Wisdom literature as the Book of Proverbs:

1. The-thoughts-of the-righteous (are) just, 2. (But) the-counsels-of-the-wicked (are) treacherous. (Proverbs 12:5)

Each colon has three words in Hebrew; the second colon *contrasts* the machinations of the evil with the thoughts of the righteous in the first colon and could almost be introduced with the conjunction "but" or "however." The conduct of the wicked is the *antithesis* of the thoughts of the righteous in the first colon. Therefore the two cola in the above example contrast behavior and thus constitute antithetic parallelism.

However, in many, many cases the exact relationship between the two cola is very difficult to categorize. There often seems to be a grammatical break or pause (called a "caesura") between the two cola or clauses; however, it is impossible to

---

[3] The student should know that this is not the only characteristic of Hebrew poetry, but rather something that even the beginner can notice and make use of. Other elements require a knowledge of both Hebrew grammar and phonetics.

[4] Terminology here often varies in scholarly works. Some prefer the word used in Greek poetry: *stichos*. The colon is a "stich" (pronounced "stick"); the bicolon a "dystich," the tricolon a "tristich."

[5] In what follows I have linked with a hyphen the English words that are represented by a single Hebrew word. Thus, there are four Hebrew words in each colon. I have also translated the lines in their original Hebrew word order.

[6] Here the word "member" reflects the later "colon."

label any correspondence as either synonymous or antithetic. Scholars call this correspondence **synthetic parallelism**, although in many instances there is not even clear parallelism. The most that can be said is that the poetic line often divides naturally (grammatically) into two parts (that is, cola). Psalms 18:34, 36, 37; 19:14; 50:22–23 are examples of synthetic parallelism.

In clear cases of parallelism (synonymous and antithetic) we can also characterize the *degree* of parallelism. If every element in the first colon is echoed back or repeated, then we have **perfect parallelism**. Notice that in the examples above from the first verse of Psalm 19 we have perfect parallelism.

1.   The-Heavens are-telling the-glory-of God

2.   And-the-work-of his-hands is-proclaiming the-firmament.

1.   Day to-day pours-forth speech,

2.   And-night to-night declares knowledge.

Each element or phrase in colon 1 is picked up again in colon 2. Scholars typically assign letters of the alphabet to the elements or phrases in the first colon to track their occurrence in the second. (If there is a new element in the second colon, then this phrase is assigned the next available letter.) If the parallel phrase in the second is *exactly* like that in the first colon, then the corresponding letter is used; if different but parallel words are used (as is most often the case) then the letter used in colon 1 is reused but with a prime mark (for example, A').[7]

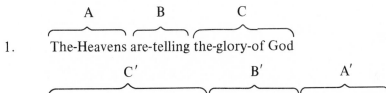

1.   The-Heavens are-telling the-glory-of God

2.   And-the-work-of his-hands is-proclaiming the-firmament.

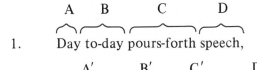

1.   Day to-day pours-forth speech,

2.   And-night to-night declares knowledge.

The placement of the letters in this last example (first line "The Heavens...") also helps the reader detect the artistic arrangement of the phrases. In the chiasm (reverse repeat) A B C// C' B' A', the two C's are placed back-to-back. This emphasizes the relationship between these two phrases. Thus the real "glory of God" is echoed in his Creation!

---

[7] Recently scholars have noticed that there seems to be a traditional list of words that frequently occur in parallelism. Thus, if a phrase is heard in the first colon, the listener anticipates a limited number of possible parallels in the subsequent colon (or cola): For example, "earth"// "heavens." There even seems to be a poetic tradition where certain phrases in a parallel set only occur in the first colon (so-called A words), whereas others are preferred in the second colon (B words). Hence, there is a preference for "Yahweh" in the first colon and its parallel "God" in the second (see Psalms 18:21).

When not all of the elements of the first colon are repeated or picked up, then we have incomplete parallelism:

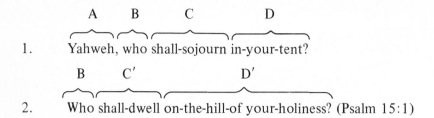

1.   Yahweh, who shall-sojourn in-your-tent?

2.   Who shall-dwell on-the-hill-of your-holiness? (Psalm 15:1)

In this example the element "Yahweh" in colon 1 is not picked up in the second colon.[8] (Further examples of incomplete parallelism: Isaiah 1:26, Psalm 6:1, Proverbs 2:18.)

Very often the second colon in incomplete parallelism will add an element to compensate for what it has omitted from the preceding colon.

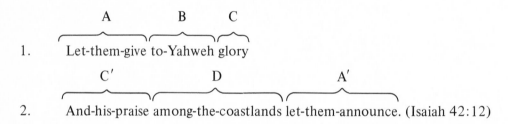

1.   Let-them-give to-Yahweh glory

2.   And-his-praise among-the-coastlands let-them-announce. (Isaiah 42:12)

Here the word "Yahweh" is not paralleled in colon 2, but this gap is compensated for by adding the phrase "among-the-coastlands."

Hebrew poetry also makes considerable use of such sound repetitions as *alliteration* and *assonance,* however these are beyond the scope of a course that relies heavily on translation. There is also research being done on the arrangement of lines in larger structures (strophes), but this also is beyond our scope.

FURTHER READINGS

Adele Berlin, *The Dynamics of Biblical Parallelism* (Bloomington: Indiana University, 1985). This is a brilliant contemporary study of the poetics of parallelism in Hebrew poetry, although it is fairly technical for the beginner.

Norman Gottwald, "Poetry, Hebrew," in *Interpreter's Dictionary of the Bible,* Vol. 3, pp. 829–838. This is a fine article for the beginning student. Although there are some excellent current studies on biblical poetry, many of these are too complicated for the beginner.

---

[8] Because the A word in the first colon was omitted in the second, the poet has achieved a balance between the cola by expanding on D′, which is longer than its parallel D.

APPENDIX F
CHRONOLOGICAL CHART

B.C.E.	PALESTINE	ANCIENT NEAR EAST
1800 TO 1500	Patriarchs (dates?)	Hammurabi
		Old Hittite Empire
1400 TO 1300	ᶜApiru Rebellion	New Hittite Empire
		Amarna Letters (Egypt)
1300 TO 1200	Exodus from Egypt (dates?) Moses (dates?) Conquest (?) of Canaan	Assyrian Dominance
1200 TO 1100	Period of the Judges and Tribal League (1200-1020) ORAL RECITALS AND G Philistine Occupation	Destruction of Hittite Empire and Ugarit
1100 TO 1000	Defeat of Tribes by Philistines at Aphek (ca. 1050)	Assyrian Revival
	Samuel and Saul found monarchy (1020-1000)	
1000 TO 900	The United Kingdom under David (1000-961) and Solomon (ca 961-922)	
	THE YAHWIST	

THE DIVIDED KINGDOM (922-722)

B.C.E.	JUDAH	ISRAEL	ANCIENT NEAR EAST
900 TO 850		ELOHIST Prophet Elijah Building of Samaria	Rise of Assyrian Power to North Aramean States
850 TO 750		AMOS (ca 750) HOSEA (ca 745)	Assyrian Dominance
750 TO 700	King Ahaz (735-715) King Hezekiah (715-687/6) MICAH ISAIAH	Fall of Samaria to Assyrians Many refugees flee to Jerusalem	

B.C.E.	JUDAH	ANCIENT NEAR EAST
700 TO 600	Sennacherib's seige of Jerusalem (701) Combination J-E BOOK OF DEUTERONOMY found by King Josiah (622) ZEPHANIAH (ca. 625) JEREMIAH (ca. 625-586) Death of King Josiah (609) HABAKKUK (ca. 605) DEUTERONOMISTIC HISTORY (1st edition)	Assyrian Empire Rise of Babylon Fall of Assyria (609)
600 TO 500	FALL OF JERUSALEM (587/6) Babylonian Exile *In Babylon:* SECOND ISAIAH P's EDITING OF JE PROPHET EZEKIEL *In Jerusalem:* HAGGAI ZECHARIAH (1-8)	Babylonian Empire Nabuchadnezzar Persian Conquest of Babylon by Cyrus (539) Cyrus allows return of Exiles and rebuilding of Temple
500 TO 400	MALACHI CHRONICLER EZRA AND NEHEMIAH (dates?) Ezra establishes the PENTATEUCH Final editing of PROVERBS BOOK OF RUTH (date?) BOOK of JONAH (date?)	Persian Empire

THE DIVIDED KINGDOM (922–722)

B.C.E.	JUDAH	ISRAEL	ANCIENT NEAR EAST
400 TO 300	BOOK OF ESTHER		Greek Alexander the Great Conquers Persia (331)
300 TO 150	Maccabean Revolt (167) GREEK ADDITIONS TO ESTHER BOOK OF DANIEL BOOK OF JUDITH		Hellenistic Empires Seleucid Oppression of Judah under Antiochus

GLOSSARY

ANTITHETIC PARALLELISM

      See PARALLELISM.

APOCALYPTIC LITERATURE

      Perhaps this type of literature is best described in terms of the community's social dynamics. The social setting for apocalyptic literature develops when a community is broken up into conflicting groups, and a minority group feels so cut off from the larger society and so disenfranchised that it no longer expects its rights to be realized within the status quo. This marginalized group can only turn to God to change the situation. Apocalyptic literature, then, focuses on the spectacular intervention of God into human history; God destroys the present order and then creates anew. Apocalyptic writings commonly describe Yahweh as a Divine Warrior and borrow heavily from ancient Creation myths in their descriptions of "re-creation" as a cosmic battle between forces of chaos and of order. In the Hebrew Bible we find apocalyptic literature in various degrees of intensity in Isaiah 24-27, 56-66; Zechariah 9-14; Daniel 7-12.

APOCRYPHA

      This is a category of ancient religious texts that did not generally acquire religious authority (canon) with the Jewish or Protestant communities. Some of these writings are, however, accepted by Greek, Russian, and Roman Catholic Christians as part of their Old Testament canon. Roman Catholics often refer to this group of books, which includes such works as Ben Sirach (Ecclesiasticus), Greek Additions to Esther and Daniel, the Wisdom of Solomon, Judith, Tobith, as the Second Canon (Deuterocanonical).

BICOLON

      See PARALLELISM.

CANON

      A canon is an authoritative list of books that have such authority because they are regarded as divinely sanctioned. As books written in ancient Israel acquired religious status in the community and became normative, they were included in the canon. This was a gradual process, which was probably completed for the Torah or Pentateuch by early postexilic times. (Ezra probably played an important role in this process.) The last section of the Hebrew Bible to become canonical probably did not become accepted as such in its present form until around 100 C.E. Protestants have generally accepted the Jewish canon as their own list for the Old Testament, whereas Catholics have a longer Old Testament canon (see APOCRYPHA).

CHRONICLER

This postexilic (ca. 350 B.C.E.?) historian wrote 1 and 2 Chronicles and perhaps portions of Ezra-Nehemiah, although the extent of the Chronicler's work here remains in dispute. The work covers the period from the creation of Adam (through genealogies) down to the fourth century B.C.E. The Chronicler is particularly interested in David and Solomon, whom he idealizes as the founders of the Jerusalem temple cult. The work stresses to the postexilic community that their restoration of the destroyed temple is the counterpart to the time of David and Solomon, whose significance would thus rest in their religious role rather than in their political structure.

CODE

A code is any kind of device used by the addresser to let the addressee know exactly how he/she wishes to be understood. It can be a body gesture (a wink), choice of vocabulary, tone, or intonation of voice. It could even be the social setting in which the communication takes place; for example, the classroom setting already suggests how a teacher's words are to be taken.

COLON

See PARALLELISM.

CONATIVE

See FUNCTIONS OF COMMUNICATION.

CRITICISMS

Another name for the tools used by the scholar for studying the Bible: *literary, historical-cultural, form, source,* and *redaction* criticisms.

D WRITER

The Deuteronomist was a reformer who lived during the dark period of Assyrian domination over Judah (about 680–650 B.C.E.). The Deuteronomist's most important literary contribution was the Book of Deuteronomy, which was found by King Josiah in the Jerusalem Temple around 622 B.C.E. This document purports to be the last words of Moses before his death and the passage of the Israelites across the Jordan River to conquer the promised land. In actuality, the book is a proposal for reform of the kingdom, which incorporates elements from both northern theology (emphasis on Moses, prophecy, personal accountability of the people) and southern Judahite theology (the monarchy and Jerusalem as center of true worship). This movement also retold Israelite history (Deuteronomistic History) in the books of Joshua, Judges, Samuel, and Kings to illustrate how successful leaders were who adhered to the principles of the Deuteronomic reform.

DAVIDIC COVENANT

This covenant (Hebrew **BERIT**) was the one-sided agreement between Yahweh and the Davidic dynasty in Jerusalem whereby Yahweh pledged to maintain the dynasty forever. This divine promise was modelled after the ancient Near Eastern "royal grants" in which a sovereign would reward a faithful vassal by making an unconditional gift. Here Yahweh pledges support for David and his sons no matter what they do; they may be punished, but the dynasty itself would not fall. See 2 Samuel 7, Psalm 132, Psalm 89. This theology, which stressed Yahweh's obligations to David, was often in conflict with the Mosaic or Sinai Covenant theology, which emphasized the people's obligations in the relationship.

DEUTEROCANONICAL

See APOCRYPHA.

DEUTERONOMIST

See D WRITER.

DEUTERONOMISTIC HISTORY (DH)

The school responsible for the Book of Deuteronomy also retold Israelite history to show how its reform determined whether Israel's leaders were successful or failures. This historical work includes the books of Joshua, 1 and 2 Samuel, 1 and 2 Kings. The DH does not seem to have used J or E material, although some scholars claim traces of J and E in the Conquest storeis of the Book of Joshua and of Judges 1. The DH emphasized a very straightforward ethic: Those who followed theology of reform prospered; those who didn't, failed. The original history culminated in the reign of King Josiah. After his untimely death in 609 B.C.E. and the destruction of Judah by the Babylonians in 586 B.C.E., there was a new edition of the history, which blamed the destruction on the kings (especially Manasseh) before good king Josiah.

DIASPORA

The Diaspora refers to Jews living outside of Palestine. Beginning in the sixth century B.C.E., Jews began to settle in colonies outside of Palestine; this spread was of course intensified in the years after the destruction of Jerusalem. Eventually Jewish communities could be found all around the Mediterranean.

E SOURCE

See ELOHIST.

ELOHIST (E)

The Elohist (ca. 900–750 B.C.E.) lived in the northern Kingdom of Israel after the breakup of Solomon's Empire. The Elohist returned to the older tribal account of Israel's origins so that the Davidic monarchy and Jerusalem—so stressed in J—played no role. Like the older tribal accounts, the E account emphasized Moses, the Sinai Covenant, and the personal accountability of the covenanted people. Its history must have extended from the Promise to the Patriarchs up to the Conquest of the Land of Canaan under Joshua.

EMOTIVE

See FUNCTIONS OF COMMUNICATION.

EZRA

Ezra was the Jewish scribe who was sent by the Persian authorities around 440 B.C.E. (?) to reform the Jewish postexilic religion in Palestine in order to restore stability to the region. (In the Bible his reform is linked with that of the governor Nehemiah, who was also dispatched by the Persian kings.) Ezra probably brought with him a version of the Law (Torah), which integrated the work of JEP with the Deuteronomist. He also probably decided to make the first five books (Genesis through Deuteronomy) the heart of Judaism. By ending the account with the death of Moses (Book of Deuteronomy), Ezra made Judaism under Persian domination predominantly a religion of the Diaspora, which still awaits the fulfillment of God's promise of the Land.

FORM CRITICISM

Form criticism is interested in speech patterns (forms) (primarily oral) and the social setting behind them. Form critics know that the written Bible had generations of oral tradition behind it and that orally transmitted material is not passed on haphazardly, but in defined units called *forms* (for example, myths of origins, hymns, funeral songs, royal chronicles, etc.). The form critic studies the literary shape of the form, the content associated with a specific form, and the social setting (*Sitz Im Leben*) in which it would normally be recited.

FUNCTIONS OF COMMUNICATION

The purpose or function of communication is based on which part of the communication process (addresser, addressee, referent, etc.) is being emphasized. If the communication focuses on the addresser, it is called *emotive* (frequent use of "I/We"); if it emphasizes the addressee (use of "You" and the imperative or vocative), it is *conative*. If communication centers on the referent, it functions as *referential* communication. If the function is to stress the means of communication, it is called *poetry*. In any case, even though all of the elements of the process of communication are present, one element is usually being stressed over (not instead of) the others, depending on the function of the communication.

HISTORICAL-CULTURAL CRITICISM

This tool investigates questions about the historical context in which a work was written. Who was the author? When did he or she live? What historical events are either referred to in the work or else might have influenced the writing of the piece? Will a knowledge of other contemporary literatures from elsewhere in the ancient Near East help better our understanding of the biblical passage? Archaeology and comparative literatures can be of considerable help in this criticism. (This criticism is usually just called "historical criticism," but I have added "cultural" in order to remind the student that this criticism uses "history" in its broadest sense to encompass features of comparative cultures in the ancient world.)

INCOMPLETE PARALLELISM

See PARALLELISM.

J WRITER

The Yahwist writer, spelled "*J*ahwist" by the German scholars who first studied the Yahwist, was so named because he prefers to call the deity by the proper name "Yahweh." J, who lived around the time of David and Solomon's Empire (ca. 950 B.C.E.), retold the ancient tribal stories about Israel's origins in such a way that the new empire with its Davidic dynasty would play a role in that story. According to J the borders of the territory promised to the Patriarchs corresponded to the extensive territories of Solomon's Empire. The J account started with Creation (Genesis 2:4b) in order to place the story of Israel on a broader stage as befitted a new cosmopolitan state. Originally the Yahwist probably extended to an account of David's kingship, but presently there is no clear evidence of J materials after the Book of Numbers.

LITERARY CRITICISM

This tool, also called *rhetorical criticism*, treats a biblical passage like any other literary passage. Literary criticism is only interested in the text itself and how it functions; it ignores such historical questions as when it was written and by whom. In studying how a literary passage conveys its meaning, the literary critic is particularly interested in the structure or arrangement of its parts, which can serve to focus the reader's attention on the important sections of the piece. Literary critics generally follow three steps: First, they determine the critical literary features, (2) they try to trace the pattern in these features, and (3) they then try to discern the meaning coveyed by that structure. (In older books on the Bible, "literary criticism" is used as the name for *source criticism*, although this usage is becoming less common.)

MYTH

A myth is a story that reflects that most basic values and notions underlying a society. Because these presuppositions are so fundamental, they cannot easily be talked about directly; they are usually expressed in terms of a story about the origins of basic elements in a society: the nature of humankind, sexuality, evil, etc. These myths often function *conatively*, for they seek to share and reenforce the common ideas that hold together a society. Readers outside the tradition must be careful not to focus on the often outlandish externals of the myth, but rather to look for the presuppositions behind it.

P WRITER

This writer, probably a Priest—hence the name (P)riestly Writer—lived in Babylon during the Exile (ca. 550 B.C.E.). Although he incorporates much older material into his work, he is mainly responsible for editing the earlier J and E material in such a way as to show that God is once again about to deliver on his threefold promise of the land, progeny, and a special relationship. The P Writer does not seem to have used any material from the Deuteronomist.

PARALLELISM

Each line of Hebrew poetry is made up of two or even three clauses called *cola*. (A two-clause line is a *bicolon*; a three-clause line is a *tricolon*.) The second colon (and third, if present) usually echoes or somehow picks up on or develops the ideas and phrases in the first colon. This relationship between the cola in a poetic line is called *parallelism*. If every element in the first colon is developed in the second, then we have *perfect parallelism*; if some elements are deleted and not picked up, then there is *imperfect parallelism* (with or without compensation). If the cola continue the same thought, then there is *synonymous parallelism*; if the two cola are contrasted (A contrasted by B), then there is *antithetic parallelism* (most often found in Wisdom sayings contrasting two behaviors). The relationship between cola that fail to fit either of these two categories is called *synthetic parallelism*.

PERFECT PARALLELISM

See PARALLELISM.

POETRY, BIBLICAL

See PARALLELISM.

PRIESTLY WRITER

See P WRITER.

PROCESS OF COMMUNICATION

This refers to an outline of all the elements present in any type of communication, whether written or spoken. There is always a communicator, the *addresser*; the person addressed, the *addressee*; the topic of communication, the *referent*; and finally the physical method by which the communication takes place (sound waves, black marks on a printed page, etc.) called the *means*.

REDACTION CRITICISM

Redaction criticism takes over where source criticism leaves off. Once a passage has been broken down into its written components (source criticism), the question remains, Why were these documents or sources arranged in their final form? According to what editorial principles were they joined together? The redaction critic looks for the blueprint according to which the source documents have been structured.

RHETORICAL CRITICISM

See LITERARY CRITICISM.

ROYAL GRANT

In the ancient Near East an appreciative king would often reward a vassal or servent by bestowing a gift. This grant was a one-sided promise on the part of the monarch toward the recipient. This was probably the model for the Davidic Covenant, in which Yahweh is portrayed as giving the monarchy in Jerusalem to David and his sons. The promise binds Yahweh, the giver, and not the recipient. See 2 Samuel 7; Psalm 132.

SINAI COVENANT

Also called the *Mosaic Covenant*, this agreement between God and the Israelite people was formalized in the desert on Mount Sinai during their flight from Egypt (Books of Exodus and Leviticus). This covenant formed the most basic relationship between the deity and the people of Israel, and it was often perceived by the prophets to be at odds with the Davidic Covenant. The Sinai Covenant stressed that the people had obligations toward God if their relationship were to be maintained. According to some it was patterned after the ancient Near Eastern Suzerainty Treaty (see below).

SOURCE CRITICISM

This critism investigates whether a finished passage has been made up from earlier writen documents (sources). Source criticism tries to isolate these sources and to uncover information about each source such as: When was each composed? What is the viewpoint or theology of each? Is there evidence of the existence of these sources elsewhere in the Bible? The source critic uses such clues as repetition, internal contradictions, different vocabulary, etc. The results of source criticism are always theoretical, because there is little hope of ever discovering proof of their existence.

SUZERAINTY TREATY

This type of international treaty was entered into by an overlord (suzerain) with a vassal state. It governed such issues as extradition, support for the vassal's successor, help in time of crisis, etc. These treaties followed a certain pattern: Preamble, Historical Prologue, Stipulations, Rules for Publication, Lists of Gods for Witnesses, Curses and Blessings for disobedience and obedience. Many think that such treaties formed the model for God's relationship to Israel in the Sinai Covenant (Treaty).

SYNONYMOUS PARALLELISM

See PARALLELISM.

SYNTHETIC PARALLELISM

See PARALLELISM.

TRADITION CRITICISM

Tradition criticism is the critical tool that studies the evolution of a biblical tradition such as the Exodus from Egypt from its earliest recoverable oral stages, through its incorporation into early written documents, on to its final form in the canonical books of the Bible. Some tradition critics continue their research beyond the "canonization stage," when books were accepted as authoritative by Jews and Christians, into the later postbiblical reuses of these traditions. Form and redaction criticisms are interested in phases of this evolution; but tradition criticism studies the entire process from oral stage to canonical book.

TRICOLON

See PARALLELISM.

YAHWIST (J)

See J WRITER.

ZION TRADITION

This tradition was probably created during the United Monarchy of David or Solomon. It glorified the status of the royal capital of Jerusalem by linking it and its temple on Mount Zion intimately with Yahweh's earthly presence. The Zion Tradition had five components that are often, but not always, found together: (1) Zion is the Mountain of God; (2) Zion is the source of the waters that fertilize the earth; (3) Zion is the site on which Yahweh destroyed the powers of chaos; (4) no enemy could ever triumph over this city; (5) the nations of the world would stream in pilgrimage to Zion to recognize its God.

INDEX

INDEX OF BIBLICAL PASSAGES (in alphabetical order)

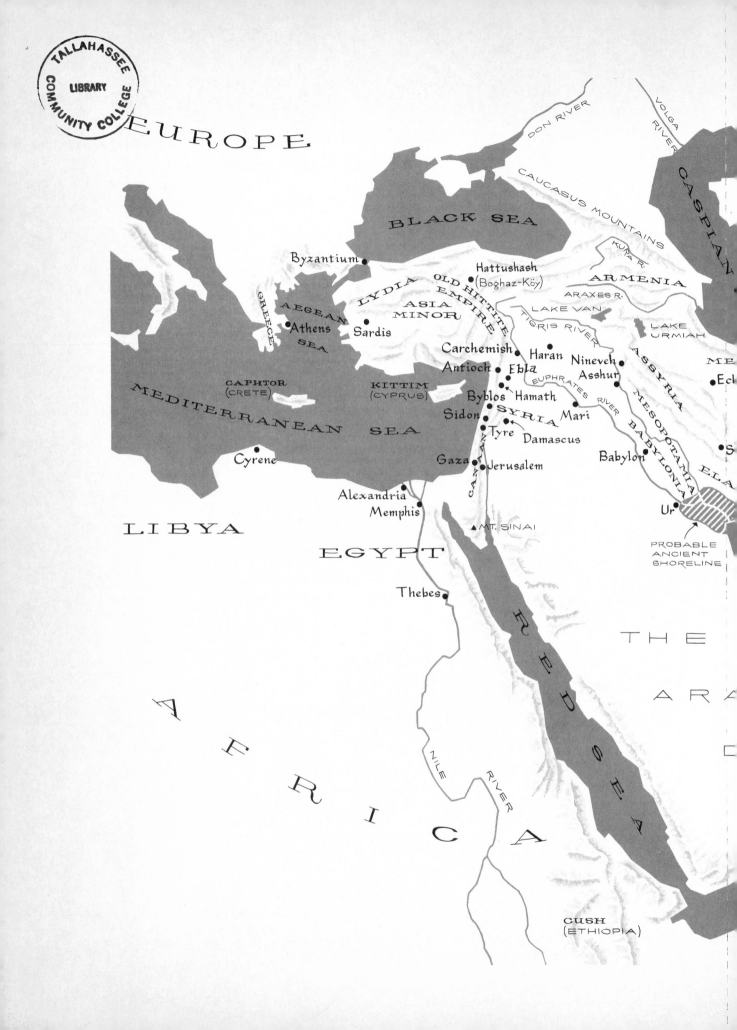

EUROPE

BLACK SEA

DON RIVER

VOLGA RIVER

CAUCASUS MOUNTAINS

CASPIAN

Byzantium

Hattushash
(Boghaz-Köy)

ARMENIA

KURA R.

ARAXES R.

LAKE VAN

LYDIA

OLD HITTITE
EMPIRE

ASIA
MINOR

GREECE

AEGEAN
SEA

Athens

Sardis

TIGRIS RIVER

LAKE
URMIAH

Carchemish

Haran

Nineveh

ME

Antioch

Ebla

Asshur

Eck

ASSYRIA

CAPHTOR
(CRETE)

KITTIM
(CYPRUS)

Byblos

Hamath

EUPHRATES

RIVER

MESOPOTAMIA

S

MEDITERRANEAN SEA

Sidon

SYRIA

Mari

Tyre

Damascus

BABYLONIA

ELA

Cyrene

Gaza

Jerusalem

Babylon

CANAAN

Ur

PROBABLE
ANCIENT
SHORELINE

Alexandria

Memphis

LIBYA

MT. SINAI

EGYPT

THE

Thebes

RED SEA

ARA

D

AFRICA

NILE

RIVER

CUSH
(ETHIOPIA)

THE ANCIENT NEAR EAST

LAKE
ARAL

OXUS RIVER

ASIA

(AFGHANISTAN)

INDUS RIVER

PERSIA
(IRAN)

•Persepolis

(PAKISTAN)

IAN GULF

INDIA

IAN

SERT

INDIAN OCEAN